W9-BNB-249

Hamlet

WITHDRAWN

TEXT EDITOR
TERRI BOURUS

ADVISORY EDITORS
DAVID BEVINGTON AND PETER HOLLAND

SERIES EDITORS
MARIE MACAISA AND DOMINIQUE RACCAH

William Shakespeare

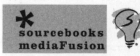

sourcebooks
mediaFusion

An Imprint of Sourcebooks Inc.®
Naperville, Illinois

Copyright © 2007 by Sourcebooks, Inc.
Cover and internal design © 2007 by Sourcebooks, Inc.
Cover illustration © 2007 Bruce Roberts, www.brucerobertsart.com
Sourcebooks and the colophon are registered trademarks of Sourcebooks, Inc.

All rights reserved. No part of this book may be reproduced in any form or by any electronic or mechanical means including information storage and retrieval systems—except in the case of brief quotations embodied in critical articles or reviews—without permission in writing from its publisher, Sourcebooks, Inc.

Audio and photo credits are at the end of the book.

Published by Sourcebooks MediaFusion, an imprint of Sourcebooks, Inc.
P.O. Box 4410, Naperville, Illinois 60567-4410
(630) 961-3900
Fax: (630) 961-2168
www.sourcebooks.com
www.sourcebooksshakespeare.com
For more information on The Sourcebooks Shakespeare, email us at shakespeare@sourcebooks.com.

Library of Congress Cataloging-in-Publication Data

Shakespeare, William, 1564-1616.
  Hamlet / text editor, Terri Bourus ; advisory editors, David Bevington and Peter Holland.
     p. cm.
  ISBN-13: 978-1-4022-0776-1
  ISBN-10: 1-4022-0776-X
  1. Hamlet (Legendary character)--Drama. 2. Murder victims' families--Drama. 3. Fathers--Death--Drama. 4. Princes--Drama. 5. Revenge--Drama. 6. Denmark--Drama. I. Bourus, Terri A. II. Bevington, David M. III. Holland, Peter, 1951- IV. Title.

PR2807.A2B68 2006
822.3'3--dc22

2006036879

                    Printed and bound in the United States of America.
                         LB 10 9 8 7 6 5 4 3 2 1

To students, teachers, and lovers of Shakespeare

Contents

About Sourcebooks MediaFusion

Launched with the 1998 *New York Times* bestseller
We Interrupt This Broadcast and formally founded in 2000,
Sourcebooks MediaFusion is the nation's leading publisher
of mixed-media books. This revolutionary imprint is dedicated
to creating original content—be it audio, video, CD-ROM,
or Web—that is fully integrated with the books we create.
The result, we hope, is a new, richer, eye-opening,
thrilling experience with books for our readers.
Our experiential books have become both bestsellers
and classics in their subjects, including poetry (*Poetry Speaks*),
children's books (*Poetry Speaks to Children*),
history (*We Shall Overcome*), sports (*And The Crowd Goes Wild*),
the plays of William Shakespeare, and more.
See what's new from us at www.sourcebooks.com.

About the Text

There were three different versions of *Hamlet* printed in the early seventeenth century. The first, printed in the late spring of 1603 by Valentine Simmes and published by Nicholas Ling, is the First Quarto (Q1), sometimes referred to during the twentieth century as the "bad" quarto.

The next one, the Second Quarto (Q2), was printed by James Roberts and published by Nicholas Ling in 1604-05; this version was also referred to as the "good" quarto. Thus, Ling was responsible for setting before the public both quarto editions. The third version of *Hamlet* appeared in the First Folio (F1), published by Isaac Jaggard and Edward Blount in 1623, seven years after Shakespeare's death. In spite of significant differences between the texts, they each have a "Hamlet" story to tell, each one making a valuable contribution to our understanding of the play.

Q1 is the least familiar of the three versions, being little more than half the length of the other two. There is also a difference in language, action, and character names, such as Gertred instead of Gertrude, Corambis instead of Polonius, Montano instead of Reynaldo, and the apt (because they suit the characters' personalities) Rossencraft and Gilderstone instead of the more familiar Rosencrantz and Guildenstern of Q2. However, it is the variation in language that is most troublesome. The differences have caused many scholars to theorize that Q1 is a faulty and unreliable text, possibly reconstructed from the memory of a Player, and therefore "bad." However, because of its likely connection to contemporary performance and proven performative qualities, this theory has now been called into question.

Q2, printed within a year or so of Q1, is the longest of the three texts. It introduces the characters and the plot line in the form that *Hamlet* audiences and readers have come to recognize. The title page of Q2 tells the reader that this is the "Newly imprinted and enlarged" version of the play, but that kind of title page advertisement was a common marketing strategy in the book trade of the Early Modern period in England. Still, this quarto has long been regarded as an authoritative text of this work.

F1 was compiled by two of Shakespeare's fellow sharers in the King's Men, John Heminge and Henry Condell. The text of *Hamlet* in F1 lacks about 200 lines from Q2, but has some eighty-five added lines not found in the earlier text. The quality and the practical brevity of the stage directions indicate that the manuscript copy for F1 was almost certainly a theatrical document. F1 is, like Q2, a familiar *Hamlet* and has been used frequently as the basis for the scripts used in staged and filmed versions of the play. Because the First Folio likely reflects a theatrical document and is therefore intrinsically linked to the stage, and because the Sourcebooks Shakespeare editions are focused on performance, F1 serves as the copy-text for the present edition. In addition, because of the authority of the Second Quarto and the performance qualities of the First Quarto, this edition is informed by both of those texts.

In all early printed texts, verse lines were normally set flush left. In performance, it becomes clear that some of the lines are shared. That is, one line continues the dialogue introduced by the previous line and is metrically connected to it as well. In this text, part lines are shared when one character is answering, responding to, or completing the thought of another; when this does not seem to be the case, these lines are treated as unshared single lines. In 1.2, when Horatio reveals the apparition of the Ghost to Hamlet, the dialogue as it appears in the Folio reads:

> *Hor*. A countenance more in sorrow then in anger.

> *Ham*. Pale, or red?

> *Hor*. Nay very pale.

> *Ham*. And fixt his eyes vpon you?

> *Hor*. Most constantly.

> *Ham*. I would I had beene there.

> *Hor*. It would haue much amaz'd you.

In this book, as in most modern editions, the same dialogue reads:

HORATIO
  A countenance more in sorrow than in anger.

HAMLET
  Pale or red?

HORATIO
  Nay, very pale.

HAMLET
                    And fixed his eyes upon you?

HORATIO
  Most constantly.

HAMLET
                    I would I had been there.

HORATIO
  It would have much amazed you.

Although the three early versions of *Hamlet* provide fascinating textual and theatrical evidence for scholars to examine and discuss, their differences have created vexing questions for editors and critics. Primarily, those differences lie in the variations of words and in the construction of the verse: the language of the play. One well-known example is Hamlet's soliloquy in 1.2, when Hamlet questions the worth of his "too too solid flesh," as it reads in the Folio. Both Q1 and Q2 read "sallied flesh." "Sallied" is not defined in the *Oxford English Dictionary*, the primary reference used for word clarification in this edition. Most editors who choose Q2 as their copy-text use the word "sullied," meaning "defiled," even though that word does not appear in any of the three early texts. The present edition reproduces the Folio version of this soliloquy, which reads "solid."

I use words and passages from Q1 and Q2 if and when they seem to clarify or expand upon a phrase or a scene: In act 4.4, for example, the soliloquy beginning "How all occasions" is included here as it is in Q2. This scene anticipates the arrival of Fortinbras at the end of the play and provides insight into Hamlet's character. I also use passages and/or stage directions from Q1 and Q2 when they allow us to better imagine or prepare a performance. The stage direction for the appearance of the Ghost "in his nightgown" is unique to Q1 and does much to set the tone for his appearance in Gertrude's chambers in 3.4. Q1, scene 14, although not included, is described in the notes because it provides a world of performance possibilities.

The F1 text has been silently modernized, but any significant differences are noted; passages and stage directions from Q1 or Q2 are recorded in the notes as well. The character names follow F1, but all speech prefixes have been regularized without notation; and I follow the punctuation in F1 as closely as possible, unless the original punctuation would confuse or mislead a modern reader.

This edition numbers every line of dialogue but, as in the other plays in this series, not stage directions or act and scene divisions. Through-Line-Numbering (TLN), a system devised by Charlton Hinman for *The Norton Facsimile: The First Folio of Shakespeare* (1968) numbers every line of type in F1, providing a fixed and reliable system of reference. Since critics, scholars, and editors increasingly use TLNs in their references, sometimes in conjunction with conventional act-scene-line references and sometimes without, the inclusion of them in this edition may assist users of this edition in working their way through secondary materials. TLNs are included at the bottom of every left-hand page.

Terri Bourus

On the CD

1. Introduction to the Sourcebooks Shakespeare *Hamlet*:
   Sir Derek Jacobi

ACT 1, SCENE 2, LINES 1-16
2. Narration: Sir Derek Jacobi
3. Andrew Cruickshank as Claudius
   Naxos • 1948
4. Edward de Souza as Claudius
   Naxos • 1997

ACT 1, SCENE 2, LINES 129-159
5. Narration: Sir Derek Jacobi
6. Sir Laurence Olivier as Hamlet
   Naxos • 1948
7. Sir Derek Jacobi as Hamlet
   BBC • 1980

ACT 1, SCENE 3, LINES 55-81
8. Narration: Sir Derek Jacobi
9. Norman Rodway as Polonius
   The Complete Arkangel Shakespeare • 2003
10. Peter Jeffrey as Polonius
    Naxos • 1997

ACT 2, SCENE 2, LINES 170-210
11. Narration: Sir Derek Jacobi
12. Simon Russell Beale as Hamlet and Norman Rodway as Polonius
    The Complete Arkangel Shakespeare • 2003

ACT 2, SCENE 2, LINES 473-529
13. Narration: Sir Derek Jacobi
14. Richard Burton as Hamlet
    Onward Production Ltd. • 1964

ACT 4, SCENE 5, LINES 154-189
30. Narration: Sir Derek Jacobi
31. Ellen Terry as Ophelia
    Naxos • 1911
32. Emma Fielding as Ophelia
    Naxos • 1997

ACT 5, SCENE 1, LINES 145-153
33. Narration: Sir Derek Jacobi
34. Sir John Gielgud as Hamlet
    Naxos • 1948
35. Richard Burton as Hamlet
    Onward Production • 1964
36. Sir Derek Jacobi as Hamlet
    BBC • 1980

ACT 5, SCENE 2, LINES 314-320
37. Narration: Sir Derek Jacobi
38. Sir John Gielgud as Hamlet
    Naxos • 1948

39. Conclusion of the Sourcebooks Shakespeare *Hamlet*:
    Sir Derek Jacobi

Featured Audio Productions

THE COMPLETE ARKANGEL SHAKESPEARE (2003)

Hamlet	Simon Russell Beale
Ophelia	Imogen Stubbs
Gertrude	Jane Lapotaire
Claudius	Bob Peck
Polonius	Norman Rodway
Ghost/Gravedigger	Paul Jesson
Horatio	Alan Cox
Laertes	Damian Lewis
Rosencrantz	John McAndrew
Guildenstern	Clarence Smith
Player King	Clifford Rose
Fortinbras	Chook Sibtain
Marcellus/Osric	Nicholas Rowe
Cornelius/Reynaldo	Alex Boyd-Williams
Prologue/Lucianus/Doctor	Nicholas Murchie
Player Queen	Steven O'Neill
Bernardo	Alan Westaway
Francisco	Alex McSweeney
Voltemand	Nick Monu

JOHN GIELGUD'S CLASSIC 1948 RECORDING PRESENTED BY NAXOS

Bernardo	Richard Williams
Francisco	Stanley Groome
Horatio	Sebastian Shaw
Marcellus	Anthony Jacobs
Claudius	Andrew Cruickshank
Voltimand	Hugh Manning
Laertes	Hugh Burden
Polonius	Baliol Holloway
Hamlet	John Gielgud
Gertrude	Marian Spencer
Ophelia	Celia Johnson
Ghost	Leon Quartermaine
Reynaldo	Frank Atkinson
Rosencrantz	Bryan Coleman
Guildenstern	John Chandos
First Player	Hugh Griffith
Player Queen	Denise Bryer
Fortinbras	Andrew Faulds
Captain	Denis McCarthy
Gravediggers	Charles Leno/Preston Lockwood
Priest	Arthur Ridley
Osric	Esme Percy
Gentleman	Alastair Duncan

NAXOS AUDIOBOOKS (1997)

Hamlet	Anton Lesser
Claudius	Edward de Souza
Gertrude	Susan Engel
Ophelia	Emma Fielding
Polonius	Peter Jeffrey
Horatio	Sean Baker
Laertes	Jamie Glover
Ghost/Player King	Geoffrey Whitehead

CBC RADIO (1961)

Ghost Of King Hamlet	Sam Payne
King Claudius	Ian Thorne
Queen Gertrude	Joy Coghill
Prince Hamlet	Peter Haworth
Polonius	Ivor Harries
Laertes	Patricia Williams
Horatio	Donald Monat
Francisco	Edward Stidder
Barnardo	John Harding
Marcellus	Roy Brimson
Osric	Edward Greenhaigh
Priest	Peter Ajello
Fortinbras	Roy Cooper
Captain Of Fortinbras' Army	Roland Hunter
1st Player	John Emerson
2nd Player	John Brinson
3rd Player	David Hughes
Gravedigger	Jack Ammon

Sir Laurence Olivier in an excerpt from the film soundtrack of *Hamlet* (1948), from Naxos AudioBooks' *Great Historical Shakespeare Recordings*

John Barrymore in an excerpt made as a "promotion" from Naxos AudioBooks' *Great Historical Shakespeare Recordings*

Richard Burton from John Gielgud's production of *Hamlet* at the Lunt-Fontanne Theatre in New York City on April 9, 1964

Sir Derek Jacobi from the BBC TV production, originally transmitted on May 25, 1980

Simon Russell Beale in *William Shakespeare's Great Speeches and Soliloquies* from Naxos

Note from the Series Editors

For many of us, our first and only encounter with Shakespeare was in school. We may recall that experience as a struggle, working through dense texts filled with unfamiliar words. However, those of us who were fortunate enough to have seen a play performed have altogether different memories. It may be of an interesting scene or an unusual character, but it is most likely a speech. Often, just hearing part of one instantly transports us to that time and place. "Friends, Romans, countrymen, lend me your ears," "But, soft! What light through yonder window breaks?," "To sleep, perchance to dream," "Tomorrow, and tomorrow, and tomorrow."

The Sourcebooks Shakespeare series is our attempt to use the power of performance to help you experience the play. In it, you will see photographs from various productions, on film and on stage, historical and contemporary, known worldwide or in your community. You may even recognize some actors you don't think of as Shakespearean performers. You will see set drawings, costume designs, and scene edits, all reproduced from original notes. Finally, on the enclosed audio CD, you will hear scenes from the play as performed by some of the most accomplished Shakespeareans of our times. Often, we include multiple interpretations of the same scene, showing you the remarkable richness of the text. Hear Derek Jacobi, John Barrymore, and Simon Russell Beale each perform the most famous soliloquy in the Shakespearean canon, "To be or not to be." Hear John Gielgud and Richard Burton lament, "O, what a rogue and peasant slave am I!" The actors create different worlds, different characters, different meanings.

As you read the text of the play, you can consult explanatory notes for definitions of unfamiliar words and phrases or words whose meanings have changed. These notes appear on the left pages, next to the text of the play. The audio, photographs, and other production artifacts augment the notes and they too are indexed to the appropriate lines. You can use the pictures to see how others have staged a particular scene and get ideas on costumes, scenery, blocking, etc. As for the audio, each track represents a particular interpretation of a scene. Sometimes, a passage that's difficult to comprehend opens up when you hear it out loud. Furthermore, when you hear more than one version, you gain a keener understanding of the characters. Why did Hamlet spare Claudius' life when he came upon him praying? Why did Gertrude and Claudius marry so soon after Old Hamlet's death? The actors made their choices and so can you. You may even come up with your own interpretation.

The text of the play, the definitions, the production notes, the audio–all of these work together, and they are included for your enjoyment. Because the audio consists of performance excerpts, it is meant to entertain. When you see a passage with an associated clip, you can read along as you hear the actors perform the scenes for you. Or, you can sit back, close your eyes, and listen, and then go back and reread the text with a new perspective. Finally, since the text is actually a script, you may find yourself reciting the lines out loud and doing your own performance!

You will undoubtedly notice that some of the audio does not exactly match the text. Also, there are photographs and facsimiles of scenes that aren't in your edition. There are many reasons for this, but foremost among them is the fact that Shakespeare scholarship continues to move forward and the prescribed ways of dealing with and interpreting text is always changing. Thus a play that was edited and published in the 1900s will be different from one published in 2007. Also, as explained in "About the Text," three different versions of *Hamlet* were printed in the early 1600's, with significant differences among them. Finally, artists have their own interpretation of the play and they too cut and change lines and scenes according to their vision.

The ways in which *Hamlet* has been presented have varied considerably through the years. We've included essays in the book to give you glimpses into the range of the productions, showing you how other artists have approached the play and providing examples of just what changes were made and how. Russell Jackson writes of Kenneth Branagh's 1996 movie, discussing the world he created and the effect of using the "full text" as the basis for the screenplay. "In Production," an essay by our text editor, Terri Bourus, provides an overview of how the play has been performed through the years, from Garrick's radically changed ending, to Sarah Siddon's female Hamlet (beginning a long tradition), to modern productions such as Almereyda's 2000 film, set in high-tech world of glass and chrome. In "Caviar to the General," Douglas Lanier cites a myriad of examples of pop appropriations, including music, film noir, and television. He also discusses Ophelia's extensive afterlife in popular adaptations, from being a jilted lover in Millais' 1852 painting, to an unjust victim of patriarchy in *Ophelia Speaks* (2002) and *Surviving Ophelia* (2001). Finally, for the actor in you, (and for those who want to peek behind the curtain), we have two essays that you may find especially intriguing. Andrew Wade, voice coach of the Royal Shakespeare Company for sixteen years, shares his point of view on how to understand the text and speak it. Perhaps you too can learn the art of speaking Shakespeare. The last essay is from an interview we conducted: we talked to each member of a cast and asked the actors about their characters and relationships. We found it fascinating to hear what they had to say on various topics; for instance, why Gertrude married Claudius, and what Hamlet and Ophelia's relationship was like. The characters come to life in a way that's different from reading the book or watching a performance.

One last note: we are frequently asked why we didn't include the whole play, either in audio or video. While we enjoy the plays and are avid theatergoers, we are trying to do something more with the audio (and the production notes and the essays) than just presenting them to you. In fact, our goal is to provide you tools that will enable you to explore the play on your own, from many different directions. Our hope is that the different pieces of audio, the voices of the actors, and the old production photos and notes will all engage you and illuminate the play on many levels, so that you can construct your own understanding and create your own "production," a fresh interpretation unique to you.

Though the productions we referenced and the audio clips we have included are but a miniscule sample of the play's history, we hope they encourage you to further delve into the works of Shakespeare. New editions of the play come out yearly; movie adaptations are regularly being produced; there are hundreds of theater groups in the U.S. alone; and performances could be going on right in your backyard. We echo the words of noted writer and poet Robert Graves, who said, "The remarkable thing about Shakespeare is that he is really very good—in spite of all the people who say he is very good."

We welcome you now to The Sourcebooks Shakespeare edition of *Hamlet*.

Dominique Raccah and Marie Macaisa
Series Editors

Introduction to the Sourcebooks Shakespeare *Hamlet*
Sir Derek Jacobi

track 1

In Production:

Hamlet THROUGH THE YEARS

Terri Bourus

On September 5, 1607, the English merchant ship *Dragon* lay off the coast of Sierra Leone, a province on Africa's west coast. On board, the ship's commander Captain William Keeling arranged for some of the crew to perform two plays in order to divert them: one of them was *Hamlet*, the other was *Richard III*. As far as we can tell, this was the earliest performance of *Hamlet* outside of England. The fact that it was aboard a ship in an exotic location some 2700 nautical miles from its origins is symbolic of *Hamlet's* journey as it moved out of England and developed a presence on the world stage.

The earliest version of *Hamlet* staged within England might have been around 1589, in "the Cittie of London." Though we cannot definitively connect William Shakespeare to that early performance, and no text survives to tell us what it was, there are intriguing clues. One of them comes from the preface of Robert Greene's prose romance, *Menaphon*, published in 1589. Here, the writer Thomas Nashe, surveying the London literary environment of the day, includes a reference to what appears to be a performance of *Hamlet*. Nashe tells of an "English *Seneca* read by candlelight" and suggests "if you should entreat him fair in a frosty morning, he will afford you whole Hamlets–I should say handfuls of tragical speeches." Five years later, the theatrical entrepreneur Philip Henslowe recorded in his ledger (now called *Henslowe's Diary*), that there was a play called *"hamlet"* being acted at Newington Butts on June 9, 1594, noting two playing companies in his entry, the Lord Admiral's Men and the Lord Chamberlain's Men. Perhaps it was that production that caused Nashe to later write in 1596 that he witnessed, in performance, a devil "looking as pale as the vizard of the ghost, which cried so miserably...like an oyster-wife, 'Hamlet, revenge.'"

By 1600, when Shakespeare was at the height of his career, *Hamlet* was certainly a permanent part of the repertoire at the Globe Theatre. Shakespeare's long-time fellow player and sharer in the Globe (sharers received part of the profits from performances but also bore financial responsibility), Richard Burbage, acted the lead role; perhaps Shakespeare himself played the part of the Ghost. History gives us little evidence about the performances themselves or about Burbage's interpretation, but upon his death on March 13, 1619, his elegist wrote:

> Oft have I seen him, leap into the Grave
> suiting the person, which he seemed to have
> of a sad Lover, with so true an Eye
> that there I would have sworn, he meant to dye,
> oft have I seen him, play this part in jest,
> so lively, that Spectators and the rest
> of his sad Crew, whist he seemed to bleed,
> amazed, thought even then he died in deed.

AFTER BURBAGE: THE POST-RESTORATION ERA

Tradition has it that Burbage himself groomed Joseph Taylor for the role of Hamlet, and Taylor played the part of the prince from 1619 until Parliament closed the theatres in 1642. They were reopened in 1660, when Charles II returned from exile on the continent; *Hamlet* returned as well. Though Taylor died in 1653 (or 1652; sources conflict) William Davenant, proprietor of London's Lincoln's Inn Fields and reportedly godson of Shakespeare, had seen him play the role. Thus, it was with some authority that Davenant cast Thomas Betterton as the first post-Restoration Hamlet, and he opened the play on August 24, 1661. Betterton was reportedly energetic and masculine in the part. Samuel Pepys saw him perform in *Hamlet* and recorded in his *Diary*, on May 28, 1663: "To the Duke of York's Playhouse and there saw 'Hamlet'...and mightily pleased with it, but above all with Betterton, the best part, I believe, that ever man acted."

Betterton's Ophelia was the actress Mary Saunderson (the reopening of the theaters also ended the prohibition of women actors on the British stage); she subsequently married Betterton in 1662. Thomas Betterton played the role right up to his death in 1709, the same year that Nicholas Rowe, who also praised Betterton's performance, published his six-volume edition of Shakespeare's *Works*.

THE EIGHTEENTH CENTURY: GARRICK TO KEMBLE

After a series of uninspired and forgettable productions, the unlicensed theater at Goodman's Fields, in 1736, offered a young David Garrick his first role in *Hamlet*, as the Ghost. It would not be until 1742 that Garrick would have a chance to play the title role, but when he did, the production quickly earned a reputation as the finest *Hamlet* ever staged.

David Garrick as Hamlet

Garrick was responsible for many innovations in the staging of the play. He began the tradition of having the mad Ophelia carry and distribute straw instead of flowers. Some of his more interesting ideas were a series of special props including a trick chair for the closet scene, which fell over when Hamlet started on seeing the Ghost, and a specially made wig that enabled his hair to stand on end in terror. And, the text was not exempt from his interpretive eye. In 1772, Garrick asserted that he had "dared to alter *Hamlet*. I have thrown away the gravediggers and all the fifth act." He purged the play of "everything that smacked of coarseness and impropriety," radically changing the play's ending. He left out Hamlet's departure for England, Laertes' plot with Claudius, and the gravediggers and Ophelia's funeral. Instead, Hamlet and Laertes quarreled before the King and when Claudius intervened, Hamlet killed him. Gertrude then went mad and died offstage. With these changes, Garrick began the refined misconception of Hamlet's character that ruled for the next two hundred years.

John Henderson followed Garrick, and although he was, by all accounts, excellent in the role, he was soon supplanted by John Philip Kemble, who opened at Drury Lane on September 30, 1783. Like Betterton and Garrick before him, Kemble continued in the role for nearly thirty-five years.

Kemble changed the essence of Hamlet, from aggressive and vengeful to "a fixed and sullen gloom." Though he reintroduced Elizabethan costuming to his productions, he also continued to change the text, moving it ever further away from its original sources, even removing the word "god" from his performances. He did reinsert some lines that had been eliminated by Davenant, but he cut the "rogue and peasant slave soliloquy" (found only in the second quarto) and made other changes as he saw fit. The publication of his acting texts heavily influenced subsequent stagings of the play.

Kemble was also "related" to another theatrical innovation: he was the brother of the famed eighteenth-century actress, Sarah Siddons, who first played Hamlet in 1775, beginning a long tradition of female Hamlets. Actresses who performed the role in the nineteenth century included Charlotte Cushman (who also tackled Romeo) and Sarah Bernhardt, in memorable performances during 1899-1901.

INTO THE NINETEENTH CENTURY: FROM KEAN TO POEL

From 1814-1833, Edmund Kean performed *Hamlet* and continued to adapt it to his own theatrical conventions. Kean furthered the notion of Hamlet as a tragic melancholic, and amazingly enough, he even removed much of the blank verse in favor of the prose that he felt was more immediate. He was the first to welcome his father's ghost; instead of terror, he reacted with affection and eagerness. He also treated Ophelia with love rather than brutality. His son, Charles Kean was, in 1840, the first to use a medieval Danish setting and costumes.

After Kean, the nineteenth century saw a string of great actors who continued to redefine and rearrange the play according to their own cultural expectations. William Charles Macready exaggerated Hamlet's "antic disposition," and Edwin Forrest continued that interpretation, but with an American flair. This opened the door to the great American actor, Edwin

Booth. Booth built his career on acting *Hamlet*, beginning at Burton's Theatre in New York City on May 12, 1857. Though he tried to restore some of the lines from the first folio that his predecessors had eliminated, he soon discovered that Victorian audiences preferred the more melodramatic and shorter versions of Kean and Kemble, so he reverted. Booth's version was introspective and gentle, described in the *New York Herald* as "tormented, borne down, and made miserable by an occasion...to which it is not equal."

In 1879, Henry Irving presented *Hamlet* at London's Lyceum Theatre. His performance was considered the best of the late nineteenth century, and his became the standard for all other stagings in his time. Though an avid student of Shakespeare, Irving adapted his productions to suit his own tastes and his perception of how those interpretations would be received by the audience. He eliminated the first four scenes of Act 4 and reintroduced Fortinbras to the play, a character who had been excluded for over two hundred years. Ellen Terry (Sir John Gielgud's great-aunt) played opposite him as Ophelia. Her realistic interpretation of Ophelia's madness would further develop in subsequent productions and continue on into twentieth-century interpretations. Irving's deeply psychological portrayal of *Hamlet* anticipated Freudian evaluations of the play.

track 31

Act 4, Scene 5, Lines 154-189
Ellen Terry as Ophelia

In 1881, William Poel, excited about performance possibilities in the first quarto (discovered in 1823), and perhaps in reaction to Irving's extravagant productions, founded the Elizabethan Stage Society. He produced and directed a much simpler version of *Hamlet* based on what he envisioned as a production much closer to Elizabethan theatrical conventions. The production was not a success in itself, but it is now considered an important part of the continuing evolution of *Hamlet*.

On Stage and On Screen:
Hamlets of the Twentieth Century

Johnston Forbes-Robertson, who began playing Hamlet in 1897, appeared in a twenty-two-minute silent filmed version of the play in 1913. After seeing him perform *Hamlet* in 1918, George Bernard Shaw wrote, "All the sentimental Hamlets have been bores. Forbes-Robertson's gallant, alert Hamlet, thoughtful but not in the least sentimental, is the *Hamlet* of today." In 1915-1916, Forbes-Robertson brought his *Hamlet* to the United States, and when John Barrymore ushered *Hamlet* into the twentieth century, it was that portrayal he emulated.

John Barrymore as Hamlet
Courtesy of Douglas Lanier

Unfortunately, Barrymore also altered the play almost beyond recognition, causing Shaw to write in 1925, "I wish you would...concentrate on acting, rather than on authorship, at which, believe me, Shakespeare can write your head off."

track 18

Act 3, Scene 1, Lines 55-87
John Barrymore as Hamlet

Reverting to tradition, Harley Granville-Barker, an actor and director, used many of William Poel's methods in an attempt to restore some of the Elizabethan staging techniques, and he redesigned the stage to allow for quick action and scene changes. Although some theater people rejected his ideas, they were generally well received by the theatrical community and perhaps most importantly, affected the interpretations of Sir John Gielgud. Gielgud was intrigued and inspired by Granville-Barker's techniques, so much so that he when he read Granville-Barker's text, *Preface to Hamlet* (1936), his interest in playing Hamlet was "rekindled." Gielgud's *Hamlet* drew increasingly away from the maudlin theatrical standards of the eighteenth and nineteenth centuries and irrevocably changed not just the nature of twentieth-century stagings of *Hamlet,* but also the nature of theater in general.

By the time Laurence Olivier took on the challenge of acting *Hamlet* in 1937, it was more focused and less melodramatic, thanks to Gielgud. Though Olivier played *Hamlet* on the stage many times, the portrayal for which he is best remembered is the one in his 1948 film, which opened at the Odeon in London on May 6 of that year. It was this film that brought *Hamlet* to more people than ever before (contributing to its longevity) and set the stage for its development in cinematic art.

track 6

Act 1, Scene 2, Lines 129-159
Laurence Olivier as Hamlet

Gielgud later directed Richard Burton in *Hamlet* at the Lunt-Fontaine Theatre on Broadway on April 9, 1964. This stripped-down production, meant to resemble a rehearsal, focused the play on the language and the action rather than the actors. According to Gielgud, "This is a *Hamlet* acted in rehearsal clothes, stripped of all extraneous trappings, so the beauty of the

Laurence Olivier as Hamlet in his 1948 film
Courtesy of Douglas Lanier

language and imagery may shine through..." Yet, it was difficult to ignore the presence of Gielgud (as the voice of the Ghost), the unmistakable and powerful voice of Burton, and the talents of actors such as Hume Cronyn and Eileen Herlie.

tracks 27-29

Act 4, Scene 4, Lines 32-66
John Gielgud as Hamlet
Richard Burton as Hamlet

The next year, on stage in England, Peter Hall directed the play at the Royal Shakespeare Theatre (RST) with a lanky, young, sixties-era Hamlet played by David Warner. Hall aimed to portray "the modern intellectual tortured by the needs of political commitment." David Warner was every inch the anti-hero, disaffected and apathetic, wearing loose black pants and draping a long red scarf around his neck he used as a prop during his soliloquies and his interaction with Rosencrantz and Guildenstern. For Ophelia, Hall introduced a novel characterization. Glenda Jackson played her as a neurotic shrew, a portrayal completely incompatible with most conceptions of Ophelia. It was, however, a *Hamlet* for its day, and young audiences lined up all night for standing-room-only tickets.

Tony Richardson's 1967 production at London's Roundhouse Theatre was filmed in 1969 with Nicol Williamson as Hamlet. Unlike the film made from Gielgud's 1964 production, Richardson's was redesigned with cinematic needs in mind and, as such, does not retain the elements of a theatrical production. The script was heavily cut, though Williamson strived to keep much of the quick action and humor of an early Elizabethan revenger. The film is also stamped with a sixties mark, with a kind of flower child Ophelia played by Marianne Faithfull.

At The Other Place Theatre in 1975, Buzz Goodbody became the first woman to direct a major British production, casting Ben Kingsley as the prince. This *Hamlet* was edgy and trendy, but it too aimed to capture the essence of an early revenge tragedy. At the bloody end of the performance, all the exits and entrances were shut, closing the audience in with the carnage. The effect was, by all reports, stunning and off-putting.

Derek Jacobi played *Hamlet* at the Old Vic in 1977, and then again on television for the BBC in 1980. Jacobi's *Hamlet* breaks from the hippies and rebels of the sixties, returning the character to a more traditional and far more elegant hero. His performance was widely praised. In a typical review, John O'Connor writes in the *New York Times* (November 10, 1980): "His is a Hamlet that demands attention and acclaim." Jacobi's "uncommonly rich emotional range" (as described by David Bevington) has influenced most subsequent portrayals including, and perhaps especially, Kenneth Branagh's.

track 19

Act 3, Scene 1, Lines 55-87
Derek Jacobi as Hamlet

Adrian Noble directed Kenneth Branagh in the RSC *Hamlet* at the Barbican Theatre in London in 1992. Clive Hershorn wrote, "Kenneth Branagh emerges resplendent. Here, at long last, is a Prince rich in nobility and intellect; an ardent lover with an ironic sense of humour and, above all, one mindful of the poetry with which he expresses himself. It is also one of the most lucid interpretations I have seen. And, in the end, the most moving." This uncut, four-and-a-half-hour production undoubtedly prepared Branagh for his ambitious film adaptation.

Before Branagh's film, however, the Italian director Franco Zeffirelli brought his vision of *Hamlet* to the big screen in 1990 with Mel Gibson playing the lead. Zeffirelli had to cut the text drastically in order to get the funding he needed to film; as a result Fortinbras is deleted, as well as any scenes of Claudius as a political diplomat. Still, although the soliloquies are cut and rearranged, this film manages to capture the essence of Hamlet as a revenge tragedy hero and is one of the most popular film versions.

Finally, in 1996, Branagh took on the gargantuan task of creating a cinematic *Hamlet* including as much of the "full text" as possible. The epic production, set in the nineteenth century and filmed at Blenheim Palace, is certainly the longest, with a playing time of 242 minutes. (See Russell Jackson's essay, "As Performed," devoted to this production.) Branagh's adaptation and his performance as Hamlet received nearly worldwide acclaim. "Branagh Creates 'A Palpable Hit'," shouted *U.S. News and World Report*, while *Paris Match* called him "A Prince in Front of and Behind the Camera." Reviews in England were less enthusiastic. The *Daily Telegraph*, one of the UK's major newspapers, reported "Branagh's epic Hamlet given cool reception." Another paper, the *Sunday Times*, attributed that reception to a cultural divide, explaining, "In America he's adored for taking Shakespeare to the masses. At home he's derided for doing just that." Whatever the differences, that a four-hour movie based on the "full text" is considered accessible to the masses, far away from its origins, is a testament to Branagh's skills and the power of the play.

THE TWENTY-FIRST CENTURY AND BEYOND

The twenty-first century has witnessed an overabundance of performance possibilities in *Hamlet* stagings. Michael Almereyda's 2000 *avant-garde*

Hamlet was filmed in a high-tech, modern world of glass and chrome. Ethan Hawke plays a deeply conflicted Hamlet, somewhat terrified by the sudden appearance of his father (played by Sam Shepard) on his apartment balcony. Then there was Stephen Pimlott's almost uncut four-hour *Hamlet* in 2001 with Sam West as Hamlet at the Royal Shakespeare Theatre. Pimlott saw the play as brutal *realpolitik*, not an intimate domestic drama; he visualized Hamlet as "uncompromising and...a killer. He wants truth at all costs, and the costs, when you think about it, are Ophelia, Claudius, Polonius, Gertrude, etc., etc." The setting was modern, grey, and minimalist. This production, like Almereyda's film, created an Elsinore that reflected the corruption and nihilism of a world gone corporate. Michael Bogdanov's 2005 *Hamlet* at the Grand Theatre Swansea portrayed a world driven mad by its continuing need for power, peopled with characters desperate for wealth and acquisition, again, a country at war, again, asking why.

CONCLUSION

Since 1599, *Hamlet* has been modernized, post-modernized, deconstructed, reconstructed, translated, and adapted for the time in which it is being performed. Enduringly popular, there are too many excellent performances and adaptations to record in this introduction, but the fact that it has been called the "master work of the millennium" is not insignificant. The image of Hamlet holding Yorick's skull is one of the most familiar icons in the world's cultural consciousness. The play has been, with only brief and politically based interruptions, continually performed in nearly every part of the globe and in nearly every language and possible setting since it first came to life on the London stage. There is an obvious explanation: more than any other play, *Hamlet* captures the human quest to understand the nature of life and death, to grasp the meanings of loss and love, and to come to terms with the tremendous contradictions inherent in the human heart.

As Performed:
Thoughts on Branagh's Hamlet

ON THE 1996 FILM DIRECTED BY KENNETH BRANAGH, WITH
SCREENPLAY BY KENNETH BRANAGH

Russell Jackson

Branagh's film, unlike any other film of the play, uses a "full" *Hamlet* text,
combining material from the first folio and the second quarto, to create the
"world" of the play[1]. It allows a greater sense of the general range of thought
and behavior in and around the court to make its impact. With the full text,
we simply hear and see more of the characters who usually suffer when the
play is cut. However, this "full" text limits the film director's choices, particularly in the construction of the play's action. For example, Branagh's "uncut"
script begins with the play's very first scene, which includes lengthy discus-
sions of Danish politics and other matters bearing on the apparition–lines
often abbreviated or cut in stage productions. Other directors can proceed
directly to demonstrations of these factors *in action*. The cinema's customary
priority of showing over telling is here reversed, even if, like Branagh, one
adds illustrations of the prior events, or of the "warlike preparation." In their
use of Act 1, Scene 2, other directors, notably Kozintsev (1964) and Zeffirelli
(1989) divide up Claudius' first speech to considerable effect, thus showing
him in several different contexts. Having chosen to play each scene in full and,
with only a few exceptions, in its original order, Branagh is obliged to have the
long first speech addressed in "real time" to the same audience of courtiers and
principals–as in a stage production. The sequence's following section, in
which Claudius and Gertrude speak privately to their son, taking him to one
side to reprove him for excessive mourning, requires the viewer not to think
too precisely about the "real" situation so elaborately created. What must the
hundreds of courtiers be thinking during all this? It is one of the moments of
tension in the film, between a text created for an Elizabethan stage and a

chosen filmic idiom ("classic" realism, continuity editing, etc.) in which the cinema implicitly shows us not only some of what is there to be seen and heard, but implicitly "knows" all of it.

Scene by scene, the film oscillates between screen realism carrying conviction, and moments when it seems under some strain. These instances include the Ghost's gothic appearance (and attendant special effects) in this rational world, the lack of telegraphs and a postal service, the oddity of old Hamlet's wintry naps in the orchard, the summer flowers accompanying Ophelia to her watery grave in winter, and so on. The issue is not so much whether these are mistakes and inconsistencies, as whether an audience will take any notice of them, though one should remember that, as Hamlet points out to his astonished friend, "There are more things in heaven and earth. Horatio, / Than are dreamt of in our philosophy." 1.5.165-166)

On the other hand, one can also identify in Branagh's film sufficient examples of the relationship between the "reality" suggested in the created environment and the necessary questions of the play. Consider the part militarism plays in Elsinore up to the very end. Not only is the court (as assembled in 1.2, the play scene in 3.2, and the fencing match in the last act) dominated by ostentatiously military men, there is also the background presence of a "cadet corps." Hamlet is seen inspecting them at fencing practice in one scene, in another he and Horatio walk briskly past them as they move along the hall gallery, and they are fencing again in the hall when Polonius leads Claudius and Gertrude to their interview with the returned ambassadors. This supports the idea that Denmark has an élite in training, but the follow-through comes later and almost by chance. As the film draws towards a close, it is not only the foppish upstart Osric who represents the kind of future Denmark seems to have in store, but the "Young Lord" who comes to ascertain whether Hamlet does indeed "hold his purpose" in agreeing to the fencing match and to announce that the Queen has asked him to behave courteously to Laertes. The military punctiliousness and implicit aggression in the young lord bring us back from the comic Osric to the more sinister threat of Claudius' militarism.

By using the "full" text in this setting and period Branagh has made the play resemble the film of an "epic" novel, a Tolstoyan or Balzacian compendium in which all sorts of unexplored corridors (to use an appropriate metaphor) offer glimpses of lives of which we see little more. The players, with their sense of Victorian touring troupe, are another example, as are the "flashbacks" to the earlier life of the principal characters. The presence of Gérard Depardieu as Reynaldo has been cited as evidence of the film's prodigality, as though it were a waste to employ him for such a small role. But as well as suggesting a degree of hypocrisy in Polonius rare in *Hamlet* productions, this Reynaldo seemed to come from a wider world–again, specifically the kind of wider world going on beyond the mirrored walls in the great historical novels, like Tolstoy's *War and Peace* or Pasternak's *Doctor Zhivago*.

Derek Jacobi as Claudius and Julie Christie as Gertrude in the 1996 film directed by Kenneth Branagh
Photo: Rolf Konow © Columbia TriStar. Courtesy of Douglas Lanier

Cinema can achieve a convincing environment for action on a scale beyond that of most theatrical productions. The principal set in Branagh's film, designed by Tim Harvey, was a large hall with a balcony running round it, and with a line of mirrored doors on both sides of the lower floor. It was this space and its nature that I remember as the first element of the planned film that the director described to me–apart, that is, from the long-cherished plan to use the "full text" of the play. In one corner was a chapel, with an inner area where the confessional was situated. The doors at one end of the hall gave onto a corridor that in turn led to the private apartments of the King, the Queen, Polonius, and Ophelia. At the other end of the main hall, on the opposite side to the chapel (and in fact adjacent to the lobby behind the royal dais with its tapestry backing), was Hamlet's study, which had its own upper level and could be entered by three doors, two of them concealed. The mirrored doors off the hall led to rooms, only two of which were identified with particular persons or scenes, that where Polonius and the King lurk to overhear Hamlet and Ophelia, and the padded cell where Ophelia is confined.

This is an account of the set as though it were a stable environment, a real palace, which one might describe as though in an estate-agent's leaflet, but in fact the various spaces indicated in the film and listed above were constantly changing. Ophelia's bedroom, seen only for one or two brief moments (when she and Hamlet appear in flashbacks, and when the guards are searching for Hamlet), was mostly an empty space on the sound stage. Polonius's room and the royal apartments were only furnished for a short time, and the partitioned rooms behind the mirrored walls were only furnished and decorated for the sequence in which Hamlet is pursued by guards after the murder of Polonius.

Most of the time the film's crew and their paraphernalia occupied these spaces. Behind the doors that Hamlet tears open, as he drags Ophelia down one side of the hall in the "nunnery" scene, are stagehands holding the piece of rope that keeps each door from opening too wide, and, behind them, the sound department's equipment, the video monitors and other squatters. In fact the film set is a construct within a working environment. As I watch the film I am conscious of the hours I spent sitting in this corner or that when it was out of shot, and of the hidden presence of several dozen crew members behind those walls and mirrors. Nor is the exterior "real," even though it the film used a genuine building (Blenheim Palace) and its grounds. The implicit relationship between one part of the environment and another is something established by the film's editing, but not corresponding to the "real" world: those walks, doors and colonnades do not lead as the film implies to this or that lobby or courtyard, still less to any of the studio-built interiors.

Kenneth Branagh as Hamlet in the 1996 film
Photo: Peter Mountain © Columbia TriStar. Courtesy of Douglas Lanier

For the crew, Branagh's Elsinore was not a prison but a place of work–more or less attractive on any one day according to whether or not you were sitting in a warm, draft-free bit of it. As for the aesthetic consequences of the work, this was a place of mirrors (with a puzzling effect of "infinity" at times) and of secret doors and passages. Every room had secret entrances, and none of the characters was safe. Hamlet, allowed a private space in film as he rarely is on stage, and certainly would not have been on the Elizabethan stage, could say, "Now I am alone" in his own library, a scholarly and intellectual fastness. Claudius could inhabit a world of rich antiques, Gertrude an airier, more fanciful room–although it was only hers in a limited sense: she was seen in the royal bedroom, not in a private and personal "closet." Polonius's room also had two secret doors, one for the prostitute and Reynaldo, and another through which Ophelia came. Fluid camera movement in long tracking shots through the public spaces connecting these rooms emphasizes the "secret" nature of the other doors and alcoves: the camera never penetrates those. In fact Hamlet's private apartment, filled with evidence of learning and artistic pursuits (including of course a model theatre) is not really secure: after his breathless chase to the secret door behind the bookshelves, he discovers that the guards are already there, as a rifle is leveled at his head.

In Branagh's film none of these rooms has windows, except for the casements that admit a chilly northern light into Hamlet's study–and the camera never looks out of those. Hamlet looks through one window and says "Now might I drink hot blood," and we see what is outside when a guard sees Fortinbras's troops approaching and tries to give the alarm. The lightness in Claudius' palace all seems to come from the chandeliers and, diffusedly, through the windows on the upper level of the hall. Neither he nor the Queen is ever seen outside, nor do they look out from their palace.

Some of the exteriors, shot at Blenheim, give a sense of spaciousness, threatening or liberating: these include the vast courtyard, the parkland

Derek Jacobi as Claudius in the 1996 film directed by Kenneth Branagh
Photo: Rolf Konow © Columbia TriStar. Courtesy of Douglas Lanier

where Rosencrantz and Guildenstern arrive by miniature train, the various colonnades and porches, and the path alongside the palace leading to the water garden where Laertes and Ophelia walk and meet their father. Others, more confined and disturbing, and seen only at night, are the more restricted space down by the gates where the sentries keep watch (Blenheim) and the woods where Hamlet speaks with the ghost and where Ophelia is buried (a set on a sound stage).[2] Wide shots of landscape accompany both Fortinbras' and the ghost's first appearance. Both are associated with the view into the distance from the palace gates and with the vast landscape (not especially characteristic of Denmark!) against which Hamlet stands to watch Fortinbras's troops in the soliloquy that ends the first section of the film.

All this amounts to an *emotional* geography of Branagh's Elsinore: a glittering, spacious version of the "prison" that is Denmark, beyond which we glimpse some parkland (but only under snow) and the terrain through which hostile forces move or which is associated with the supernatural (the wood) or death (the graveyard). What might be called its political geography is less strongly present, perhaps because in the chosen period, apparently 1870s-1900s, the territorial questions of northern and central Europe cannot be invoked too clearly. Fortinbras is seen tearing down a map of Scandinavia and North Germany, but not for long enough (we hoped) to remind audiences of such real geopolitical issues as the Schleswig-Holstein Question, and a scripted scene in which he was shown smashing through an identifiable Polish border post was not filmed (would the signs have said "Welcome to Poland"?). Fortinbras' invasion is effected by troops in rough grey greatcoats who look like guerillas, even though he and his officers are more grandly turned out, and Claudius inhabits what is clearly a palace rather than a castle. There are echoes of David Lean's *Doctor Zhivago*, and not merely in the casting of Julie Christie, though there is no precise correspondence with the political and social events with which it deals.

Claudius appears to be an accomplished politician, but the only male courtiers we see, apart from the visitors Rosencrantz, Guildenstern, and Horatio, are officers: this is a militaristic regime–even Ophelia gets a uniform for the first court scene–and a small assembly of the bourgeoisie is briefly seen watching events from a spectator's gallery on the bridge across the hall[3]. Although we are told of "warlike preparation," and even see some of it taking place in what seem to be the cellars of the palace, the military in Claudius' court are more decorative than formidable: the emphasis is on the panache, complacency, and superficial brilliance of the regime. Also, its Machiavellian dimension, which is particularly devoted to Claudius' containment of the Hamlet problem and his manipulation of Laertes, is given full effect by including their entire long scene together. Claudius' possession of the throne and the queen, and his defense of both, are the central issues of politics as depicted in the film, and the collapse of Denmark as a power is subordinate to this–a consequence of the rottenness at the heart of the court. Old Hamlet seems, from what we are told in the first scene, to have belonged to a more primitive political age, when personal combat between monarchs before their armies might decide dynastic rivalries, and which pre-dated the nation-state. This could hardly be associated with the earlier decades of the nineteenth century, and the guise of his statue and his ghost as a stylized medieval warrior has no real bearing on the life of the court we are shown. Like all productions that shift the play so far from the sixteenth century, this one has problems relating events at Elsinore with the saga-world of the story that is one of the play's sources. Branagh's concluding sequence juxtaposes a grand (some have said, grandiose) lying in state for the prince with the literal destruction of the old, ideally martial Hamlet by hammer-blows from the invader's troops. The image recalls news footage of statues being toppled by jubilant crowds after the fall of a dictatorial regime: shattering an illusion of power, and underlining the futility of Hamlet's act of vengeance. It has to be admitted that the strategies adopted may have disadvantages: while the chosen period facilitates an audience's engagement with the personal relationships of the play, it diminishes the sense of its in-built dynastic politics, by substituting a necessarily vague version of more recent issues and events.

Grigori Kozintsev's 1964 film offers–perhaps more than Branagh's–an impressively comprehensive view of the play's physical and moral world. Its effectiveness lies not merely in its inclusion of the "society" beyond the court, but in the extent to which this is a necessary part of the psychology of the central characters. In this respect it is both deeply romantic *and* bracingly post-romantic, and relates directly to the situation of the thinking person (or most people) in Soviet Russia during the period when the film was made. *Anyone* might be "the observed of all observers." In its own way, Branagh's

1996 *Hamlet* shares with Kozintsev's the ability to suggest that what we are seeing is only a corner of a real world in which men and women live and breathe, and in which problems of identity and personal morality are related to a wider, political context.

NOTES:

(1) On the detail of the textual choices, see my article in *Shakespeare Bulletin*, 15/2 (Spring 1997) 37-38. Branagh discusses his reasons for making a "full text" version in a foreword to the published screenplay (New York, W.W. Norton, 1996; London, Chatto and Windus, 1997).

(2) We also see the orchard where (in flashback) Claudius kills his brother. The shooting script included a riverside scene in which Laertes would be seen leaving by boat on the first stage of his journey to Paris, but this was not filmed.

(3) These were referred to during production (and on call-sheets) as "the Commoners." It may be significant that they appear only on the bridge, so that in some of what he says, Claudius–a master of the theater of politics–is literally "playing to the gallery."

"Caviar to the General"

Hamlet IN POPULAR CULTURE

Douglas Lanier

Hamlet: QUINTESSENTIAL SHAKESPEARE

If we judge by the sheer number of popular works in which it somehow figures, there is a case to be made that *Hamlet* is popular culture's favorite Shakespeare play. It is indicative of *Hamlet*'s popular status as *the* quintessentially Shakespearean play that when the Klingon Language Institute [1] turned to translating Shakespeare, it chose not the play that perhaps best matches Klingon culture–*Macbeth*–but rather *Hamlet*, a play that has the cultural stature of the Institute's other object of translation: the Bible. Only *Romeo and Juliet* rivals *Hamlet* in the number of adaptations, parodies, and homages it has prompted, and like *Romeo and Juliet*, *Hamlet*'s influence shapes our very image of Shakespeare as a playwright. Whereas the Shakespeare of *Romeo and Juliet* is popularly regarded as a poet of love, *Hamlet* is often invoked in popular culture to convey a very different impression of Shakespeare's work–as highbrow art. The play features many elements identified with this conception of Shakespearean theater: a courtly setting, a tone of tragic seriousness, a conflicted, highly self-conscious protagonist, and numerous emotionally wrought soliloquies. Hamlet, a college boy so intellectually inclined that nearly everything he confronts becomes an occasion for philosophical commentary, serves in popular culture to exemplify those qualities that modern audiences find most difficult in Shakespeare's writing: its high-minded philosophizing, verse dense with compacted imagery and learned allusions, and a plot short on action and long on talk.

THE MOST FAMOUS SPEECH IN THE WORLD

Two moments in *Hamlet* have become iconic in popular culture: Hamlet's "to be or not to be" soliloquy and Hamlet's address to the skull of Yorick, the dead court jester, at Ophelia's graveside. Not coincidentally, both exemplify Hamlet in his philosophizing mode. "To be or not to be," Hamlet's self-loathing contemplation of suicide and his own inaction, has become the quin-tessential soliloquy in the popular imagination, perhaps the single most rec-ognized, cited, and parodied speech in the Shakespeare canon. Because its opening lines are so very familiar, the speech has been a particular favorite of advertisers throughout the twentieth century, though allusions to this speech rarely get beyond its opening line. Because it is regarded as so quin-tessentially Shakespearean, "to be or not to be" has become a favorite for pop parodists. Ernst Lubitsch's anti-war comedy *To Be Or Not to Be* (1942), for example, makes comic hay of the solemn reverence that surrounds this famous speech. The self-important actor Joseph Tura tries again and again to perform "to be or not to be" only to be interrupted in mid-speech. Though Tura presents himself as a great Shakespearean, the only evidence the film offers of his status is his ever-thwarted attempt to perform this soliloquy. Ironically, his speaking of the phrase "to be or not to be" becomes the signal for a young airman in the audience to meet Tura's wife backstage for a tryst. A fantasy sequence in *The Last Action Hero* (1993) cleverly plays upon the disjunction between Shakespeare's highbrow theater and the conventions of contemporary action films. Arnold Schwarzenegger plays the role of the melancholy Dane who, unlike Shakespeare's protagonist, pummels and machine-guns everyone in sight. At the end of the sequence, he provides an action-movie riff on Hamlet's speech about inaction, offering the line "to be or not to be...not to be!" as he tosses a bomb that blows Elsinore to smithereens. The scene may be a wry response to Franco Zeffirelli's film *Hamlet* (1990) which cast action star Mel Gibson as Hamlet and cut nearly half of Shakespeare's text in favor of a less ruminative conception of the character.

"Alas, poor Yorick"

The play's second famous moment–Hamlet's address to Yorick's skull–rivals the balcony scene from *Romeo and Juliet* as the most widely evoked Shake-spearean image in popular culture. The image of Hamlet holding a skull aloft has become so iconic that a pop character need only hold up a skull-shaped object to bring the reference to mind. Its familiarity helps explain why this image too appears in advertisements, despite the fact that the scene from which it springs stresses the transitory nature of all earthly things. Sometimes the image is intended to evoke matters Shakespearean. Such is the case with Poor Yorick, a web-based company that specializes in Shakespearean educational materials; the company's original logo was a skull raised in hand. In other examples, the connection between pop references to Yorick's skull and Shakespeare's *Hamlet* are somewhat looser. Examples from comic book covers illustrate the point. The cover of the June 1992 issue of *Justice League Europe* features a villain holding the severed head of the superhero Power Girl (aka Kara), with the caption, "Alas–poor Kara!" The allusion seems gratuitous until we learn that the villain is Deconstructo, devoted to destroying revered objects, including superheroes and classic art such as Shakespeare, both of which here Deconstructo mutilates. On the cover of *Lobo* 36 (1997) we see the ultra-violent Lobo hovering over Shakespeare himself as he types out a script for *Lobo*, the very comic we will be reading. In the foreground is a skull with "Yorick" incised on its forehead, a reminder of Shakespeare's tragedy but also a wry foreshadowing of the blood-and-guts violence to come. Hamlet's words as he addresses Yorick's skull are often misquoted in popular culture: he says not "Alas, poor Yorick, I knew him well" but rather "Alas poor Yorick, I knew him, Horatio." The difference is subtle but important. The popular (mis)quotation treats Hamlet's speech as a solitary address–a soliloquy–rather than Hamlet's remembrance of the court jester in the company of Horatio and the gravedigger. Perhaps this explains why this moment is so often conflated with "to be or not to be," Hamlet's most famous soliloquy.

Hamlet AND *Film Noir*

Hamlet has also provided many motifs for *film noir*, that distant generic relative of Renaissance revenge tragedy, of which *Hamlet* is the most famous example. Central to *Hamlet* and *film noir* are the following:

- an alienated protagonist (Hamlet) pitted against systematic corruption, the scope of which he discovers in the course of the plot;
- an antagonist (Claudius) who appears benign but who is in fact sinister;
- a woman (Gertrude) somehow implicated in the corruption;
- a spectacular moment in which the antagonist is confronted with his crime;

- the protagonist's erratic, mad, or ill-judged behavior as he pursues justice;
- an innocent or naive woman (Ophelia) who pays a price for her devotion to the protagonist;
- the protagonist's spectacular revenge upon the antagonist, often completed with an ironic twist.
- a fatalistic tone;
- the protagonist's melancholic introspection (in *film noir*, this is supplied by voiceover; in Shakespeare, by soliloquy).

Though *Hamlet*'s influence upon the contemporary thriller tends to be oblique, sometimes elements from Shakespeare's play appear in relatively direct form. *Strange Illusion* (1945), a film by the much-admired Poverty Row director Edgar Ulmer, tells the *Hamlet*-inspired tale of Paul Cartwright, whose father, a judge, is tragically and mysteriously murdered. As Paul's widowed mother prepares to marry the suave stranger Brett Curtis, Paul has nightmares warning him that Brett is not to be trusted. Eventually Paul pieces together that Brett is really Claude Barrington, a murderous con-man and his father's killer, and Paul gathers his friends Hardy-Boys style to expose the villain. The film is noteworthy not only for its creative adaptation of Shakespeare's play and resourcefulness on a very low budget, but also for its interest in psychoanalysis. Indeed, Paul's Hamlet-like "madness" leads him at one point to be confined in an asylum where he is menaced by an evil analyst. The film's emphasis upon the Oedipal content in Paul's dreams testifies both to the twentieth-century interest in psychoanalytic approaches to *Hamlet* and to *film noir*'s fascination with nightmare imagery and pop Freudianism. Michelle Manning's *Blue City* (1986) deals with somewhat similar material with a bigger budget and much less panache. The influence of *film noir* also runs in the other direction. As if in recognition of the connection between Shakespeare's play and this popular genre, Laurence Olivier's 1948 *Hamlet* borrows heavily from *film noir*'s cinematic style, using such techniques as voiceover, angular compositions, unusual camera angles, and stark lighting to tell Shakespeare's story.

Several other adaptations of *Hamlet* exhibit an affinity for the sub-genre of corporate *noir*, that is, *film noir* set in the realm of big business. *The Bad*

Sleep Well (1960), a little-known film by acclaimed Japanese director Akira Kurosawa, freely reimagines the narrative of *Hamlet* within the world of a corrupt Japanese corporation. In Kurosawa's version, Koishi Nichi, the Hamlet figure of the story, emerges as a mysterious avenger of his father's forced suicide who battles post-war Japanese corporate corruption from the bombed-out ruins of a munitions factory. Though Nichi dies in the end–the result of one of many double-crosses in the film–his nemesis, Iwabuchi, receives a phone call at film's end that indicates the pyrrhic nature of his victory. *The Rest is Silence*, Helmut Käutner's film of the year before, offers a similar transposition of *Hamlet* to a business environment–here Hamlet is the son of a German industrialist supposedly killed during the war–and is equally interested in using the play to address post-war national guilt. Aki Kaurismäki's *Hamlet Goes Business* (1987) treats his corporate *noir* adaptation with icily black humor, situating the plot in a timber company that turns to manufacturing rubber ducks. *Strange Brew* (Dave Thomas and Rick Moranis, 1983), starring the beer-swilling Canadian duo Bob and Doug Mackenzie, treats its *Hamlet* subtext with an even lighter touch, though it too concerns a corrupt corporation–the Elsinore Brewery. *Let the Devil Wear Black* (Stacy Title, 1999) and Michael Almereyda's slacker tragedy *Hamlet* (2000) also use motifs derived from corporate *noir*.

Hamlet AND POPULAR GENRES

Hamlet has also been adapted to musical form, though the fit has typically been less than ideal. Though several operatic versions predate it, Ambroise Thomas's opera *Hamlet*, first performed in 1868, is the only *Hamlet* opera that has secured a place, albeit minor, in the classical music repertory. Several orchestral suites and tone poems based upon *Hamlet* have also appeared. Of these Hector Berlioz's *Tristia* (1848), Franz Liszt's *Hamlet* (1858), Peter Tchaikovsky's *Hamlet* (1888), and Frank Bridge's "Lament for Strings" (1915) and "There Is a Willow Grows Aslant a Brook" (1928) are the best known, though none rank among the composers' best works. By and large popular musical versions have been even less successful. Cliff Jones's *Rockabye Hamlet* (1974) and Pierre Groscolas's *Halliday Hamlet* (1976, featuring French rock star Johnny Halliday) sought to graft Shakespeare's play to the rock opera format, but they garnered small audiences and little critical acclaim, a fate shared by more recent examples. Only *Musikal Hamlet* (2000), an adaptation written by and starring Czech pop idol Janek Ledecky, has enjoyed any lasting notoriety, and then only thus far in Eastern Europe. It is indicative of the uneasy relationship between *Hamlet* and music that so many musical parodies of the play exist. One notable example is "The Producer" (1966), an episode of *Gilligan's Island* in which the castaways perform Shakespeare's play to the tunes of famous operatic arias. Rap versions such as Moe Moskowitz and the Punsters' "Hamlet Rap" (1994) and Robert Krakovski's *The Trage-D of Hammy-T* (1999) play their adaptations for comedy, suggesting the incompatibility of *Hamlet* and contemporary hip-hop. One of the more curious musicalized *Hamlet*s is Orpheus's 1997 version featuring cult film star Richard E. Grant's overwrought performance of "to be or not to be" set to house music. By turns danceable, dreamlike, and campy, Orpheus's dance mix exemplifies post-modern deadpan parody, at once flaunting the absurdity of combining Shakespeare with club music while offering a surprisingly effective piece which uses the phrase "perchance to dream" as its focus.

Transpositions of *Hamlet* to other genres have provided more interesting results. For example, the conventions of the spaghetti Western have proved surprisingly amenable to *Hamlet*, for three such adaptations appeared in the genre's heyday (*Apocalypse Joe*, dir. Leopoldo Savona, 1971; *Lust in the Sun*, dir. Richard Balducci, 1971; and the best of the lot, *Johnny Hamlet*, dir. Enzo G. Castellari, 1972). "To be or not to be" even makes a small but thematically crucial appearance in John Ford's classic Western, *My Darling Clementine* (1946), when Doc Holliday and Wyatt Earp save a bumbling Shakespearean actor from being harassed by the Clantons. Holliday's troubled nature is revealed by the fact that he completes the speech when the Shakespearean runs dry. Because a devotion to Shakespeare seems quixotic in the modern age, another group of adaptations make *Hamlet*, in its role as the quintessential Shakespearean tragedy, the centerpiece of stories about idealists determined to perform the role or teach the play in the face of considerable obstacles. This plotline underpins, for example, Penny Marshall's film *Renaissance Man* (1994), which chronicles the struggles of Bill Rago, a downwardly-mobile former executive, to teach *Hamlet* to underprivileged army recruits; Kenneth Branagh's film *In the Bleak Midwinter* (aka *A Mid-*

winter's Tale, 1995), in which Joe Harper, a down-on-his-luck actor, gathers a rag-tag troupe to perform *Hamlet* in a small village during the Christmas season; Paul Rudnick's play *I Hate Hamlet* (1994), which portrays Andrew Rally, an insecure sitcom actor, as he attempts Shakespeare's most demanding role with the help of John Barrymore's ghost; or the Canadian TV series *Slings and Arrows* (2003), which in its first season details the trials of a dramatic company struggling to mount a production of *Hamlet*. Heroic versions of this motif, both set in prison camps and using *Hamlet* as a medium for resistance, can be found in Don Chaffey's *Breakout* (1958) and David L. Cunningham's *To End All Wars* (2001).

Hamlet FROM OTHER PERSPECTIVES

Perhaps because Shakespeare so strongly emphasizes Hamlet's perspective on the events at Elsinore and even the play's minor characters are vivid in the popular consciousness, several writers have been prompted to imagine how the plot of *Hamlet* might look from other characters' points of view. Though other Shakespeare plays have prompted the same kind of reimagining, *Hamlet* is by far the most popular choice for such adaptations. The variety of points of view is remarkable. Claudius's perspective is featured in John Turing's novel *My Nephew Hamlet* (1967) and Ken Gass's play *Claudius* (1993); Gertrude is the main character in Lillie Buffum Chase Wyman's novel *Gertrude of Denmark: An Interpretive Romance* (1924) and Margaret Atwood's delightfully acid short story "Gertrude Talks Back" (in *Good Bones*, 1992). Both are the protagonists of John Updike's novel *Gertrude and Claudius* (2000). Fortinbras's point of view is offered in two surreal plays, Janusz Glowacki's *Fortinbras Gets Drunk* (1990), and Lee Blessing's *Fortinbras* (1991). In Terrence Ortwein's play *And Flights of Angels* (1991), Horatio directs a group of players in telling Hamlet's story, and Alethea Hayter's novel *Horatio's Version* (1972) provides exactly what its title promises. Even Yorick gets his say in Salman Rushdie's short story "Yorick" (in *East and West*, 1994). Perhaps the most beloved of these adaptations is Tom Stoppard's extraordinary play *Rosencrantz and Guildenstern Are Dead* (1966; the 1990 film version was directed by Stoppard himself). In Stoppard's adaptation, Rosencrantz and Guildenstern are hapless minor characters caught up in a predetermined sequence of events they never fully understand and in which they are powerless to intervene. The two reflect upon the absurdity of their fated condition as they participate in bits and pieces of Shakespeare's play that rush them to their deaths. Stoppard's play is, however, not the first version to elevate Rosencrantz and Guildenstern to prominence within a *Hamlet* adaptation. W. S. Gilbert (of Gilbert and Sullivan fame) wrote a Shakespearean burlesque entitled *Rosencrantz and Guildenstern* in 1874 (first performed in 1891). In Sullivan's version, Rosencrantz is in love with Ophelia, who, betrothed to Hamlet, conspires with Guildenstern and his friend to break the engagement. Their plan involves tricking Hamlet, a serial soliloquizer, into performing a tragedy which Claudius (Hamlet's father in this version) wrote in his youth and which out of embarrassment he banned all mention of at court.

Versions of Ophelia

Of all of the subsidiary characters in *Hamlet*, Ophelia has had the most vigorous afterlife in popular adaptations, where she serves as a symbol of the jilted lover. Ophelia was a favorite subject for nineteenth -century painters. Of these paintings the most famous is John Everett Millais's 1852 depiction of Ophelia as she floats briefly in the brook before her billowing dress pulls her under the water. Typical of nineteenth-century portraits of Ophelia, Millais's emphasis falls upon her helpless madness and tragic beauty. The image is of fallen innocence, a moment of young erotic awakening followed almost immediately by madness and martyr-like death. Millais's image–and the conception of Ophelia that informs it–has had wide influence, providing, for example, the model for staging Ophelia's death in Olivier's 1948 film *Hamlet*. Prompted by Shakespeare's scenes of Ophelia's singing, several Ophelia-themed song cycles–most famously by Johannes Brahms–also partake of this theme of melancholic beauty. Avant-garde composers such as John Cage and Oliver Knussen also used Ophelia as compositional inspiration, finding in her mad music a metaphor for their own unconventional works. The close association of Ophelia and music may also explain why "Ophelia" is one of the most frequent Shakespeare-themed song titles in popular music.

After the advent of the feminist movement, Ophelia has taken on a different resonance, that of an unjust victim of patriarchy. Mary Pipher's influential book *Reviving Ophelia: Saving the Selves of Adolescent Girls*

(1994) uses Shakespeare's character as a metaphor for teenage girls who, Pipher argues, are psychologically maimed by a "girl-poisoning" culture. One measure of the book's influence is that it has spawned a number of related "Ophelia" titles on similar subjects–Sara Shandler's *Ophelia Speaks* (2000) and Cheryl Dellasega's *Surviving Ophelia* (2001). A feminist re-envisioning of Ophelia found wide cultural expression in art as well, underpinning such diverse works as Jean Betts' comedy *Ophelia Thinks Harder* (1993), Byrony Lavery's play *Ophelia* (1997), Natalie Merchant's song "Ophelia" (from the 1998 album *Ophelia*), Jurgen Vsych's strange but rewarding film *Ophelia Learns to Swim* (2000), and Stephen Berkoff's epistolary play *The Secret Love Life of Ophelia* (2001).

Somewhat related to this reconception of Ophelia are examples of Hamlet reimagined as a woman. Several nineteenth-century actresses–Charlotte Cushman and Sarah Bernhardt among them–played the role of Hamlet to demonstrate their theatrical talents. One of the finest silent films of the play, Sven Gade and Heinz Schall's *Hamlet* (1921, starring Asta Neilsen) takes

Hans Junkermann as Polonius, Lilly Jacobson as Ophelia, and Asta Nielsen as Hamlet in Sven Gade and Heinz Schall's 1921 silent film
Courtesy of Douglas Lanier

cross-gender casting further, rewriting Shakespeare's plot to accommodate a feature-length story about a female Hamlet. In this version, in an effort to hide the fact that the heir to the Danish throne is female, Hamlet, a woman, is forced to pretend to be a man even as s/he later pursues revenge against the usurping Claudius. Complicating matters, this Hamlet falls in love with Horatio but dare not reveal her secret. This film resonates in fascinating ways with women's movements of the twenties and with lesbian subculture, a subject of periodic interest in early German cinema.

For a more contemporary example of a female Hamlet, one might look to Daniel Sackheim's *The Glass House* (2001), a "grrl-power" thriller inspired by elements from Shakespeare's play.

The Glass House reminds us of another important link between *Hamlet* and the youth culture of post-World War II generations. It is striking that so many of the *Hamlet* adaptations of this period use Shakespeare's play as a vehicle for expressing intergenerational tensions, reconceiving of Hamlet as an icon for youthful rebellion against or alienation from the older generation. That theme emerges in works as different in tone and audience as *Strange Illusion*, *The Bad Sleep Well*, and *Let the Devil Wear Black*, to name a few. It is particularly strong in Claude Chabrol's *Ophélia* (1963). In Chabrol's film, Yvan Lesurf, a young man whose businessman father dies and whose mother quickly remarries, becomes obsessed with the *Hamlet* narrative, convincing himself–erroneously, it turns out–that his own life mirrors Shakespeare's play. Chabrol's elliptical film both evokes Hamlet as an emblem for a vague sense of youthful disaffection from elders and critiques that connection at the very same time. Hamlet's status as a symbol for the alienation of modern youth has strongly influenced performances on film and stage of the character from the mid-twentieth-century on. Richard Burton's justly famous 1964 stage portrayal emphasized Hamlet's savage, ironic intelligence, his caustic contempt for authority, and his anguished and angry sense of entrapment in a situation not of his own making. Burton's Hamlet provided a powerful analogue for the feelings of alienation of the emerging sixties' generation. Nicol Williamson's performance in Tony Richardson's 1969 film of *Hamlet* strikes similar chords.

This conception of the character remains just as powerful with the current generation. Hamlet is now routinely considered a young actor's role,

Ethan Hawke as Hamlet, Diane Venora as Gertrude, and Kyle MacLachlan as Claudius in the 2000 film
directed by Michael Almereyda
Courtesy of Douglas Lanier

rather than, as it was in previous centuries, a role for the mature Shake-spearean. Michael Almereyda's *Hamlet* (2000) reimagines Hamlet as a disaffected slacker engulfed by the trappings of postmodern culture–anonymous cityscapes, corporate business, and media saturation. Epitomizing that culture is his glib uncle Claudius, mogul of Denmark Corporation, against whom Hamlet instinctively rebels. That this Hamlet desires to carve out a mode of expression of his own–he is an independent filmmaker–from the media products that surround him speaks to the difficult contradictions an aspiring young artist–and a Shakespearean filmmaker–must navigate in contemporary culture.

To take an example farther afield, the notion that *Hamlet* concerns a young man coming of age also suffuses the Shakespearean borrowings in *The Lion King* (1994), where the young lion Simba must rebel against his usurping uncle Scar in order to grow into maturity and take his rightful role as king. Though *The Lion King* plays down the darker elements of Hamlet's youthful disaffection, the sense that *Hamlet* provides the film with a plot about intergenerational strife testifies yet again to how contemporary culture views the play.

Shamlet: Pop Parodies

Hamlet's status as the quintessential Shakespeare play has prompted all manner of lampoons in popular culture. Indeed, it was John Poole's *Hamlet Travestie* in 1810 that is widely credited for starting the Victorian Shakespearean burlesque craze. In the twentieth century, parodies of *Hamlet* often exploit the perceived divide between elite and popular culture, treating Shakespeare's play as an exemplar of highbrow culture that becomes absurd when transposed into the current pop idiom of the day. There are myriad examples. A short interlude in Woody Allen's *Everything You Wanted to Know About Sex (But Were Afraid To Ask)* (1972) recasts bits of the "to be or not to be" soliloquy in terms of a bad stand-up comedy routine; *Green Eggs and Hamlet* (1995), an amateur film directed by Michael O'Neal, retells the events of Shakespeare's play in Dr. Seuss rhymes; and *The Skinhead Hamlet* (1982), a short play by Richard Curtis, writer for the *Blackadder* TV series and *Bridget Jones* films, converts Shakespeare's dialogue into a series of comically inarticulate "oi"'s and expletives. In several cases, the parody targets less Shakespeare's play than its reputation or performance. "Another Point of View, or Hamlet Revisited," an episode of the classic radio show *CBS Radio Workshop* (broadcast 1956), offers an elaborate mock-argument concluding that Hamlet is the real villain of the play, sending up the penchant of scholars to offer perverse interpretations of the play; the second act of the Reduced Shakespeare Company's *The Compleat Works of Wllm Shkspr (abridged)* (1994), devoted entirely to *Hamlet*, lampoons the burden of the past faced by any performer of the play–one of the actors runs away when he hears the group will attempt it–as well as the vogue for psychoanalytic interpretation–the audience is invited to enact Ophelia's unconscious by portraying her ego, superego, and id. Curiously, political lampoons using *Hamlet* are relatively rare. One exception is "Shamlet," a 1988 comedy routine by political parodists The Capitol Steps concerning the inability of a Democratic candidate to decide to run for the presidency.

Hamlet GOES GLOBAL

As one might expect of a play so widely regarded as quintessentially Shake-spearean, popular adaptations of *Hamlet* have appeared in nearly every culture in which Shakespeare has been performed. Many adaptors have creatively transposed the play to their native cultures. To offer but a sampling:

- Dev Virahsawmy, a noted Mauritian translator of Shakespeare, has written two adaptations, *Hamlet 2* (1995) and *Dokter Hamlet* (1997).
- The opera *Revenge of the Prince* (2005, produced by the Shanghai Peking Opera) shifts the action to ancient China and adds musical, acrobatic, and dance sequences.
- Ozualda Ribiera Candeias's film *A Herança* (1970) reimagines the narrative as a tale of rural Brazil.
- Metin Erksan's film *Intikam Melegi - Kadin Hamlet* (1977) offers a surreal modernization of the play and stars Turkish film siren Fatma Girik cross-dressed in the title role.
- Eldar Ryazanov's *Beregis avtomobilya* (1966) examines how an insurance agent's pursuit of a car thief comes to mirror Laertes's pursuit of Hamlet.
- Krsto Papic's film *Predstava Hamleta u Mrdusi Donjoj* (aka *Acting Hamlet in the Village of Mrdusa Donja*) (1974), an adaptation of Ivo Bresan's 1971 play, chronicles a village performance of Shakespeare's play led by a local commissar, a performance which ends up exposing the commissar's crimes and precipitating revenge against him.

Though the number and variety of *Hamlet* performances and adaptations worldwide precludes any easy survey, certain distinctive traditions of adapting *Hamlet* have developed in some cultures. In Western Europe, the non-English-speaking avant-garde has often been attracted to *Hamlet* as an example of modernism *avant la lettre*, and it has been willing to treat the play more subversively than their English-speaking counterparts, as is exemplified by the work of Carmelo Bene, Celestino Coronado, Heiner Müller and Giovanni Testori, to name a few. Moreover, whereas recently the West has tended to treat *Hamlet* as a play about intergenerational conflict or Oedipal psychology, Eastern Europe has tended to treat the play as a political work, using performances of *Hamlet* as a vehicle for covert protest against repressive regimes. *Hamlet* is now firmly established as a classic of world literature, and the sheer range of interpretations and adaptations it has inspired ensure that its long, vibrant cultural afterlife is sure to continue.

NOTES:

(1) http://www.kli.org/

Dramatis Personae

THE GHOST

HAMLET, Prince of Denmark, son of the late King Hamlet and Queen Gertrude

CLAUDIUS, King of Denmark, brother of the late King Hamlet, and uncle to Hamlet

GERTRUDE, Queen of Denmark, wife of King Claudius, widow of the old King Hamlet, and mother to Hamlet

HORATIO, Hamlet's university friend from Wittenberg

POLONIUS, father of Laertes and Ophelia and counselor to the king

LAERTES, son of Polonius and brother of Ophelia

OPHELIA, daughter of Polonius and sister of Laertes

REYNALDO, servant of Polonius

Danish Ambassadors to Norway:
VOLTEMAND
CORNELIUS

OSRIC, a foppish courtier
A Lord
A Gentleman

Friends of Hamlet in his youth:
ROSENCRANTZ
GUILDENSTERN

Sentinels:
MARCELLUS
BERNARDO
FRANCISCO

FORTINBRAS, Prince of Norway
CAPTAIN in Fortinbras's army

English Ambassadors

FIRST CLOWN, a gravedigger
SECOND CLOWN, the gravedigger's assistant

A Priest

Players

Lords, Ladies, Sailors, Soldiers, Messengers, Guards, Attendants, the mob who follow Laertes, and the reported Pirates

[Hamlet

Act 1

0: Location: A guard platform at Elsinore Castle in Denmark.

0: Scene: This opening scene is conventionally staged on either constructed castle ramparts or on a bare platform, but whatever the set, the time is midnight and the two sentinels come upon one lone soldier standing guard. The soldiers are apprehensive and there is an air of anxiety and expectancy about them. The opening line, "Who's there!" might have called the noisy audience at the Globe to attention. Zeffirelli cut this scene from his 1990 film, beginning instead with the funeral of the king as Hamlet (Mel Gibson), dressed rather like a monk in a black, hooded cloak, hovers over and around the center of the action, watching. Michael Bogdanov, working with The Wales Theatre Company in 2005, opened the play at a military base where the country was being threatened with invasion by an unseen enemy force. Helicopters took off and landed, radar screens loomed over the stage like images of Big Brother, and the ominous glare of searchlights moved in full circle, sweeping over the characters on stage as well as the faces of the audience.

2: **Stand and unfold**: step forward and identify yourself

4: **carefully**: right on time

7: **sick at heart**: feeling uneasy to the point of illness

11: **rivals**: partners

13. **Friends to this ground**: allies of Denmark, not threatening

Act 1, Scene 1]

BERNARDO
Who's there?

FRANCISCO
Nay, answer me. Stand, and unfold yourself.

BERNARDO
Long live the King!

FRANCISCO
        Bernardo?

BERNARDO
          He.

FRANCISCO
You come most carefully upon your hour.

BERNARDO
'Tis now struck twelve. Get thee to bed, Francisco.   5

FRANCISCO
For this relief much thanks. 'Tis bitter cold,
And I am sick at heart.

BERNARDO
Have you had quiet guard?

FRANCISCO
        Not a mouse stirring.

BERNARDO
Well, goodnight.
If you do meet Horatio and Marcellus,   10
The rivals of my watch, bid them make haste.

FRANCISCO
I think I hear them. Stand, ho! Who's there?
        Enter HORATIO and MARCELLUS

HORATIO
Friends to this ground.

13: **liegeman to the Dane**: loyal subjects to the King of Denmark

14: **Give you**: God grant you

20: **piece**: his physical body

24: **fantasy**: imagination

30: **approve our eyes**: validate, confirm

Costume rendering for Francisco from the 1934 production at the New Theatre directed by Sir John Gielgud
Photo: Rare Book and Special Collections Library, University of Illinois at Urbana-Champaign

MARCELLUS
        And liegemen to the Dane.

FRANCISCO
  Give you good night.

MARCELLUS
  O, farewell, honest soldier.   15
  Who hath relieved you?

FRANCISCO
  Bernardo has my place.
  Give you good night.

                                      Exit FRANCISCO

MARCELLUS
  Holla, Bernardo!

BERNARDO
  Say, what, is Horatio there?

HORATIO
                A piece of him.   20

BERNARDO
  Welcome, Horatio; welcome, good Marcellus.

MARCELLUS
  What, has this thing appeared again tonight?

BERNARDO
  I have seen nothing.

MARCELLUS
  Horatio says 'tis but our fantasy,
  And will not let belief take hold of him   25
  Touching this dreaded sight, twice seen of us.
  Therefore I have entreated him along
  With us to watch the minutes of this night,
  That if again this apparition come,
  He may approve our eyes and speak to it.   30

HORATIO
  Tush, tush, 'twill not appear.

BERNARDO
                Sit down awhile,
  And let us once again assail your ears
  That are so fortified against our story,
  What we have two nights seen.

37: **the pole**: Polaris, the North Star (part of the constellation *Ursa Minor*), long used as a navigational aid.

41: Scene: ***Enter GHOST***: Many performances, especially on film, follow Horatio's description of the Ghost in 1.1.48, "that fair and warlike form." One notable exception is Paul Scofield in the 1990 Franco Zeffirelli production. There, the Ghost appears to Hamlet dressed in a long, dark gown with no military accoutrements and no kingly ornamentation. In Michael Almereyda's 2000 film, the Ghost (Sam Shepard) is first spotted on an elevator, his image captured by a security camera.

43: **scholar**: Latin was the language of scholars and the Church; as a scholar, Horatio, it was hoped, could converse with the spirit

44: **Mark**: look at

45: **harrows**: torments

47: **usurp'st**: disturbs

49: **buried Denmark**: the dead King

50: **sometimes**: formerly

HORATIO
                    Well, sit we down,
    And let us hear Bernardo speak of this.   35

BERNARDO
    Last night of all,
    When yond same star that's westward from the pole
    Had made his course to illume that part of heaven
    Where now it burns, Marcellus and myself,
    The bell then beating one–   40

MARCELLUS
    Peace, break thee off.

                                                    Enter GHOST

                    Look, where it comes again!

BERNARDO
    In the same figure like the King that's dead.

MARCELLUS
    Thou art a scholar; speak to it, Horatio.

BERNARDO
    Looks it not like the King? Mark it, Horatio.

HORATIO
    Most like. It harrows me with fear and wonder.   45

BERNARDO
    It would be spoke to.

MARCELLUS
                    Question it, Horatio.

HORATIO
    What art thou that usurp'st this time of night,
    Together with that fair and warlike form
    In which the majesty of buried Denmark
    Did sometimes march? By Heaven I charge thee, speak!   50

MARCELLUS
    It is offended.

BERNARDO
                    See, it stalks away!

HORATIO
    Stay, speak, speak! I charge thee, speak!

                                                    Exit GHOST

56: **on't**: of it

58: **avouch**: proof

62: **Norway**: King of Norway (Fortinbras's father)

63: **parle**: meeting, debate

64: **smote**: attacked; **sledded Polacks**: The Polish army traveled on sleds in the winter.

66: **jump**: exactly

68: **In what...to work**: how this might have happened

69: **gross and scope**: general drift

71: **Good now**: If you please

73: **toils the subject**: wearies the citizens (subjects) of Denmark

74: **daily cast of brazen cannon**: constant production of armaments (Denmark is mobilizing for war)

75: **foreign mart**: international trade in weapons

76: **impress**: enforced military service

78: **toward**: in preparation

MARCELLUS
  'Tis gone and will not answer.

BERNARDO
  How now, Horatio! You tremble and look pale.
  Is not this something more than fantasy?   55
  What think you on't?

HORATIO
  Before my God, I might not this believe
  Without the sensible and true avouch
  Of mine own eyes.

MARCELLUS
                    Is it not like the King?

HORATIO
  As thou art to thyself.   60
  Such was the very armor he had on
  When he th' ambitious Norway combated.
  So frowned he once, when, in an angry parle
  He smote the sledded Polacks on the ice.
  'Tis strange.   65

MARCELLUS
  Thus twice before, and jump at this dead hour,
  With martial stalk hath he gone by our watch.

HORATIO
  In what particular thought to work I know not,
  But in the gross and scope of my opinion
  This bodes some strange eruption to our state.   70

MARCELLUS
  Good now, sit down, and tell me, he that knows,
  Why this same strict and most observant watch
  So nightly toils the subject of the land,
  And why such daily cast of brazen cannon
  And foreign mart for implements of war,   75
  Why such impress of shipwrights, whose sore task
  Does not divide the Sunday from the week.
  What might be toward, that this sweaty haste
  Doth make the night joint-laborer with the day?
  Who is't that can inform me?

HORATIO
                    That can I.   80
  At least, the whisper goes so. Our last king,
  Whose image even but now appeared to us,

84: **Thereto...pride**: inspired by his competitive nature to combat

87: **sealed compact**: mutually agreed upon contract

88: **heraldry**: the laws of combat

91: **moiety competent**: equal or appropriate portion

92: **gagèd**: engaged, pledged

95: **carriage of the article**: execution of the contract

97: **unimprovèd**: untried

98: **skirts**: outlying areas, borders

99: **Sharked up...resolutes**: gathered together men with motive to fight

101: **That hath a stomach in't**: requires courage

108: **post-haste and rummage**: feverish activity and commotion

112: **question**: cause

109-126: **I think...countrymen**: From the Second Quarto, these lines are included here because they explain the possibility of impending war with Norway, the appearance of Fortinbras, and the mobilization that has set the Danish soldiers on edge; it also helps to explain the mood of the castle and the country.

113: **mote**: a speck of dust, and thus negligible

114: **palmy**: flourishing

119: **Disasters in the sun**: threatening omens; **moist star**: the moon, which controls the tides

120: **Neptune's empire**: the sea (Neptune is the Roman god of the sea)

123: **harbingers**: heralds

124: **omen**; foretells evil to come

126: **climatures**: regions

Was, as you know, by Fortinbras of Norway
Thereto pricked on by a most emulate pride,
Dared to the combat; in which our valiant Hamlet–   85
For so this side of our known world esteemed him–
Did slay this Fortinbras, who by a sealed compact,
Well ratified by law and heraldry,
Did forfeit, with his life, all those his lands
Which he stood seized of, to the conqueror.   90
Against the which, a moiety competent
Was gagèd by our king, which had returned
To the inheritance of Fortinbras,
Had he been vanquisher, as, by the same covenant
And carriage of the article designed,   95
His fell to Hamlet. Now, sir, young Fortinbras,
Of unimprovèd mettle hot and full,
Hath in the skirts of Norway here and there
Sharked up a list of landless resolutes,
For food and diet, to some enterprise   100
That hath a stomach in't; which is no other–
As it doth well appear unto our state–
But to recover of us, by strong hand
And terms compulsatory those foresaid lands
So by his father lost. And this, I take it,   105
Is the main motive of our preparations,
The source of this our watch and the chief head
Of this post-haste and rummage in the land.

BERNARDO
    I think it be no other but e'en so.
    Well may it sort that this portentous figure   110
    Comes armèd through our watch; so like the king
    That was and is the question of these wars.

HORATIO
    A mote it is to trouble the mind's eye.
    In the most high and palmy state of Rome,
    A little ere the mightiest Julius fell,   115
    The graves stood tenantless and the sheeted dead
    Did squeak and gibber in the Roman streets;
    At stars with trains of fire and dews of blood,
    Disasters in the sun; and the moist star
    Upon whose influence Neptune's empire stands   120
    Was sick almost to doomsday with eclipse.
    And even the like precurse of fierce events,
    As harbingers preceding still the fates
    And prologue to the omen coming on,
    Have heaven and earth together demonstrated   125
    Unto our climatures and countrymen–

                                        Enter GHOST again

    But soft, behold! Lo, where it comes again!

128: **cross**: confront; **blast**: destroy

138: Stage Direction: *[The cock crows]*: This stage direction is from the Second Quarto. An early seventeenth century audience would have been aware of the significance of the sound of the morning rooster. Spirits could only walk the night and never during the day.

135: **happily**: fortunately

140: **partisan**: pike (a long-handled weapon)

152: **the god of day**: i.e., the Sun god, Apollo

154: **erring:** wandering around, out of its element; **hies**: hurries

156: **made probation**: demonstrated

Costume rendering for the Ghost from the 1934 production at the New Theatre directed by Sir John Gielgud.

Photo: Rare Book and Special Collections Library, University of Illinois at Urbana-Champaign

I'll cross it, though it blast me. Stay, illusion!
If thou hast any sound, or use of voice,
Speak to me.   130
If there be any good thing to be done,
That may to thee do ease and grace to me,
Speak to me!
If thou art privy to thy country's fate,
Which, happily, foreknowing may avoid, O, speak!   135
Or if thou hast uphoarded in thy life
Extorted treasure in the womb of earth,
For which, they say, you spirits oft walk in death,

[The cock crows]

Speak of it. Stay, and speak.–Stop it, Marcellus.

MARCELLUS
Shall I strike at it with my partisan?   140

HORATIO
Do, if it will not stand.

BERNARDO
                    'Tis here!

HORATIO
                    'Tis here!

Exit GHOST

MARCELLUS
'Tis gone!
We do it wrong, being so majestical,
To offer it the show of violence,
For it is, as the air, invulnerable,   145
And our vain blows malicious mockery.

BERNARDO
It was about to speak when the cock crew.

HORATIO
And then it started like a guilty thing
Upon a fearful summons. I have heard
The cock, that is the trumpet to the morn,   150
Doth with his lofty and shrill-sounding throat
Awake the god of day, and, at his warning,
Whether in sea or fire, in earth or air,
The extravagant and erring spirit hies
To his confine, and of the truth herein   155
This present object made probation.

158: **ever 'gainst**: just before

163: **takes**: enchants; **charm**: bewitches

164: **so gracious**: blessed

166-167: Robert Frost once wrote that he thought these two lines to be the most perfect verse in the English language:

> **But look, the morn, in russet mantle clad,**
> **Walks o'er the dew of yon high eastward hill.**

173: **As needful in our loves**: what they owe each other as comrades

MARCELLUS

    It faded on the crowing of the cock.
    Some say that ever 'gainst that season comes
    Wherein our Savior's birth is celebrated,
    The bird of dawning singeth all night long,   160
    And then, they say, no spirit dares stir abroad.
    The nights are wholesome; then no planets strike,
    No fairy takes, nor witch hath power to charm,
    So hallowed and so gracious is the time.

HORATIO

    So have I heard and do in part believe it.   165
    But look, the morn, in russet mantle clad,
    Walks o'er the dew of yon high eastward hill.
    Break we our watch up and by my advice,
    Let us impart what we have seen tonight
    Unto young Hamlet; for, upon my life,   170
    This spirit, dumb to us, will speak to him.
    Do you consent we shall acquaint him with it
    As needful in our loves, fitting our duty?

MARCELLUS

    Let's do't, I pray, and I this morning know
    Where we shall find him most conveniently.   175
                               Exeunt

0: Location: Within the castle

0: Scene: Conventionally set in a hall with thrones or sometimes with simple chairs (as in Gielgud's 1964 production), this scene contrasts sharply with the previous one, moving the action from the cold gray castle ramparts to the warmth and merriment of the court. Branagh makes the most of this contrast in his 1996 film with a colorful court scene, dressing Gertrude (Julie Christie) in a white wedding dress and Claudius (Derek Jacobi) in a scarlet coat. Hamlet stands by the throne, clad head-to-foot entirely in black. Peter Brook opened his 2005 *Hamlet* at the Court scene, only there is no court; Adrian Lester (Hamlet) sits alone. There were no thrones or chairs in this minimalist production; a simple orange-red square carpet was off-center with pillows carefully placed around it. Adrian Lester began the performance with Hamlet's soliloquy, "O that this too too sullied flesh would melt," placing the focus immediately and intensely on Hamlet.

tracks 2-4

1-16:
Andrew Cruickshank as Claudius
Edward de Souza as Claudius

4: **one brow of woe**: a collective mourning

5: **nature**: natural love

7: **remembrance of ourselves**: we must consider the living now

8: **sometime sister**: former sister-in-law

9: **jointress**: ruling jointly with Claudius

11: **one auspicious and one dropping**: feeling simultaneously hopeful and sorrowful

13: **dole**: sorrow

17: **know**: should be informed

18: **supposal**: opinion

20: **disjoint**: fractured; **out of frame**: order

23: **Importing**: concerning

31: **gait**: proceeding

38: **dilated articles**: detailed letters

Act 1, Scene 2]

Enter CLAUDIUS, King of Denmark, GERTRUDE, the Queen, HAMLET, POLONIUS, LAERTES, and his sister, OPHELIA, Lords Attendant.

CLAUDIUS
   Though yet of Hamlet our dear brother's death
   The memory be green, and that it us befitted
   To bear our hearts in grief and our whole kingdom
   To be contracted in one brow of woe,
   Yet so far hath discretion fought with nature   5
   That we with wisest sorrow think on him
   Together with remembrance of ourselves.
   Therefore our sometime sister, now our queen,
   Th' imperial jointress to this warlike state,
   Have we as 'twere with a defeated joy,   10
   With one auspicious and one dropping eye,
   With mirth in funeral and with dirge in marriage,
   In equal scale weighing delight and dole,
   Taken to wife. Nor have we herein barred
   Your better wisdoms, which have freely gone   15
   With this affair along. For all, our thanks.
   Now follows that you know young Fortinbras,
   Holding a weak supposal of our worth,
   Or thinking by our late dear brother's death
   Our state to be disjoint and out of frame,   20
   Colleaguèd with the dream of his advantage,
   He hath not failed to pester us with message
   Importing the surrender of those lands
   Lost by his father, with all bonds of law,
   To our most valiant brother. So much for him.   25

Enter VOLTEMAND and CORNELIUS

   Now for ourself, and for this time of meeting,
   Thus much the business is: we have here writ
   To Norway, uncle of young Fortinbras–
   Who, impotent and bed-rid scarcely hears
   Of this his nephew's purpose–to suppress   30
   His further gait herein, in that the levies,
   The lists and full proportions, are all made
   Out of his subject; and we here dispatch
   You, good Cornelius, and you, Voltemand,
   For bearing of this greeting to old Norway,   35
   Giving to you no further personal power
   To business with the King, more than the scope
   Of these dilated articles allow.
   Farewell, and let your haste commend your duty.

44: **the Dane**: the Danish King

45: **lose your voice**: waste your words

47: **native**: naturally connected, related

50: **Dread my lord**: i.e., my revered king

51: **leave and favor**: your permission and approval

58-60: **wrung from me...my hard consent**: From the Second Quarto, these lines are more consistent with the way Polonius speaks.

60: **will**: desire **hard**: reluctant

62: **Take they fair hour**: i.e., make the most of your youth (fair hour)

63: **at thy will**: as you decide

64: **cousin**: kinsman, relative

64: **But now my cousin Hamlet, and my son**: With these words, Claudius calls attention to the change in his relationship with his nephew. Gielgud set the scene on a nearly bare stage, intentionally stripped-down to look like a rehearsal. There was only a raised platform, a table, and two chairs set on the lower of the two levels. Characteristic of Gielgud, the focus is on the language rather than anything visual.

65: **A little more than kin**: Hamlet is related to Claudius in two ways: nephew to uncle and son to stepfather; **less than kind:** less than 1) natural, and 2) beneficent

67. **i' th' sun**: i.e., the sunshine of royal favor, and a play on sun/son. Claudius refers to him as his "son," and Hamlet is also referring to being the son of Gertrude and the dead King.

VOLTEMAND
    In that and all things will we show our duty.   40

CLAUDIUS
    We doubt it nothing. Heartily farewell.
                      Exeunt VOLTEMAND and CORNELIUS
    And now, Laertes, what's the news with you?
    You told us of some suit. What is't, Laertes?
    You cannot speak of reason to the Dane
    And lose your voice. What wouldst thou beg, Laertes,   45
    That shall not be my offer, not thy asking?
    The head is not more native to the heart,
    The hand more instrumental to the mouth,
    Than is the throne of Denmark to thy father.
    What wouldst thou have, Laertes?

LAERTES
               Dread my lord,   50
    Your leave and favor to return to France,
    From whence though willingly I came to Denmark
    To show my duty in your coronation,
    Yet now, I must confess, that duty done,
    My thoughts and wishes bend again toward France   55
    And bow them to your gracious leave and pardon.

CLAUDIUS
    Have you your father's leave? What says Polonius?

POLONIUS
    He hath, my lord, wrung from me my slow leave
    By laborsome petition, and at last
    Upon his will I sealed my hard consent.   60
    I do beseech you give him leave to go.

CLAUDIUS
    Take thy fair hour, Laertes. Time be thine,
    And thy best graces spend it at thy will.
    But now, my cousin Hamlet, and my son–

HAMLET
    A little more than kin and less than kind.   65

CLAUDIUS
    How is it that the clouds still hang on you?

HAMLET
    Not so, my lord, I am too much i' th' sun.

70: **vailèd lids** downcast eyes

72: **common**: common to all humans i.e., universal

75: **particular**: personal

77: **'Tis not alone my inky cloak**: Although he wears black for mourning, Hamlet is also talking about the "blackness" of his inner turmoil, confusion, and deep grief.

79: **windy suspiration**: deep sighs

80: **fruitful river**: copious tears

81: **dejected 'havior**: sad facial expressions

92: **obsequious sorrow**: dutiful mourning

93: **obstinate condolement**: deep sorrow, unwilling to be comforted

95: **most incorrect to heaven**: that goes against divine will

96: **unfortified**: not prepared for grief; **impatient**: not used to suffering

105: **first corse**: first corpse (referred to as "corse" during the Early Modern Period); a reference to Abel, the first human to die, murdered by his brother Cain

107: **unprevailing woe**: futile grief

GERTRUDE
    Good Hamlet, cast thy nightly color off,
    And let thine eye look like a friend on Denmark.
    Do not forever with thy vailèd lids   70
    Seek for thy noble father in the dust.
    Thou know'st 'tis common–all that lives must die,
    Passing through nature to eternity.

HAMLET
    Ay, madam, it is common.

GERTRUDE
                If it be,
    Why seems it so particular with thee?   75

HAMLET
    "Seems," madam? Nay it is. I know not "seems."
    'Tis not alone my inky cloak, good mother,
    Nor customary suits of solemn black,
    Nor windy suspiration of forced breath,
    No, nor the fruitful river in the eye,   80
    Nor the dejected 'havior of the visage,
    Together with all forms, moods, shapes of grief,
    That can denote me truly. These indeed "seem,"
    For they are actions that a man might play.
    But I have that within which passeth show,   85
    These but the trappings and the suits of woe.

CLAUDIUS
    'Tis sweet and commendable in your nature, Hamlet,
    To give these mourning duties to your father;
    But, you must know, your father lost a father;
    That father lost, lost his, and the survivor bound   90
    In filial obligation for some term
    To do obsequious sorrow. But to persever
    In obstinate condolement is a course
    Of impious stubbornness. 'Tis unmanly grief.
    It shows a will most incorrect to heaven,   95
    A heart unfortified, a mind impatient,
    An understanding simple and unschooled;
    For what we know must be and is as common
    As any the most vulgar thing to sense,
    Why should we in our peevish opposition   100
    Take it to heart? Fie, 'tis a fault to heaven,
    A fault against the dead, a fault to nature,
    To reason most absurd, whose common theme
    Is death of fathers, and who still hath cried,
    From the first corse till he that died today,   105
    'This must be so.' We pray you, throw to earth
    This unprevailing woe, and think of us

109: **most immediate**: next in line to succeed

113: **Wittenberg**: a famous German Protestant university founded in 1502 and site of the histori-cal posting of Martin Luther's treatises on 31 Oct.1517. After Luther, the University of Wittenberg became a well-known center for Reformation scholars and theologians.

114: **retrograde**: contrary; also to bend back on oneself, as in the orbit of Mars.

115: **bend**: yield, incline

124: **Sits smiling:** pleases; **in grace**: honor

125: **jocund**: merry

129: **solid**: substantial, living; the first and Second Quartos read "sallied," a word that is unde-fined in the *Oxford English Dictionary* [OED]. Many editors choose "sullied" as in "defiled."

129-159: **O, that this too...hold my tongue**: Other than "To be or not to be," this is possibly Hamlet's best known soliloquy. Directors (like editors) have to choose one of the two variant readings of the word in the opening line: Olivier, Burton, Jacobi, Gibson, and Branagh all chose the Folio reading "solid." Director Peter Brook chose "sullied" and had his Hamlet (Adrian Lester) mouth it carefully and precisely, as if to draw attention to the choice.

129-159:
Laurence Olivier as Hamlet
Sir Derek Jacobi as Hamlet

tracks 5-7

132: **canon**: law

134: **uses**: customs

137: **merely**: entirely

140: **Hyperion to a satyr**: as the sun god (a model of perfection) is to a satyr (a lustful half-goat creature and companion to Bacchus, the Roman god of wine)

141: **beteem**: permit

147: **ere**: before

As of a father, for let the world take note,
You are the most immediate to our throne,
And with no less nobility of love   110
Than that which dearest father bears his son
Do I impart toward you. For your intent
In going back to school in Wittenberg,
It is most retrograde to our desire.
And we beseech you, bend you to remain   115
Here, in the cheer and comfort of our eye,
Our chiefest courtier, cousin, and our son.

GERTRUDE
Let not thy mother lose her prayers, Hamlet.
I pray thee, stay with us. Go not to Wittenberg.

HAMLET
I shall in all my best obey you, madam.   120

CLAUDIUS
Why, 'tis a loving and a fair reply.
Be as ourself in Denmark. Madam, come.
This gentle and unforced accord of Hamlet
Sits smiling to my heart; in grace whereof,
No jocund health that Denmark drinks today,   125
But the great cannon to the clouds shall tell,
And the King's rouse the heavens shall bruit again,
Respeaking earthly thunder. Come, away.

Exeunt all but HAMLET

HAMLET
O, that this too too solid flesh would melt,
Thaw, and resolve itself into a dew,   130
Or that the Everlasting had not fixed
His canon 'gainst self-slaughter! O God! God!
How weary, stale, flat and unprofitable,
Seem to me all the uses of this world!
Fie on't! O fie, fie. 'Tis an unweeded garden   135
That grows to seed. Things rank and gross in nature
Possess it merely. That it should come to this!
But two months dead—nay, not so much, not two.
So excellent a king that was, to this,
Hyperion to a satyr, so loving to my mother   140
That he might not beteem the winds of heaven
Visit her face too roughly. Heaven and earth,
Must I remember? Why, she would hang on him,
As if increase of appetite had grown
By what it fed on, and yet, within a month—   145
Let me not think on't—frailty, thy name is woman—
A little month, or ere those shoes were old
With which she followed my poor father's body,

129-159:
Laurence Olivier as Hamlet
Sir Derek Jacobi as Hamlet

Colleen Dewhurst as Gertrude and James Earl Jones as Claudius in the 1971-72 Public Theater production directed by Gerald Freedman
Photo: George E. Joseph

149: **Niobe**: In Greek mythology, Niobe's grief at her children's death was so deep, she could not stop crying, even after she was turned to stone.

150: **wants discourse of reason**: lacks the ability to reason

153: **Hercules**: a Greek mythological hero of great strength

155: **gallèd**: inflamed and red

156: **post**: hurry

157: **incestuous**: refers to a forbidden sexual relationship between close relatives. Henry VIII based his divorce from Katharine of Aragon on a passage from Leviticus 18:16 forbidding marriage between a widow and her brother-in-law. However, this sort of remarriage was quite common in Germanic cultures.

163: **change**: exchange; that is, we will call each other "friend"

164: **what make you**: what are you doing away from

Like Niobe, all tears, why she, even she–
O, Heaven! a beast, that wants discourse of reason,   150
Would have mourned longer–married with my uncle,
My father's brother, but no more like my father
Than I to Hercules. Within a month,
Ere yet the salt of most unrighteous tears
Had left the flushing in her gallèd eyes,   155
She married. O, most wicked speed, to post
With such dexterity to incestuous sheets!
It is not, nor it cannot come to good.
But break my heart, for I must hold my tongue.

Enter HORATIO, BERNARDO, and MARCELLUS

HORATIO
Hail to your lordship!

HAMLET
                    I am glad to see you well–   160
Horatio–or I do forget myself.

HORATIO
The same, my lord, and your poor servant ever.

HAMLET
Sir, my good friend; I'll change that name with you.
And what make you from Wittenberg, Horatio?
Marcellus.   165

MARCELLUS
My good lord.

HAMLET
I am very glad to see you. Good even, sir.
But what, in faith, make you from Wittenberg?

HORATIO
A truant disposition, good my Lord.

HAMLET
I would not hear your enemy say so,   170
Nor shall you do mine ear that violence,
To make it truster of your own report
Against yourself. I know you are no truant.
But what is your affair in Elsinore?
We'll teach you to drink deep ere you depart.   175

HORATIO
My lord, I came to see your father's funeral.

179: **hard upon**: soon after

180-181: **The funeral...marriage tables**: Leftover food from the funeral was fresh enough to serve to guests at the wedding.

182: **dearest foe**: greatest enemy

193: **Season your admiration**: control your disbelief and astonishment

194: **attent**: attentive

HAMLET
I pray thee, do not mock me, fellow student;
I think it was to see my mother's wedding.

HORATIO
Indeed, my lord, it followed hard upon.

HAMLET
Thrift, thrift, Horatio! The funeral baked meats   180
Did coldly furnish forth the marriage tables.
Would I had met my dearest foe in heaven
Ere I had ever seen that day, Horatio!
My father! Methinks I see my father.

HORATIO
Where, my lord?

HAMLET
                    In my mind's eye, Horatio.   185

HORATIO
I saw him once; he was a goodly king.

HAMLET
He was a man. Take him for all in all,
I shall not look upon his like again.

HORATIO
My lord, I think I saw him yesternight.

HAMLET
Saw? Who?   190

HORATIO
My lord, the King your father.

HAMLET
The King my father?

HORATIO
Season your admiration for awhile
With an attent ear till I may deliver,
Upon the witness of these gentlemen,   195
This marvel to you.

HAMLET
For Heaven's love, let me hear.

201: Scene: **A figure like your father**: Since Sir John Gielgud's 1930 Hamlet, there has been an on-again, off-again tradition of doubling the roles of the Ghost and Claudius. One notable example is Peter Brook's 2005 Hamlet with Adrian Lester. Jeffery Kissooner played both roles and, under Brook's direction, he played them as not only brothers, but twin brothers, yet twins who were no more like each other "than I to Hercules." The effect was startling.

202: **point**: to the smallest detail; **cap-à-pie**: from head-to-foot

206: **truncheon**; a short staff as an officer might carry

207:**with the act of fear**: in the ways that fear affects them

220: **even**: just

224: **writ down**: prescribed

HORATIO
  Two nights together had these gentlemen,
  Marcellus and Bernardo, on their watch,
  In the dead waste and middle of the night,   200
  Been thus encountered. A figure like your father,
  Armed at point exactly, cap-à-pie,
  Appears before them, and with solemn march
  Goes slow and stately. By them thrice he walked,
  By their oppressed and fear-surprisèd eyes,   205
  Within his truncheon's length, whilst they, distilled
  Almost to jelly with the act of fear,
  Stand dumb and speak not to him. This to me
  In dreadful secrecy impart they did.
  And I with them the third night kept the watch,   210
  Where, as they had delivered, both in time,
  Form of the thing, each word made true and good,
  The apparition comes. I knew your father;
  These hands are not more like.

HAMLET
               But where was this?

MARCELLUS
  My lord, upon the platform where we watched.   215

HAMLET
  Did you not speak to it?

HORATIO
               My lord, I did,
  But answer made it none. Yet once methought
  It lifted up its head and did address
  Itself to motion, like as it would speak;
  But even then the morning cock crew loud,   220
  And at the sound it shrunk in haste away,
  And vanished from our sight.

HAMLET
              'Tis very strange.

HORATIO
  As I do live, my honored lord, 'tis true;
  And we did think it writ down in our duty
  To let you know of it.   225

HAMLET
  Indeed, indeed, sirs, but this troubles me.
  Hold you the watch tonight?

231: **beaver**: the front piece of head armor that lifts like a visor

232: **What**: How

Set rendering from the 1958 production at the Shakespeare Memorial Theatre directed by Glen Byam Shaw
Photo: Rare Book and Special Collections Library, University of Illinois at Urbana-Champaign

MARCELLUS and BERNARDO
                    We do, my lord.

HAMLET
  Armed, say you?

MARCELLUS and BERNARDO
                    Armed, my lord.

HAMLET
                              From top to toe?

MARCELLUS and BERNARDO
  My lord, from head to foot.

HAMLET
  Then saw you not his face?   230

HORATIO
  O, yes, my lord; he wore his beaver up.

HAMLET
  What, looked he frowningly?

HORATIO
  A countenance more in sorrow than in anger.

HAMLET
  Pale or red?

HORATIO
                  Nay, very pale.

HAMLET
  And fixed his eyes upon you?

HORATIO
                  Most constantly.   235

HAMLET
  I would I had been there.

HORATIO
  It would have much amazed you.

HAMLET
  Very like, very like. Stayed it long?

239: **tell**: count

241: **grisly**: gray

243: **sable silvered**: black sprinkled with white

244: **warrant**: guarantee

250: **hap**: occur

257: **doubt**: suspect

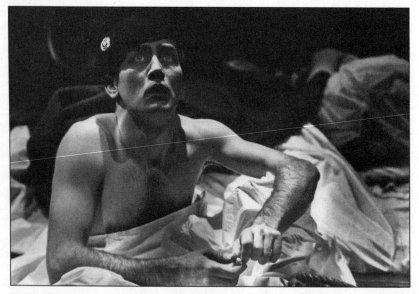

Martin Sheen as Hamlet in the 1967-68 Public Theater production directed by Joseph Papp
Photo: George E. Joseph

HORATIO
While one with moderate haste might tell a hundred.

MARCELLUS and BERNARDO
Longer, longer.   240

HORATIO
Not when I saw't.

HAMLET
                    His beard was grisly, no?

HORATIO
It was, as I have seen it in his life,
A sable silvered.

HAMLET
                    I will watch tonight;
Perchance 'twill walk again.

HORATIO
                    I warrant you it will.

HAMLET
If it assume my noble father's person,   245
I'll speak to it, though hell itself should gape
And bid me hold my peace. I pray you all,
If you have hitherto concealed this sight,
Let it be tenable in your silence still;
And whatsoever else shall hap tonight,   250
Give it an understanding, but no tongue.
I will requite your loves. So, fare you well.
Upon the platform, 'twixt eleven and twelve,
I'll visit you.

All
                    Our duty to your honor.

HAMLET
Your loves, as mine to you. Farewell.   255
                                            Exeunt all but HAMLET

My father's spirit in arms! All is not well.
I doubt some foul play. Would the night were come!
Till then sit still, my soul; foul deeds will rise,
Though all the earth o'erwhelm them, to men's eyes.

                                                            Exit

0: Location: Polonius' chambers

0: Scene: This domestic scene, often played with humor, is sometimes staged with a sense of sorrow, for this is the last time that Polonius's family will be together.

1: **embarked**: aboard ship

3: **convoy is assistant**: the ship is ready

6: **a toy in blood**: idle fancy, "toy" connotes childlike

7: **primy**: in its prime (youthful)

8: **Forward**: eager

9: **perfume and suppliance:** (from the Second Quarto) that which makes the moment sweet and pleasurable

11: **crescent**: growing

12: **thews**: muscles and sinews

14: **withal**: at the same time

15: **soil**: stain; **cautel**: deception

17: **greatness**: high rank

19. **unvalued**: common

20: **Carve**: choose

22: **circumscribed**: restricted

23: **voice...body**: vote and consent of the nation

25: **fits**: suits

26: **sect and force**: rank and power

27: **give his saying deed**: act on his word

28: **main voice**: collective voice. Denmark is (and was) an elected monarchy. Monarchs are elected from the nobility and though usually a direct descendent of the king, it is not always the case. Claudius was elected King by majority vote.

30. **If with too...list his songs**: i.e., if you believe everything he says

32: **unmastered**: uncontrolled

Act 1, Scene 3]

LAERTES
My necessaries are embarked. Farewell.
And, sister, as the winds give benefit
And convoy is assistant, do not sleep,
But let me hear from you.

OPHELIA
                    Do you doubt that?

LAERTES
For Hamlet and the trifling of his favors,   5
Hold it a fashion and a toy in blood,
A violet in the youth of primy nature,
Forward, not permanent, sweet, not lasting,
The perfume and suppliance of a minute,
No more.

OPHELIA
                    No more but so?

LAERTES
                              Think it no more.   10
For nature crescent does not grow alone
In thews and bulk, but as this temple waxes,
The inward service of the mind and soul
Grows wide withal. Perhaps he loves you now,
And now no soil nor cautel doth besmirch   15
The virtue of his will. But you must fear,
His greatness weighed, his will is not his own;
For he himself is subject to his birth.
He may not, as unvalued persons do,
Carve for himself, for on his choice depends   20
The sanctity and health of this whole state;
And therefore must his choice be circumscribed
Unto the voice and yielding of that body
Whereof he is the head. Then if he says he loves you,
It fits your wisdom so far to believe it   25
As he in his particular sect and force
May give his saying deed, which is no further
Than the main voice of Denmark goes withal.
Then weigh what loss your honor may sustain,
If with too credent ear you list his songs,   30
Or lose your heart, or your chaste treasure open
To his unmastered importunity.

34: **keep you...affection**: control your feelings

36: **chariest**: most careful

39: **The canker...spring**: the cankerworm destroys new blossoms

42: **Contagious blastments**: withering blights

44: **Youth...near**: young people are often rebellious even without temptation

47: **ungracious**: ungodly

49: **puffed and reckless libertine**: proud and unconstrained womanizer

57-81: In Gielgud's production, Polonius, brilliantly acted by Hume Cronyn (the first actor to receive a Tony Award in a Shakespearean role), delivers this advice to Laertes with a clipped business-like tone, emphasizing Polonius's craftiness and cunning.

51: **recks not his own rede**: heeds not his own advice

54: **Occasion...leave**: we have an opportunity to say good-bye again

tracks 8-10

55-81:
Norman Rodway as Polonius
Peter Jeffrey as Polonius

56: **sits in the shoulder of your sail**: is favorable for sea travel

57: **you are stayed for**: i.e., they are waiting for you

59: **See thou character**: i.e., take note, remember this

60: **unproportioned**: unruly

61: **familiar**: friendly; **vulgar**: indiscriminate

65: **unfledged**: immature

67: **Bear't**: accept with conviction

69: **censure**: opinion

70: **habit**: dress

71: **in fancy**: in excess

73-74: **they in France...chief in that**: i.e., the French Nobility display their taste and breeding in their apparel

Fear it, Ophelia, fear it, my dear sister,
And keep you in the rear of your affection,
Out of the shot and danger of desire.   35
The chariest maid is prodigal enough
If she unmask her beauty to the moon.
Virtue itself 'scapes not calumnious strokes.
The canker galls the infants of the spring
Too oft before their buttons be disclosed,   40
And in the morn and liquid dew of youth
Contagious blastments are most imminent.
Be wary then; best safety lies in fear;
Youth to itself rebels, though none else near.

OPHELIA
I shall th' effect of this good lesson keep   45
As watchman to my heart. But, good my brother,
Do not, as some ungracious pastors do,
Show me the steep and thorny way to heaven,
Whiles, like a puffed and reckless libertine
Himself the primrose path of dalliance treads,   50
And recks not his own rede.

LAERTES
                    O, fear me not.

                                              Enter POLONIUS

I stay too long. But here my father comes.
A double blessing is a double grace,
Occasion smiles upon a second leave.

POLONIUS
Yet here, Laertes? Aboard, aboard, for shame!   55
The wind sits in the shoulder of your sail,
And you are stayed for. There—my blessing with thee!
And these few precepts in thy memory
See thou character. Give thy thoughts no tongue,
Nor any unproportioned thought his act.   60
Be thou familiar, but by no means vulgar.
Those friends thou hast, and their adoption tried,
Grapple them to thy soul with hoops of steel,
But do not dull thy palm with entertainment
Of each unhatched, unfledged comrade. Beware   65
Of entrance to a quarrel, but being in,
Bear't that the opposèd may beware of thee.
Give every man thy ear, but few thy voice.
Take each man's censure, but reserve thy judgment.
Costly thy habit as thy purse can buy,   70
But not expressed in fancy; rich, not gaudy;
For the apparel oft proclaims the man,
And they in France of the best rank and station
Are of a most select and generous chief in that.
Neither a borrower nor a lender be,   75

55-81:
Norman Rodway as Polonius
Peter Jeffrey as Polonius

77: **husbandry**: thrift

78: "This above all, to thine own self be true.": David Sabin as Polonius and Bo Foxworth as Laertes in the Shakespeare Theatre Company's 2001 production directed by Gale Edwards
Photo: Carol Rosegg

81: **season**: ripen, mature

83: **tend**: wait

91: **Marry**: By the Virgin Mary

94: **audience**: attentive company

95: **'tis put on me**: it is reported to me

100: **tenders**: offers

102: **green**: inexperienced

103: **Unsifted**: untested, naive

104: **"tenders"**: counters used in gambling (note contrast in use of "tenders" in 1.3.108 and 1.3.110)

For loan oft loses both itself and friend,
And borrowing dulls the edge of husbandry.
This above all, to thine own self be true,
And it must follow, as the night the day,
Thou canst not then be false to any man.   80
Farewell. My blessing season this in thee.

LAERTES
Most humbly do I take my leave, my lord.

POLONIUS
The time invites you. Go, your servants tend.

LAERTES
Farewell, Ophelia, and remember well
What I have said to you.   85

OPHELIA
'Tis in my memory locked,
And you yourself shall keep the key of it.

LAERTES
Farewell.

Exit [LAERTES]

POLONIUS
What is't, Ophelia, he hath said to you?

OPHELIA
So please you, something touching the Lord Hamlet.   90

POLONIUS
Marry, well bethought.
'Tis told me, he hath very oft of late
Given private time to you, and you yourself
Have of your audience been most free and bounteous.
If it be so—as so 'tis put on me,   95
And that in way of caution—I must tell you,
You do not understand yourself so clearly
As it behooves my daughter and your honor.
What is between you? Give me up the truth.

OPHELIA
He hath, my lord, of late made many tenders   100
Of his affection to me.

POLONIUS
Affection, puh! You speak like a green girl,
Unsifted in such perilous circumstance.
Do you believe his "tenders," as you call them?

108: **sterling**: true currency; **Tender**: regard

110: **Running...a fool**; i.e., if you keep acting this way, you'll make me look foolish; **tender me:** 1) show me, and 2) make me look like

113: **"fashion"**: a whim; **Go to**: i.e., enough of this (an expression of impatience)

116: **springes...woodcocks**: traps to easily catch stupid and foolish birds

119: **extinct**: extinguished

120-121: **Even...for fire**: i.e., don't mistake the fire of passion for true love

123-124: **Set...parley**: i.e., do not surrender your virginity to his sweet talk

125: **in**: concerning

126: **a larger tether**: i.e., more freedom, referring to men having more freedom to act on their impulses than women.

127: **In few**: In short

128: **brokers**: go-betweens

129: **investments**: clerical vestments

130: **implorators**: solicitors

134: **slander**: disgrace

133-135: "I would not, in plain terms, from this time forth / Have you so slander any moment leisure / As to give words or talk with the Lord Hamlet.": Bill Murray as Polonius and Julia Stiles as Ophelia in the 2000 film directed by Michael Almereyda
Photo: Larry Riley © Miramax Films. Courtesy of Douglas Lanier

OPHELIA
I do not know, my lord, what I should think.   105

POLONIUS
Marry, I'll teach you. Think yourself a baby
That you have ta'en these tenders for true pay
Which are not sterling. Tender yourself more dearly,
Or—not to crack the wind of the poor phrase,
Running it thus—you'll tender me a fool.   110

OPHELIA
My lord, he hath importuned me with love
In honorable fashion.

POLONIUS
Ay, "fashion" you may call it. Go to, go to.

OPHELIA
And hath given countenance to his speech, my lord,
With almost all the holy vows of heaven.   115

POLONIUS
Ay, springes to catch woodcocks. I do know,
When the blood burns, how prodigal the soul
Gives the tongue vows. These blazes, daughter,
Giving more light than heat, extinct in both,
Even in their promise, as it is a-making,   120
You must not take for fire. From this time daughter,
Be somewhat scanter of your maiden presence.
Set your entreatments at a higher rate
Than a command to parley. For Lord Hamlet,
Believe so much in him, that he is young   125
And with a larger tether may he walk
Than may be given you. In few, Ophelia,
Do not believe his vows, for they are brokers,
Not of that dye which their investments show,
But mere implorators of unholy suits,   130
Breathing like sanctified and pious bawds
The better to beguile. This is for all:
I would not, in plain terms, from this time forth
Have you so slander any moment leisure
As to give words or talk with the Lord Hamlet.   135
Look to't, I charge you. Come your ways.

OPHELIA
I shall obey, my lord.
                                                    Exeunt

0: Location: The guard platform

0: Scene: As in 1.1, this scene is often staged on a platform or a set that resembles a castle tower or walkway. Zeffirelli constructed a castle for the film with a Germanic-style hall reminiscent of a medieval mead-hall. His Hamlet, like Olivier's, looks down on the King and Queen through an opening in the ceiling designed to act as a vent to the open-pit fire below, and comments on the fatal flaw of Denmark–wassailing. Ironically, it is wassailing cup that will hold the poisoned drink in 5.2.

1: **shrewdly**: sharply. The Second Quarto's word order "it is very cold" suits the modern ear; the First Folio reads, "is it very cold?"

2: **eager**: bitter

7: **wont**: custom

10: **wassail**: drinking party; **upspring reels**: German dances associated with heavy drinking

11: **Rhenish**: Rhine wine

13: **The triumph of his pledge**: the king's ability to drain his cup in one draft

16: **to the manner born**: i.e., born into the customs of his country

17: **breach**: breaking (of the custom)

18-39: **This heavy-handed...scandal**: These lines appear only in the Second Quarto; they may have been cut in performance in deference to the English Queen, Anne of Denmark.

19: **taxed**: blamed

20: **clepe**: call

21: **addition**: reputation (literally a title of honor)

22: **at height**: excellently

Act 1, Scene 4]

Enter HAMLET, HORATIO, and MARCELLUS

HAMLET
The air bites shrewdly; it is very cold.

HORATIO
It is a nipping and an eager air.

HAMLET
What hour now?

HORATIO
I think it lacks of twelve.

HAMLET
No, it is struck.   5

HORATIO
Indeed? I heard it not. Then it draws near the season
Wherein the spirit held his wont to walk.

[Noise within the castle]

What does this mean, my lord?

HAMLET
The king doth wake tonight and takes his rouse,
Keeps wassail, and the swaggering upspring reels,   10
And, as he drains his draughts of Rhenish down,
The kettle-drum and trumpet thus bray out
The triumph of his pledge.

HORATIO
                          Is it a custom?

HAMLET
Ay, marry, is't,
And to my mind, though I am native here   15
And to the manner born, it is a custom
More honored in the breach than the observance.
This heavy-headed revel east and west
Makes us traduced and taxed of other nations.
They clepe us drunkards, and with swinish phrase   20
Soil our addition; and indeed it takes
From our achievements, though performed at height,

23: **pith...attribute**: essence of our reputation

25: **mole of nature**: natural fault, blemish

27: **his**: its

28: **o'ergrowth of some complexion**: refers to the increase of one of the four "humours," the controlling essences of man's psychological and physical well-being

29: **pales and forts**: fences and ramparts (castle defenses)

30: **o'erleavens**: mixes with and corrupts

31: **plausive**: pleasing

33: **Being Nature's livery**: having an identifying mark; **Fortune's star**: chance astrological events

35: **undergo**: sustain

37-39: **The dram...scandal**: i.e., one significant fault can ruin an otherwise good reputation and negatively stereotype an entire group

43: **airs**: gentle breezes; **blasts**: pestilent winds

49: **canonized**: consecrated; **hearsèd**: coffined

51: **enurned**: entombed

54: **complete steel**: armor (referring to the Ghost's dress and appearance). The Ghost is usually dressed as Horatio describes him here.

55: **glimpses of the moon**: flickering moonlight

56: **we fools of Nature**: us mere mortals

57: **shake our disposition**: disturb us

61: **impartment**: communication

The pith and marrow of our attribute.
So, oft it chances in particular men,
That for some vicious mole of nature in them,   25
As in their birth wherein they are not guilty–
Since Nature cannot choose his origin–
By the o'ergrowth of some complexion,
Oft breaking down the pales and forts of reason,
Or by some habit that too much o'erleavens   30
The form of plausive manners, that these men,
Carrying, I say, the stamp of one defect,
Being Nature's livery, or Fortune's star,
His virtues else, be they as pure as grace,
As infinite as man may undergo,   35
Shall in the general censure take corruption
From that particular fault. The dram of evil
Doth all the noble substance of a dout
To his own scandal.

Enter GHOST

HORATIO
    Look, my lord, it comes!   40

HAMLET
    Angels and Ministers of grace defend us!
    Be thou a spirit of health or goblin damned,
    Bring with thee airs from heaven or blasts from hell,
    Be thy intents wicked or charitable,
    Thou comest in such a questionable shape   45
    That I will speak to thee. I'll call thee Hamlet,
    King, Father, Royal Dane. Oh, oh, answer me,
    Let me not burst in ignorance, but tell
    Why thy canonized bones, hearsèd in death,
    Have burst their cerements; why the sepulcher,   50
    Wherein we saw thee quietly enurned,
    Hath oped his ponderous and marble jaws,
    To cast thee up again. What may this mean
    That thou, dead corse, again in complete steel
    Revisits thus the glimpses of the moon,   55
    Making night hideous, and we fools of Nature
    So horridly to shake our disposition
    With thoughts beyond the reaches of our souls?
    Say, why is this? Wherefore? What should we do?

[GHOST beckons HAMLET]

HORATIO
    It beckons you to go away with it,   60
    As if it some impartment did desire
    To you alone.

64: **waves**: beckons

68: **pin's fee**: practically worthless

72-77: **What if it...madness:** Because Horatio does not know what the apparition is, he tries to warn Hamlet that the Ghost may be threatening his life, perhaps by drawing him to the edge of a cliff where he could fall and drown, or by dragging him into madness.

73: **summit**: from the Second Quarto; the First Folio reads "sonnet," which doesn't fit in this description

74: **beetles o'er**: juts out, an overhang

76: **deprive...Reason**: i.e., make you mad

78-81: **The very place...beneath:** These four lines appear only in the Second Quarto; they are included here because they complete Horatio's thought about the lure and danger of the sea.

78: **desperation**: frantic impulses

79: **motive**: cause

82: **wafts**: wave, as in to beckon

86: **artery**: In Elizabethan times, arteries were thought to carry vital spirits.

Nicholas Farrell as Horatio, Kenneth Branagh as Hamlet, and Jack Lemmon as Marcellus in the 1996 film directed by Kenneth Branagh
Photo: Rolf Konow © Columbia TriStar. Courtesy of Douglas Lanier

MARCELLUS
Look with what courteous action
It waves you to a more removèd ground.
But do not go with it.

HORATIO
No, by no means.   65

HAMLET
It will not speak. Then I will follow it.

HORATIO
Do not, my lord.

HAMLET
Why, what should be the fear?
I do not set my life at a pin's fee;
And for my Soul, what can it do to that,
Being a thing immortal as itself?   70
It waves me forth again. I'll follow it.

HORATIO
What if it tempt you toward the flood, my lord,
Or to the dreadful summit of the cliff
That beetles o'er his base into the sea,
And there assume some other horrible form,   75
Which might deprive your sovereignty of Reason
And draw you into madness? Think of it.
The very place puts toys of desperation,
Without more motive, into every brain
That looks so many fathoms to the sea   80
And hears it roar beneath.

HAMLET
It wafts me still. Go on. I'll follow thee.

MARCELLUS
You shall not go, my lord.

HAMLET
Hold off your hand.

HORATIO
Be ruled, you shall not go.

HAMLET
My fate cries out,   85
And makes each petty artery in this body

87: **Nemean lion**: In Greek mythology, the Nemean lion was a ferocious mythological beast slain by Hercules as one of his twelve labors.

89: **lets**: hinders, holds me back

92: **'Tis not fit thus to obey him**: In Germanic warrior society, the custom of *comitatus* would forbid men from abandoning their leader.

93: **Have after**: Go on; **issue**: end

95: **direct it**: determine the outcome

Costume rendering for Marcellus from the 1958 production at the Shakespeare Memorial Theatre directed by Glen Byam Shaw
Photo: Rare Book and Special Collections Library, University of Illinois at Urbana-Champaign

As hardy as the Nemean lion's nerve.
Still am I called? Unhand me, gentlemen.
By heaven, I'll make a ghost of him that lets me!
I say away! Go on, I'll follow thee.   90

Exeunt GHOST and HAMLET

HORATIO
He waxes desperate with imagination.

MARCELLUS
Let's follow. 'Tis not fit thus to obey him.

HORATIO
Have after. To what issue will this come?

MARCELLUS
Something is rotten in the state of Denmark.

HORATIO
Heaven will direct it.

MARCELLUS
                    Nay, let's follow him.   95

Exeunt

0: Location: The castle battlements

0: Scene: The apparition scene can be interpreted in many different ways. For Olivier, the Ghost was a specter in armor with a hint of a death mask flashing as he nodded his head. Olivier carries his hilted sword in front of him as he follows the Ghost, as if the cross-shape of the hilt will protect him from the peril the night holds. Mel Gibson does the same thing. Sir John Gielgud is the voice of the Ghost in his 1964 Broadway production. Gielgud's Ghost remains unseen by the audience, but it casts a large shadow over the dark stage. Tony Richardson's (1969) Ghost is neither an apparition nor a shadow. Rather we view him only through Hamlet's (Nicole Williamson) eyes, his face blanched with the white and hoary reflection cast by the spirit. The Ghost's voice is Williamson's, a choice that makes us wonder if the Ghost is not simply a voice in Hamlet's mind. Paul Scofield's interpretation in Zeffirelli's 1992 film is riveting, and his is one of the few Ghosts to appear without armor, his face and head uncovered and visible. His hand, hovering over his face, cries out in anguish about the horrors of the unredeemed and unforgiven dead. In Almereyda's film, Sam Shepard enters his son's modern New York-style apartment dressed in a long black trench coat and looking very human. He can touch his son (Ethan Hawke) and they embrace at the end of the scene while Shepard voices a desperate, "Remember me," as do Lester (Hamlet) and Kissooner (the Ghost) in Brook's *Hamlet*.

12: **to fast in fires:** to do penance in Purgatory. In the Elizabethan Christian belief system, people who died without being confessed, or shriven, had to spend time in Purgatory where their sins could be burned away or "purged."

13: **crimes...days of Nature:** sins committed during my natural life

8: "So art thou to revenge, when thou shalt hear.": Clifford Rose as Ghost and Kenneth Branagh as Hamlet in the Royal Shakespeare Company's 1992 production directed by Adrian Noble
Photo: Donald Cooper

Act 1, Scene 5]

HAMLET
  Where wilt thou lead me? Speak. I'll go no further.

GHOST
  Mark me.

HAMLET
                I will.

GHOST
                              My hour is almost come
  When I to sulphurous and tormenting flames
  Must render up myself.

HAMLET
                Alas, poor ghost!

GHOST
  Pity me not, but lend thy serious hearing   5
  To what I shall unfold.

HAMLET
  Speak, I am bound to hear.

GHOST
  So art thou to revenge, when thou shalt hear.

HAMLET
  What?

GHOST
  I am thy father's spirit,   10
  Doomed for a certain term to walk the night,
  And for the day confined to fast in fires,
  Till the foul crimes done in my days of Nature
  Are burnt and purged away. But that I am forbid
  To tell the secrets of my prison house,   15
  I could a tale unfold whose lightest word
  Would harrow up thy soul, freeze thy young blood,
  Make thy two eyes, like stars, start from their spheres,
  Thy knotted and combinèd locks to part
  And each particular hair to stand on end,   20
  Like quills upon the fretful porcupine.

22: **eternal blazon**: display of the afterlife
23: **List**: listen

25: Scene: In Gielgud's 1964 production, Burton reacted to the Ghost with an instantly recognizable kind of madness. He shifted between mockery, laughter, and misery from one line to the next and the audience reacted in kind.

With respect to Sarah Bernhardt's flighty and "comic" portrayal of Hamlet to Edwin Booth's more serious performance, the feminist critic Elizabeth Robbins wrote in a December 1900 review that, "Madame Bernhardt took the story of the apparition with less surprise than Booth. He stood during the scene, alert, keen to his finger tips, to listen to so strange a story. Madam Bernhardt sat and crossed her legs." Still, Robbins continued, "I think her scenes with the Ghost appealed to me more than anything else she did; particularly the first, where Hamlet's awe is shown to be modified, softened, by his great filial affection...I never got so vivid an impression of the warm, personal relationship between the buried Majesty of Denmark and his son as Madame Bernhardt."

34: **fat**: gross, ugly
35: **Lethe**: one of the four rivers in Hades; Lethe is the river of forgetfulness
39: **a forgèd process**: a lie, a tale meant to deceive
40: **abused**: deceived

41-42: "The serpent that did sting thy father's life / Now wears his crown.": Richard Easton as Ghost and Roger Rees as Hamlet in the Royal Shakespeare Company's 1984 production directed by Ron Daniels
Photo: Donald Cooper

43: **adulterate**: lustful, adulterous

But this eternal blazon must not be
To ears of flesh and blood. List, Hamlet, O, list!
If thou didst ever thy dear father love–

HAMLET
O Heaven!   25

GHOST
Revenge his foul and most unnatural murder.

HAMLET
Murder!

GHOST
Murder most foul, as in the best it is,
But this most foul, strange and unnatural.

HAMLET
Haste, haste me to know it,   30
that with wings as swift
As meditation, or the thoughts of love,
May sweep to my revenge.

GHOST
                      I find thee apt;
And duller shouldst thou be than the fat weed
That roots itself in ease on Lethe wharf,   35
Wouldst thou not stir in this. Now, Hamlet, hear.
'Tis given out that, sleeping in my orchard,
A serpent stung me. So the whole ear of Denmark
Is by a forgèd process of my death
Rankly abused. But know, thou noble youth,   40
The serpent that did sting thy father's life
Now wears his Crown.

HAMLET
                      O my prophetic soul. Mine uncle?

GHOST
Ay, that incestuous, that adulterate beast,
With witchcraft of his wit, with traitorous gifts–
O wicked wit and gifts, that have the power   45
So to seduce–won to his shameful lust
The will of my most seeming-virtuous queen.
O Hamlet, what a falling-off was there,
From me, whose love was of that dignity
That it went hand-in-hand even with the vow   50
I made to her in marriage, and to decline
Upon a wretch whose natural gifts were poor
To those of mine. But virtue, as it never will be moved,

56: **sate itself**: be unable to go further

61: **hebonon**: a deadly poisonous plant

62: **porches**: vestibules, entryways

63: **leprous distilment**: a mixture that causes leper-like scales on the skin

67: **possett**: curdle

68: **eager**: acid-like

70: **a most instant tetter barked about**: scaly, bark-like rash covered the body

71: **lazar-like**: like Lazarus, the leper

74: **dispatched**: removed

75: **blossoms of my sin**: unconfessed sins

76: **unaneled**: killed without a chance to confess his sins. The Last Rites, or *Extreme Unction*, was one of the seven Catholic sacraments, and included the absolution of sins.

82: **luxury**: lechery

84-85: **Taint not...mother aught**: i.e., do not harm your mother

88: **matin**: the earliest prayer of the day, recited just before dawn

92: **couple**: include

96: **distracted globe**: a reference to Hamlet's confused and baffled mind as well as the Globe theatre and its audience

97: **table of my memory**: references Hamlet's life; that is, what he has been taught, his expectations, and his perceptions of reality

Though lewdness court it in a shape of heaven,
So lust, though to a radiant angel linked,   55
Will sate itself in a celestial bed, and prey on garbage.
But, soft, methinks I scent the morning's air.
Brief let me be. Sleeping within my orchard,
My custom always of the afternoon,
Upon my secure hour thy uncle stole   60
With juice of cursèd hebenon in a vial,
And in the porches of mine ears did pour
The leprous distilment, whose effect
Holds such an enmity wi' th' blood of man
That swift as quicksilver it courses through   65
The natural gates and alleys of the body,
And with a sudden vigor doth posset
And curd, like eager droppings into milk,
The thin and wholesome blood. So did it mine,
And a most instant tetter barked about,   70
Most lazar-like, with vile and loathsome crust,
All my smooth body.
Thus was I, sleeping, by a brother's hand
Of Life, of Crown, of Queen, at once dispatched,
Cut off even in the blossoms of my sin,   75
Unhouseled, disappointed, unaneled,
No reckoning made, but sent to my account
With all my imperfections on my head.
O horrible, O horrible, most horrible!
If thou hast nature in thee, bear it not;   80
Let not the royal bed of Denmark be
A couch for luxury and damnèd incest.
But, howsoever thou pursuest this act,
Taint not thy mind, nor let thy soul contrive
Against thy mother aught. Leave her to heaven   85
And to those thorns that in her bosom lodge
To prick and sting her. Fare thee well at once.
The glow-worm shows the matin to be near,
And 'gins to pale his uneffectual fire.
Adieu, adieu, Hamlet. Remember me.   90
                                                                            Exit

HAMLET
O all you host of heaven! O earth! What else?
And shall I couple hell? O, fie! Hold, my heart,
And you, my sinews, grow not instant old,
But bear me stiffly up. Remember thee?
Ay, thou poor ghost, while memory holds a seat   95
In this distracted globe. Remember thee?
Yea, from the table of my memory
I'll wipe away all trivial fond records,

99: **all saws...past**: all advice and custom, and all expectations

101: **thy commandment**: i.e., the charge to revenge his father's murder

106: **My tables...down**: i.e., my memories and plans for the future are now replaced with a new reality upon the Ghost's charge, "Remember me."

This scene is often interpreted literally–as if the "tables" are tablets or notebooks that Hamlet carries around writing impressions or events, much like a diary. However, it seems that he is talking about his memory ("tables" being metaphorical) and the changes in his perceptions of the world because of the shock of the apparition, the tale of murder, and the subsequent demand for revenge, a revenge that will now change the course of Hamlet's life. Burton is one of the few performers to "wipe away" his memories, not by writing in a "tablet" or notebook, but by sweeping his hand across his brow as if to erase something there.

109: **word**: promise

115: **Hillo...come**: the common cry of the falconer, meant to bring a hunting bird back to the arm (or other roost)

All saws of books, all forms, all pressures past,
That youth and observation copied there,   100
And thy commandment all alone shall live
Within the book and volume of my brain,
Unmixed with baser matter. Yes, yes, by heaven!
O most pernicious woman!
O villain, villain, smiling, damnèd villain!   105
My tables, my tables–meet it is I set it down,
That one may smile, and smile, and be a villain.
At least I'm sure it may be so in Denmark.
So, uncle, there you are. Now to my word–
It is "Adieu, adieu, remember me."   110
I have sworn't.

HORATIO and MARCELLUS
[*Within*] My lord. My Lord.

                              Enter HORATIO and MARCELLUS

MARCELLUS
                    Lord Hamlet!

HORATIO
                         Heaven secure him.

HAMLET
  So be it.

HORATIO
  Illo, ho, ho, my Lord!

HAMLET
  Hillo, ho, ho, boy! Come, bird, come.   115

MARCELLUS
  How is't, my noble Lord?

HORATIO
                    What news, my Lord?

HAMLET
  O, wonderful!

HORATIO
  Good my Lord, tell it.

HAMLET
                    No, you'll reveal it.

123: **arrant**: complete

126: **circumstance**: details, elaborate speech

135: **St. Patrick**: in the Roman Catholic belief system, St. Patrick was thought to be the keeper of the Gate to Purgatory (as St. Peter is to Heaven's gate). This is particularly noteworthy when one realizes that Hamlet has been attending Wittenberg, one of the centers for the Protestant Reformation. Here, and in other places, Hamlet refers to a particularly Roman Catholic belief.

136: **offense**: referring to offenses against the welfare of the kingdom and against moral sensibilities

137: **an honest ghost**: a genuine or truthful apparition

HORATIO
    Not I, my Lord, by heaven–

MARCELLUS
                Nor I, my Lord.

HAMLET
    How say you, then? Would heart of man once think it?   120
    But you'll be secret?

HORATIO and MARCELLUS
                Ay, by heaven, my Lord.

HAMLET
    There's ne'er a villain dwelling in all Denmark
    But he's an arrant knave.

HORATIO
    There needs no ghost, my lord, come from the grave
    To tell us this.

HAMLET
                Why, right; you are i' th' right.   125
    And so, without more circumstance at all,
    I hold it fit that we shake hands and part.
    You, as your business and desires shall point you,
    For every man has business and desire,
    Such as it is; and for mine own poor part,   130
    Look you, I'll go pray.

HORATIO
    These are but wild and whirling words, my Lord.

HAMLET
    I'm sorry they offend you, heartily–
    Yes, 'faith, heartily.

HORATIO
                There's no offense, my Lord.

HAMLET
    Yes, by Saint Patrick, but there is, Horatio,   135
    And much offense too. Touching this vision here,
    It is an honest ghost, that let me tell you,
    For your desire to know what is between us,
    O'ermaster't as you may. And now, good friends,
    As you are friends, scholars and soldiers,   140
    Give me one poor request.

145: In...not I: i.e., I swear to never reveal this

146: Upon my sword: Swearing on a sword was common for Christians because the hilt forms a cross: it was common for Germanic people because of the sacred nature of warrior society.

Staging of the Ghost scene
Drawing by C. Walter Hodges by permission of Cambridge University Press

149: truepenny: trusty fellow

150: cellerage: an area beneath the stage; this is a direct reference to the performance space

155: *Hic et ubique*: Latin for here and everywhere

HORATIO
What is't, my Lord? We will.

HAMLET
Never make known what you have seen tonight.

HORATIO and MARCELLUS
My lord, we will not.

HAMLET
                    Nay, but swear't.

HORATIO
In faith, my Lord, not I.

MARCELLUS
                    Nor I, my Lord, in faith.   145

HAMLET
Upon my sword.

MARCELLUS
                    We have sworn, my Lord, already.

HAMLET
Indeed, upon my sword, indeed.

GHOST
Swear—

                                        GHOST cries under the stage

HAMLET
Ah, ha, boy! Sayest thou so? Art thou there, truepenny? Come on—you
hear this fellow in the cellarage—consent to swear.   150

HORATIO
Propose the oath, my lord.

HAMLET
Never to speak of this that you have seen.
Swear by my sword.

GHOST
Swear–

HAMLET
Hic et ubique? Then we'll shift our ground.   155
Come hither, gentlemen,

162: **pioner**: foot soldier who marches in advance of the army to dig trenches; **remove**: to move to another spot

164: **And therefore...welcome**: Welcoming strangers (including travelers) was an old custom in most societies; it is the root of what the Greeks called *xenia* and what is now called hospitality.

166: **our philosophy**: i.e., what was usually comprehended as being "real"

170: **antic disposition**: behavior of a madman

172: **encumbered**: folded

173: **doubtful**: nonsensical

174: **an if**: if

175: **list**: liked

177: **aught**: anything

184: **friending**: friendship

185: **not lack**: be left undone

186: **still**: keep

187: **out of joint**: disordered, irregular

And lay your hands again upon my sword.
Never to speak of this that you have heard,
Swear by my sword.

GHOST
Swear–   160

HAMLET
Well said, old mole! Canst work i' th' ground so fast?
A worthy pioner! Once more remove, good friends.

HORATIO
O day and night, but this is wondrous strange!

HAMLET
And therefore as a stranger give it welcome.
There are more things in heaven and earth, Horatio,   165
Than are dreamt of in our philosophy. But come,
Here, as before, never, so help you mercy,
How strange or odd so e'er I bear myself,
As I perchance hereafter shall think meet
To put an antic disposition on–   170
That you, at such time seeing me, never shall,
With arms encumbered thus, or this headshake,
Or by pronouncing of some doubtful phrase,
As "Well, well, we know," or "We could, an if we would,"
Or "If we list to speak," or "There be, an if they might,"   175
Or such ambiguous giving out, to note
That you know aught of me–this not to do,
So grace and mercy at your most need help you,
Swear.

GHOST
Swear!   180
                                              [They swear]

HAMLET
Rest, rest, perturbed spirit! So, gentlemen,
With all my love I do commend me to you.
And what so poor a man as Hamlet is
May do, t'express his love and friending to you,
God willing, shall not lack. Let us go in together;   185
And still your fingers on your lips, I pray.
The time is out of joint. O cursèd spite,
That ever I was born to set it right!
Nay, come, let's go together

                                              Exeunt

[Hamlet

Act 2

0: Location: In Polonius's chambers

8: **Inquire me**: inquire for me; **Danskers**: Danish people

9: **keep:** live

11: **drift of question**: roundabout questioning

14: **Take you**: pretend

20: **put on**: attribute to

21: **forgeries**: deceptions, lies; **rank**: foul

Act 2, Scene 1]

POLONIUS
Give him this money and these notes, Reynaldo.

REYNALDO
I will, my Lord.

POLONIUS
You shall do marvelous wisely, good Reynaldo,
Before you visit him, to make inquiry
Of his behavior.   5

REYNALDO
My lord, I did intend it.

POLONIUS
Marry, well said, very well said. Look you, sir,
Inquire me first what Danskers are in Paris,
And how, and who, what means, and where they keep,
What company, at what expense; and finding   10
By this encompassment and drift of question
That they do know my son, come you more nearer
Than your particular demands will touch it.
Take you, as 'twere, some distant knowledge of him,
As thus, "I know his father and his friends,   15
And, in part, him." Do you mark this, Reynaldo?

REYNALDO
Ay, very well, my Lord.

POLONIUS
"And in part him, but," you may say, "not well,
But, if't be he I mean, he's very wild,
Addicted so and so"; and there put on him   20
What forgeries you please. Marry, none so rank
As may dishonor him–take heed of that–
But, sir, such wanton, wild, and usual slips
As are companions noted and most known
To youth and liberty.

REYNALDO
                        As gaming, my Lord?   25

27: **drabbing**: whoring

29: **season**: initiate, begin

31: **incontinency**: licentiousness

35: **unreclaimèd**: not restrained; **of general assault**: common to all young men

40: **a fetch of warrant**: a justifiable and clever trick

41. **sullies**: gossip

42: **i' th' working**: as it is being worked on

43: **party**: partner

44: **prenominate crimes**: aforementioned wrongdoings

46: **closes...consequence**: confides in you like this

48: **phrase**: expression; **addition**: title of address

POLONIUS
Ay, or drinking, fencing, swearing,
Quarrelling, drabbing—you may go so far.

REYNALDO
My Lord, that would dishonor him.

POLONIUS
Faith, no, as you may season it in the charge,
You must not put another scandal on him;   30
That he is open to incontinency,
That's not my meaning, but breathe his faults so quaintly
That they may seem the taints of liberty,
The flash and outbreak of a fiery mind,
A savageness in unreclaimèd blood, of general assault.   35

REYNALDO
But, my good Lord—

POLONIUS
Wherefore should you do this?

REYNALDO
Ay, my Lord, I would know that.

POLONIUS
Marry, sir, here's my drift,
And I believe it is a fetch of warrant.   40
You laying these slight sullies on my son,
As 'twere a thing a little soiled i' th' working,
Mark you, your party in converse, him you would sound,
Having ever seen in the prenominate crimes
The youth you breathe of guilty, be assured   45
He closes with you in this consequence;
"Good sir," or so, or "friend," or "gentleman,"
According to the phrase or the addition
Of man and country.

REYNALDO
                    Very good, my Lord.

POLONIUS
And then, sir, does he this—he does—what was I about to say? By the mass,   50
I was about to say something. Where did I leave?

REYNALDO
At "closes in the consequence," at "friend or so," and "gentleman."

58: **falling out**: a quarreling

60: *Videlicet*: that is to say; namely

62: **reach**: wide understanding

63: **windlasses**: circuitous routes (in hunting); **assays**: attempts; **bias**: (from the game of bowls) the weighting of the bowl that directs it to a certain point

64: **By indirections...out**: i.e., to slyly question in a roundabout way, and through that, come to the truth

65: **former**: preceding

66: **You have me**: i.e., you get my meaning

69: **in**: for

71: **ply**: practice

Costume rendering for Reynaldo from the 1934 production at the New Theatre directed by Sir John Gielgud
Photo: Rare Book and Special Collections Library, University of Illinois at Urbana-Champaign

POLONIUS
  At "closes in the consequence," ay, marry!
  He closes with you thus: "I know the gentleman.
  I saw him yesterday, or th'other day,   55
  Or then, or then, with such, or such, and, as you say,
  "There was he gaming, there o'ertook in's rouse,
  There falling out at tennis", or perchance,
  "I saw him enter such a house of sale,"
  Videlicet, a brothel, or so forth. See you now—   60
  Your bait of falsehood takes this carp of truth;
  And thus do we of wisdom and of reach,
  With windlasses and with assays of bias,
  By indirections find directions out.
  So, by my former lecture and advice,   65
  Shall you my son. You have me, have you not?

REYNALDO
  My Lord, I have.

POLONIUS
                God be wi'you. Fare you well.

REYNALDO
  Good my Lord.

POLONIUS
  Observe his inclination in yourself.

REYNALDO
  I shall, my Lord.   70

POLONIUS
  And let him ply his music.

REYNALDO
                Well, my Lord.

POLONIUS
  Farewell!

                                          Exit REYNALDO
                                          Enter OPHELIA

  How now, Ophelia! What's the matter?

OPHELIA
  Alas my Lord, I have been so affrighted!

77: **unbraced**: unfastened

79: **down-gyvèd to his ankles**: fallen down around his ankles, like a prisoners fetters or chains, called "gyves"

99: **their light**: Light was thought to be the source of sight; the eyes took in light and released it again.

101: **ecstasy**: insanity

102: **property fordoes**: quality destroys

POLONIUS
    With what, in the name of Heaven?   75

OPHELIA
    My lord, as I was sewing in my chamber,
    Lord Hamlet, with his doublet all unbraced,
    No hat upon his head, his stockings fouled,
    Ungartered, and down-gyvèd to his ankle,
    Pale as his shirt, his knees knocking each other,   80
    And with a look so piteous in purport
    As if he had been loosèd out of hell
    To speak of horrors, he comes before me.

POLONIUS
    Mad for thy love?

OPHELIA
                 My lord, I do not know,
    But truly, I do fear it.

POLONIUS
                 What said he?   85

OPHELIA
    He took me by the wrist and held me hard.
    Then goes he to the length of all his arm,
    And, with his other hand thus o'er his brow,
    He falls to such perusal of my face
    As he would draw it. Long stayed he so.   90
    At last, a little shaking of mine arm
    And thrice his head thus waving up and down,
    He raised a sigh so piteous and profound
    That it did seem to shatter all his bulk
    And end his being. That done, he lets me go,   95
    And, with his head over his shoulder turned,
    He seemed to find his way without his eyes,
    For out o' doors he went without their help,
    And to the last bended their light on me.

POLONIUS
    Go with me. I will go seek the King.   100
    This is the very ecstasy of love,
    Whose violent property fordoes itself
    And leads the will to desperate undertakings
    As oft as any passion under heaven
    That does afflict our natures. I am sorry.   105
    What, have you given him any hard words of late?

108-109: "I did repel his letters and denied / His access to me.": Kate Winslet as Ophelia and Richard Briers as Polonius in the 1996 film directed by Kenneth Branagh
Photo: Rolf Konow © Columbia TriStar. Courtesy of Douglas Lanier

111: **coted**: observed

112: **wreck**: ruin through seduction; **beshrew my jealousy**: curse my suspicions

113: **It seems...age**: i.e., it is natural to old people

114: **To cast**: to go too far

117: **close**: secret

118: **More grief...love**: i.e., cause more sorrow if kept hidden than cause hatred if revealed

OPHELIA
    No, my good lord, but, as you did command,
    I did repel his letters and denied
    His access to me.

POLONIUS
                That hath made him mad.
    I am sorry that with better heed and judgment   110
    I had not coted him. I feared he did but trifle
    And meant to wreck thee. But, beshrew my jealousy!
    It seems it is as proper to our age
    To cast beyond ourselves in our opinions
    As it is common for the younger sort   115
    To lack discretion. Come, go we to the king.
    This must be known, which, being kept close, might move
    More grief to hide than hate to utter love.

                                      Exeunt

0: Location: The castle

0: Scene: In a clear break from the Romantic era interpretation of Hamlet and the court, the Birmingham Repertory Theatre (1925) created a 1920s image of a wealthy family, reminiscent of the way we might imagine that time through the lens of 1920s movies or a Noel Coward play. Act 2.2 opened in a richly decorated living room with "The Charleston" playing on a gramophone, a chain-smoking and sullen Hamlet, and the queen placed downstage nonchalantly playing bridge with an older woman and the court chaplain.

4: **sending**: summons

7: **that**: what

12: **neighbored:** familiar; **'havior:** temperament

16: **occasion**: opportunity

18: **opened**: revealed

21: **adheres**: is attached

22: **gentry**: courtesy

23-24: **expend your time...hope**: i.e., your staying longer gives us hope (because of what you might find out)

27: **of**: over

28: **dread**: revered

30: **full bent**: fullest extent, as when an arrow is drawn full and bends the bow

Act 2, Scene 2]

CLAUDIUS
Welcome, dear Rosencrantz and Guildenstern.
Moreover that we much did long to see you,
The need we have to use you did provoke
Our hasty sending. Something have you heard
Of Hamlet's transformation–so I call it,   5
Since nor th' exterior nor the inward man
Resembles that it was. What it should be,
More than his father's death, that thus hath put him
So much from the understanding of himself
I cannot dream of. I entreat you both,   10
That being of so young days brought up with him,
And since so neighbored to his youth and 'havior,
That you vouchsafe your rest here in our court
Some little time, so by your companies
To draw him on to pleasures, and to gather,   15
So much as from occasion you may glean,
Whether aught, to us unknown, afflicts him thus,
That, opened, lies within our remedy.

GERTRUDE
Good gentlemen, he hath much talked of you,
And sure I am two men there are not living   20
To whom he more adheres. If it will please you
To show us so much gentry and good will
As to expend your time with us awhile,
For the supply and profit of our hope,
Your visitation shall receive such thanks   25
As fits a king's remembrance.

ROSENCRANTZ
                Both your majesties
Might, by the sovereign power you have of us,
Put your dread pleasures more into command
Than to entreaty.

GUILDENSTERN
                We both obey,
And here give up ourselves, in the full bent   30
To lay our service freely at your feet,
To be commanded.

38: **practices**: actions

42: **still**: always

44-45: "I hold my duty, as I hold my soul, / Both to my God and to my gracious King.": Felix Aylmer as Polonius, Basil Sydney as Claudius, Eileen Herlie as Gertrude, and ensemble in the 1948 film directed by Laurence Olivier
Courtesy of Douglas Lanier

47: **policy**: cleverness

52: **fruit**: (from the Second Quarto) dessert

55: **head**: the source

CLAUDIUS
Thanks, Rosencrantz and gentle Guildenstern.

GERTRUDE
Thanks, Guildenstern and gentle Rosencrantz.
And I beseech you instantly to visit   35
My too much changèd son. Go, some of you,
And bring these gentlemen where Hamlet is.

GUILDENSTERN
Heavens make our presence and our practices
Pleasant and helpful to him!

GERTRUDE
                    Amen!

                              Exeunt ROSENCRANTZ, GUILDENSTERN
                                                    Enter POLONIUS

POLONIUS
The ambassadors from Norway, my good Lord,   40
Are joyfully returned.

CLAUDIUS
Thou still hast been the father of good news.

POLONIUS
Have I, my Lord? I assure my good liege,
I hold my duty, as I hold my soul,
Both to my God and to my gracious King.   45
And I do think—or else this brain of mine
Hunts not the trail of policy so sure
As it hath used to do—that I have found
The very cause of Hamlet's lunacy.

CLAUDIUS
O, speak of that, that do I long to hear.   50

POLONIUS
Give first admittance to the ambassadors.
My news shall be the fruit to that great feast.

CLAUDIUS
Thyself do grace to them, and bring them in.

                                          Exit POLONIUS

He tells me, my sweet Queen, he hath found
The head and source of all your son's distemper.   55

56: **doubt...main**: suspect it is the primary subject

58: **sift**: subtly question, perhaps through a process of elimination

59: **brother Norway**: fellow King

60: **desires**: good wishes

61: **Upon our first**: i.e., when we first arrived

63: **Polack**: the King of Poland

67: **falsely borne**: systematically deceived

67-68: **sends out ...Fortinbras:** i.e., orders Fortinbras to stop his preparations

69: **in fine**: in conclusion

71: **assay of arms**: military campaign

79: **regards of...allowance**: terms of safety for Denmark and permission for Fortinbras

80: **likes**: pleases

81: **considered**: convenient (when he has had time to think about it)

86: **expostulate**: speak about the matter

GERTRUDE
    I doubt it is no other but the main,
    His father's death, and our o'erhasty marriage.
                    Enter POLONIUS, VOLTEMAND, and CORNELIUS

CLAUDIUS
    Well, we shall sift him. Welcome, my good friends!
    Say, Voltemand, what from our brother Norway?

VOLTEMAND
    Most fair return of greetings and desires.   60
    Upon our first, he sent out to suppress
    His nephew's levies, which to him appeared
    To be a preparation 'gainst the Polack;
    But, better looked into, he truly found
    It was against your highness; whereat grieved   65
    That so his sickness, age, and impotence
    Was falsely borne in hand, sends out arrests
    On Fortinbras, which he, in brief, obeys,
    Receives rebuke from Norway, and, in fine,
    Makes vow before his uncle never more   70
    To give the assay of arms against your majesty.
    Whereon old Norway, overcome with joy,
    Gives him three thousand crowns in annual fee
    And his commission to employ those soldiers,
    So levied as before, against the Polack,   75
    With an entreaty, herein further shown,
    That it might please you to give quiet pass
    Through your dominions for this enterprise,
    On such regards of safety and allowance
    As therein are set down.

CLAUDIUS
                    It likes us well;   80
    And at our more considered time we'll read,
    Answer, and think upon this business.
    Meantime we thank you for your well-took labor.
    Go to your rest; at night we'll feast together.
    Most welcome home!
                 Exeunt VOLTEMAND, CORNELIUS and others

POLONIUS
               This business is very well ended.   85
    My liege, and madam, to expostulate
    What majesty should be, what duty is,
    Why day is day, night, night, and time is time,
    Were nothing but to waste night, day, and time.
    Therefore, since brevity is the soul of wit,   90

91: **flourishes**: ornaments

96: **More matter, with less art**: i.e., get to the matter (the point) quickly

99: **a foolish figure**: referring to a foolish figure of speech and the foolish figure speaking

104: **For this...by cause**: i.e., a lack of love caused a lack of reason

105: **Perpend**: consider this

106: **she is mine**: An unmarried daughter "belonged" to her father; sometimes referred to as "bridling."

111: **a vile phrase**: Polonius is criticizing Hamlet's composition skills.

114: **stay**: wait; **I will be faithful**: i.e., I'll read it as I promised

115-119: **Doubt**: can be read several ways: "Do you think?" Do you believe?" "Do you suspect?"

115-122: Scene: In the film, *Shakespeare in Love*, Joseph Fiennes (as Shakespeare) recites this verse to Philip Henslowe (Geoffrey Rush), proving to Henslowe that the poet is suffering a terrible case of writer's block. In Almereyda's 2000 film, Hamlet (Ethan Hawke) recites the verse before he writes it down. The scene begins with Hamlet walking the city streets, and ends in a coffee shop/ diner where he sits, with a voice over reciting, while he writes down, "Doubt that the stars are fire."

119: **reckon my groans**: count my lover's sighs (a fairly frank reference to sex)

121-122: **whilst this machine is to him**: i.e., as long as I live

124: **more above**: in addition

125: **fell out**: happened

And tediousness the limbs and outward flourishes,
I will be brief. Your noble son is mad.
Mad call I it, for to define true madness,
What is't but to be nothing else but mad.
But let that go.   95

GERTRUDE
More matter, with less art.

POLONIUS
Madam, I swear I use no art at all.
That he is mad 'tis true; 'tis true 'tis pity;
And pity it is true–a foolish figure.
But farewell it, for I will use no art.   100
Mad let us grant him, then; and now remains
That we find out the cause of this effect,
Or rather say, the cause of this defect,
For this effect defective, comes by cause.
Thus it remains, and the remainder thus. Perpend,   105
I have a daughter–have while she is mine–
Who, in her duty and obedience, mark,
Hath given me this. Now gather, and surmise.
                              The Letter.
To the celestial and my soul's idol, the most beautified Ophelia–   110
That's an ill phrase, a vile phrase; "beautified" is a vile phrase.
But you shall hear these, in her excellent white bosom, these.

GERTRUDE
Came this from Hamlet to her?

POLONIUS
Good madam, stay awhile, I will be faithful.
    "Doubt thou the stars are fire,   115
    Doubt that the sun doth move,
    Doubt truth to be a liar,
    But never doubt I love."
O dear Ophelia, I am ill at these numbers. I have not art to reckon my groans.
But that I love thee best, O most best, believe it. Adieu.   120
        Thine evermore most dear lady, whilst
            this machine is to him, Hamlet.

This, in obedience, hath my daughter shown me,
And more above, hath his soliciting,
As they fell out by time, by means, and place,   125
All given to mine ear.

130: **fain**: gladly

135: **If...table-book**: i.e., if I had kept this to myself

136: **mute and dumb**: without reacting outwardly

138: **round**: directly

139: **bespeak**: address

140: **out of thy star**: above your social rank; yet another reference to the stars (heavenly bodies) and how they dominate humankind's movements

146-150: **Fell into...wail for:** Polonius describes the decline into love-madness: from sadness, to loss of appetite, to insomnia, to lightheadedness, to insanity.

151: "It may be very likely.": Glenn Close as Gertrude and Alan Bates as Claudius in the 1990 film directed by Franco Zeffirelli

Copyright © 1990 Icon Distribution, Inc. Courtesy of Douglas Lanier

CLAUDIUS
But how hath she received his love?

POLONIUS
What do you think of me?

CLAUDIUS
As of a man faithful and honorable.

POLONIUS
I would fain prove so. But what might you think,   130
When I had seen this hot love on the wing,
As I perceived it, I must tell you that,
Before my daughter told me, what might you,
Or my dear majesty, your queen here, think,
If I had played the desk or table-book,   135
Or given my heart a winking, mute and dumb,
Or looked upon this love with idle sight.
What might you think? No, I went round to work,
And-my young mistress-thus I did bespeak,
"Lord Hamlet is a prince, out of thy star.   140
This must not be." And then I precepts gave her,
That she should lock herself from his resort,
Admit no messengers, receive no tokens,
Which done, she took the fruits of my advice;
And he, repulsèd-a short tale to make-   145
Fell into a sadness, then into a fast,
Thence to a watch, thence into a weakness,
Thence to a lightness, and, by this declension,
Into the madness wherein now he raves,
And all we wail for.

CLAUDIUS
                    Do you think 'tis this?   150

GERTRUDE
It may be very likely.

POLONIUS
Hath there been such a time-I'd fain know that-
That I have positively said 'tis so,
When it proved otherwise?

CLAUDIUS
                    Not that I know.

155: **Take this...from this:** Usually directors chose to have Polonius point from his head to his shoulder to clarify the meaning of this line.

158: **the center:** the middle of the earth, **try:** test

162: **arras:** a heavy wall hanging or tapestry hung on castle walls intended to keep out cold drafts

164: **thereon:** on that amount

166: **carters:** wagon drivers

Sam Waterston as Hamlet in the 1975-76 Public Theatre production directed by Michael Rudman
Photo: George E. Joseph

167: **sadly:** gravely, seriously

169: **board him:** accost him

tracks 11-12

170-210:
Simon Russell Beale as Hamlet and Norman Rodway as Polonius

171: **God 'a mercy:** thank you

POLONIUS
    Take this from this, if this be otherwise.   155
    If circumstances lead me, I will find
    Where truth is hid, though it were hid indeed
    Within the center.

CLAUDIUS
                How may we try it further?

POLONIUS
    You know, sometimes he walks four hours together
    Here in the lobby.

GERTRUDE
                So he has indeed.   160

POLONIUS
    At such a time I'll loose my daughter to him.
    [*To CLAUDIUS*] Be you and I behind an arras then.
    Mark the encounter. If he love her not,
    And be not from his reason fallen thereon,
    Let me be no assistant for a state,   165
    But keep a farm and carters.

CLAUDIUS
                We will try it.

                      Enter HAMLET, reading on a book

GERTRUDE
    But look where sadly the poor wretch comes reading.

POLONIUS
    Away, I do beseech you, both away.
    I'll board him presently.

                  Exeunt CLAUDIUS and GERTRUDE
    Oh give me leave. How does my good Lord Hamlet?   170

HAMLET
    Well, God-a-mercy.

POLONIUS
    Do you know me, my lord?

HAMLET
    Excellent, excellent well. Y'are a fishmonger.

POLONIUS
    Not I, my lord.

tracks 11-12

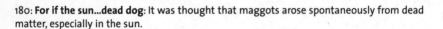

170-210:
Simon Russell Beale as Hamlet and Norman Rodway as Polonius

180: **For if the sun...dead dog**: It was thought that maggots arose spontaneously from dead matter, especially in the sun.

183-184: **Let her not...may conceive**: If a woman walked outdoors (in the sun), she might very well meet a man (and get pregnant). Hamlet is also referring to conceiving an idea as well as a child.

189: "Words, words, words.": David Sabin as Polonius and Wallace Acton as Hamlet in the Shakespeare Theatre Company's 2001 production directed by Gale Edwards
Photo: Carol Rosegg

190: **matter**: the matter that he reads, and the matter (or issue) that has changed Hamlet

194: **purging**: discharging; **amber**: resin or thick liquid (as in rheumy eyes)

197: **honesty**: honorable

HAMLET
Then I would you were so honest a man.   175

POLONIUS
Honest, my lord?

HAMLET
Ay, sir. To be honest, as this world goes, is to be one man picked out of
ten thousand.

POLONIUS
That's very true, my lord.

HAMLET
For if the sun breed maggots in a dead dog, being a good kissing carrion–   180
have you a daughter?

POLONIUS
I have, my lord.

HAMLET
Let her not walk i' th' sun. Conception is a blessing, but not as your
daughter may conceive. Friend, look to't.

POLONIUS
[Aside] How say you by that? Still harping on my daughter, yet he knew   185
me not at first; he said I was a fishmonger. He is far gone, far gone. And
truly in my youth I suffered much extremity for love, very near this. I'll
speak to him again. What do you read, my lord?

HAMLET
Words, words, words.

POLONIUS
What is the matter, my lord?   190

HAMLET
Between who?

POLONIUS
I mean the matter that you read, my Lord.

HAMLET
Slanders, sir; for the satirical slave says here that old men have gray
beards, that their faces are wrinkled, their eyes purging thick amber or
plum-tree gum, and that they have a plentiful lack of wit, together with   195
weak hams. All which, sir, though I most powerfully and potently
believe, yet I hold it not honesty to have it thus set down; for yourself, sir,
should be old as I am, if like a crab you could go backward.

tracks 11-12

170-210:
Simon Russell Beale as Hamlet and Norman Rodway as Polonius

199-200: Will you...the air: Outside air was believed to be unhealthy, especially to the sick.

202: pregnant: heavy with meaning

204: prosperously: successfully

217: indifferent: ordinary, uncaring

218: Happy: fortunate

219: button: highest point

POLONIUS
[*Aside*] Though this be madness, yet there is method in't.–Will you walk
out of the air, my lord?   200

HAMLET
Into my grave?

POLONIUS
Indeed, that is out o' the air. [*Aside*] How pregnant sometimes his replies
are! A happiness that often madness hits on, which reason and sanity
could not so prosperously be delivered of. I will leave him, and suddenly
contrive the means of meeting between him and my daughter.–My   205
honorable lord, I will most humbly take my leave of you.

HAMLET
You cannot, sir, take from me anything that I will more willingly part
withal–except my life, my life.

POLONIUS
Fare you well, my lord.

HAMLET
These tedious old fools!   210

POLONIUS
You go to seek the Lord Hamlet; there he is.
                    Enter ROSENCRANTZ and GUILDENSTERN

ROSENCRANTZ
God save you, sir!

                                        [Exit POLONIUS]

GUILDENSTERN
My honored lord!

ROSENCRANTZ
My most dear lord!

HAMLET
My excellent good friends! How dost thou, Guildenstern? O, Rosencrantz!   215
Good lads, how do ye both?

ROSENCRANTZ
As the indifferent children of the earth.

GUILDENSTERN
Happy in that we are not over-happy,
On Fortune's cap we are not the very button.

223: **privates**: intimates, but also a pun on private parts (genitalia)

228-229: "What have you, my good friends, deserved at the hands of / Fortune, that she sends you to prison hither?": Andrew Long as Rosencrantz, Wallace Acton as Hamlet, and Antony Hagopian as Guildenstern in the Shakespeare Theatre Company's 2001 production directed by Gale Edwards
Photo: Carol Rosegg

233: **goodly:** vast; **confines, wards, and dungeons**: kinds of imprisonment

HAMLET
   Nor the soles of her shoe?   220

ROSENCRANTZ
   Neither, my lord.

HAMLET
   Then you live about her waist, or in the middle of her favors?

GUILDENSTERN
   Faith, her privates we.

HAMLET
   In the secret parts of Fortune? O, most true—she is a strumpet. What's
   the news?   225

ROSENCRANTZ
   None, my lord, but that the world's grown honest.

HAMLET
   Then is doomsday near. But your news is not true. Let me question more
   in particular. What have you, my good friends, deserved at the hands of
   Fortune, that she sends you to prison hither?

GUILDENSTERN
   Prison, my lord?   230

HAMLET
   Denmark's a prison.

ROSENCRANTZ
   Then is the world one.

HAMLET
   A goodly one, in which there are many confines, wards, and dungeons,
   Denmark being one o' th' worst.

ROSENCRANTZ
   We think not so, my lord.   235

HAMLET
   Why, then, 'tis none to you; for there is nothing either good or bad, but
   thinking makes it so. To me it is a prison.

ROSENCRANTZ
   Why then, your ambition makes it one; 'tis too narrow for your mind.

243: "A dream itself is but a shadow.": Roger Rees as Hamlet, Christopher Ravenscroft as Rosencrantz, and Arthur Kohn as Guildenstern in the Royal Shakespeare Company's 1984 production directed by Ron Daniels
Photo: Donald Cooper

247: **fey**: faith

248: **wait**: accompany

249: **sort**: class

250: **dreadfully attended**: carefully watched

251: **beaten way**: well-worn path

254: **too dear**: not worth

255: **free**: voluntary

259: **modesties**: sense of decency

260: **color**: disguise

HAMLET

O God, I could be bounded in a nutshell and count myself a king of
infinite space, were it not that I have bad dreams. 240

GUILDENSTERN

Which dreams, indeed, are ambition, for the very substance of the
ambitious is merely the shadow of a dream.

HAMLET

A dream itself is but a shadow.

ROSENCRANTZ

Truly, and I hold ambition of so airy and light a quality that it is but a
shadow's shadow. 245

HAMLET

Then are our beggar's bodies and our monarchs and outstretched heroes, the
beggars' shadows. Shall we to the court? For, by my fey, I cannot reason.

ROSENCRANTZ and GUILDENSTERN

We'll wait upon you.

HAMLET

No such matter. I will not sort you with the rest of my servants, for, to
speak to you like an honest man, I am most dreadfully attended. But, in 250
the beaten way of friendship, what make you at Elsinore?

ROSENCRANTZ

To visit you, my lord; no other occasion.

HAMLET

Beggar that I am, I am even poor in thanks, but I thank you, and sure,
dear friends, my thanks are too dear a halfpenny. Were you not sent for?
Is it your own inclining? Is it a free visitation? Come, deal justly with me. 255
Come, come; nay, speak.

GUILDENSTERN

What should we say, my lord?

HAMLET

Why, anything but to the purpose. You were sent for, and there is a kind
of confession in your looks, which your modesties have not craft enough
to color. I know the good King and Queen have sent for you. 260

ROSENCRANTZ

To what end, my lord?

262: **conjure**: solemnly request, think of

263: **consonancy**: friendship

269-281: Scene: In Zeffirelli's film, Hamlet (Mel Gibson) recites these lines outside, under a blue and white, cloud-filled sky. In 1600, Richard Burbage had the advantage of a "heavens" literally fretted with golden fire. The Elizabethan stage was built with a roof over it and under the roof was painted a ceiling or "heavens" with golden stars and comets shooting cross the blue background. The "groundlings" stood around the stage (as one can do today at Shakespeare's New Globe Theatre in London) and could easily look up to see the heavens to which Hamlet referred.

270: **moult no feather**: remain intact

272: **disposition**: i.e., melancholy, depression

274: **oe'rhanging firmament**: double-meaning–the heavens and the star-painted roof over-hanging the Elizabethan stage

275: **fretted**: adorned

277: **faculty**: natural gifts

278: **express**: precise

280: **quintessence of dust**: Dust was believed to be the element (the others are earth, air, fire, and water) out of which man was made. According to Genesis 2.7 and 3.19: "For thou art dust and unto dust thou shalt return."

284: **Lenten entertainment**: During Lent (the forty days before Easter in the Catholic Liturgical Calendar), the theaters in London were closed while in court, entertainment was permitted to continue as usual.

285: **coted**: passed

288: **foil and target**: sword and shield

290: **o' th' sear**: primed to laugh. A "sear" is the catch in a gunlock that keeps the hammer cocked until ready to fire.

290-291: **the Lady...halt for't**: i.e., recite the verse accurately or the poetry and performance will suffer

HAMLET

That, you must teach me. But let me conjure you by the rights of our fellowship, by the consonancy of our youth, by the obligation of our ever-preserved love, and by what more dear a better proposer could charge you withal, be even and direct with me, whether you were sent for or no?   265

ROSENCRANTZ

[*Aside to GUILDENSTERN*] What say you?

HAMLET

Nay, then, I have an eye of you.–If you love me, hold not off.

GUILDENSTERN

My lord, we were sent for.

HAMLET

I will tell you why. So shall my anticipation prevent your discovery, and your secrecy to the King and Queen moult no feather. I have of late – but   270
wherefore I know not–lost all my mirth, forgone all custom of exercises; and indeed it goes so heavily with my disposition that this goodly frame, the earth, seems to me a sterile promontory. This most excellent canopy, the air, look you, this brave o'erhanging firmament, this majestical roof fretted with golden fire–why, it appears no other thing to me than a foul   275
and pestilent congregation of vapors. What a piece of work is a man! How noble in reason, how infinite in faculty, in form and moving how express and admirable, in action how like an angel, in apprehension how like a god! The beauty of the world, the paragon of animals! And yet, to me, what is this quintessence of dust? Man delights not me–no, nor   280
woman neither, though by your smiling you seem to say so.

ROSENCRANTZ

My lord, there was no such stuff in my thoughts.

HAMLET

Why did you laugh then, when I said "Man delights not me"?

ROSENCRANTZ

To think, my lord, if you delight not in man, what Lenten entertainment the players shall receive from you. We coted them on the way, and hither   285
are they coming, to offer you service.

HAMLET

He that plays the king shall be welcome–his majesty shall have tribute of me; the adventurous knight shall use his foil and target; the lover shall not sigh gratis; the humorous man shall end his part in peace; the Clown shall make those laugh whose lungs are tickled o' th' sear; and the Lady shall say   290
her mind freely, or the blank verse shall halt for't. What players are they?

292: **tragedians**: actors (players)

293: **residence**: performance venue

295: **late innovation**: i.e., the new, popular theater

296: **estimation**: esteem

300: **keeps**: continues; **wonted**: usual

301: **eyases**: young birds of prey as in "aerie"; an eagle's nest. This refers to the company of boy actors performing at Blackfriars who were so popular that they threatened the income of London's adult playing companies.

303-304: **many wearing...quills**: Gentlemen (who wore rapiers) often fear the poet's pen.

305: **escoted**: provided for

306: **quality**: profession

309: **succession**: later employment

311-312: **There was...question**: i.e., companies couldn't even sell a play unless it addressed the current controversy between the child companies and the adult players

312: **went to cuffs**: fight

314: **much throwing about of brains**: a great battle of wits

ROSENCRANTZ
Even those you were wont to take delight in, the tragedians of the city.

HAMLET
How chances it they travel? Their residence, both in reputation and profit, was better both ways.

ROSENCRANTZ
I think their inhibition comes by the means of the late innovation. 295

HAMLET
Do they hold the same estimation they did when I was in the city? Are they so followed?

ROSENCRANTZ
No, indeed, are they not.

HAMLET
How comes it? Do they grow rusty?

ROSENCRANTZ
Nay, their endeavor keeps in the wonted pace. But there is, sir, an aerie 300
of children, little eyases, that cry out on the top of question, and are most tyrannically clapped for't. These are now the fashion, and so berattle the common stages–so they call them–that many wearing rapiers are afraid of goose-quills and dare scarce come thither.

HAMLET
What, are they children? Who maintains 'em? How are they escoted? 305
Will they pursue the quality no longer than they can sing? Will they not say afterwards, if they should grow themselves to common players–as it is most like, if their means are no better–their writers do them wrong, to make them exclaim against their own succession?

ROSENCRANTZ
Faith, there has been much to-do on both sides, and the nation holds it 310
no sin to tar them to controversy. There was, for a while, no money bid for argument, unless the poet and the player went to cuffs in the question.

HAMLET
Is't possible?

GUILDENSTERN
O, there has been much throwing about of brains.

HAMLET
Do the boys carry it away? 315

318: **mows**: faces

319: **'Sblood**: by God's blood. This is from the Second Quarto; it does not appear in the First Folio because of revised censorship rules.

323: **appurtenance**: accompanying ceremony

324: **extent**: offering

325: **fairly**: courteously; **entertainment**: welcome

328: **north-north-west**: a tiny movement from North on the compass, but in traveling this way, one will stray far from the goal of north

329: **hawk from a handsaw**: A hawk (bird of prey) and a handsaw (a small saw) are not comparable objects; Hamlet is probably alluding to his ability to distinguish between a truth and a lie.

332: **swaddling-clouts**: baby wrappings, but dead bodies were also often wrapped in linen

334: **twice a child:** in his second childhood

338: **Roscius**: a famous Roman actor in the first century BCE

ROSENCRANTZ
Ay, that they do, my lord–Hercules and his load too.

HAMLET
It is not strange; for my uncle is King of Denmark, and those that would make mows at him while my father lived, give twenty, forty, fifty, a hundred ducats apiece for his picture in little. 'Sblood, there is something in this more than natural, if philosophy could find it out.   320

Flourish for the Players

GUILDENSTERN
There are the players.

HAMLET
Gentlemen, you are welcome to Elsinore. Your hands. Come. The appurtenance of welcome is fashion and ceremony. Let me comply with you in this garb, lest my extent to the players–which, I tell you, must show fairly outward–should more appear like entertainment than yours.   325
You are welcome. But my uncle-father and aunt-mother are deceived.

GUILDENSTERN
In what, my dear lord?

HAMLET
I am but mad north-north-west; when the wind is southerly, I know a hawk from a handsaw.

Enter POLONIUS

POLONIUS
Well be with you, gentlemen!   330

HAMLET
Hark you, Guildenstern, and you too–at each ear a hearer. That great baby you see there is not yet out of his swaddling-clouts.

ROSENCRANTZ
Happily he's the second time come to them, for they say an old man is twice a child.

HAMLET
I will prophesy: he comes to tell me of the players. Mark it.–You say   335
right, sir; for o' Monday morning, 'twas so indeed.

POLONIUS
My lord, I have news to tell you.

HAMLET
My lord, I have news to tell you. When Roscius was an actor in Rome–

340: **Buzz, buzz**: a popular, but rude response to old news

343-345: "The best actors in the world, either for tragedy, comedy, history, pastoral...": Roger Rees as Hamlet and Christopher Benjamin as Polonius in the Royal Shakespeare Company's 1984 production directed by Ron Daniels
Photo: Donald Cooper

345: **Seneca:** a Roman playwright and philosopher, known for his tragedies

346: **Plautus:** A Roman writer of comedies

348: **Jepthah**: In Judges 11.29-40, Jepthah unintentionally sacrifices his only daughter because of a rash oath.

351: **passing**: surpassingly, exceedingly

355: **Nay, that follows not**: Hamlet is saying that just because Polonius has a daughter, it does not make him comparable to Jepthath

358: *"As by lot, God wot"*: i.e., by chance God knows

POLONIUS
The actors are come hither, my lord.

HAMLET
Buzz, buzz!   340

POLONIUS
Upon mine honor–

HAMLET
Then came each actor on his ass–

POLONIUS
The best actors in the world, either for tragedy, comedy, history, pastoral,
pastoral-comical, historical-pastoral, tragical-historical, tragical-
comical-historical-pastoral, scene individable, or poem unlimited. Seneca   345
cannot be too heavy, nor Plautus too light. For the law of writ and the
liberty, these are the only men.

HAMLET
O Jephthah, judge of Israel, what a treasure hadst thou!

POLONIUS
What a treasure had he, my lord?

HAMLET
Why,
    "One fair daughter and no more,   350
    The which he loved passing well."

POLONIUS
Still on my daughter.

HAMLET
Am I not i' th' right, old Jephthah?

POLONIUS
If you call me Jephthah, my lord, I have a daughter that I love passing well.

HAMLET
Nay, that follows not.   355

POLONIUS
What follows, then, my lord?

HAMLET
Why,
    "As by lot, God wot,"
and then, you know,

360: **like**: likely

361: **row**: stanza; **chanson**: ballad

362: **abridgement**: The entrance of the players cuts Hamlet short.

364: **valanced**: fringed, as with a beard

365: **beard**: confront, challenge

366: **lady and mistress**: boy actors who played the female parts; **nearer to heaven**: taller

367: **chopine**: platform high-soled shoe

368: **uncurrent gold**: sometimes coins would be cut or shaved—in this case, they were not worth their full value.

369: **French falconers**: French falconers are known for being extremely quick.

375: **caviary**: caviar; **general**: populace

376: **top of**: outweighed

377: **modesty**: restraint

378: **sallets**: seasoned dishes

381: **handsome than fine**: beautifully crafted rather than cheap and showy

382: **Aeneas' tale to Dido**: Aeneas describes the defeat of Troy to Dido in Virgil's' *Aeneid* and also Marlowe's *Dido, Queen of Carthage*.

383: **Priam's slaughter**: the story of how Pyrrhus killed Priam during the battle for Troy

387: **sable**: black

389: **couchèd**: hidden; **horse**: i.e., the Trojan horse

390: **complexion**: appearance

391: **heraldry**: heraldric colors

392: **gules**: red; **tricked**: covered, decorated

394: **impasted**: encrusted; **parching**: fiery

397: **with coagulate gore**: covered with a thick, gooey substance

398: **carbuncles**: gems that seem to glow with its own light

"It came to pass, as most like it was"– 360
the first row of the pious chanson will show you more, for look, where my
abridgement comes.

Enter four or five Players

You're welcome, masters, welcome all. I am glad to see thee well.
Welcome, good friends. O, my old friend! Thy face is valanced since I
saw thee last. Comest thou to beard me in Denmark? What, my young 365
lady and mistress! By'r lady, your ladyship is nearer to heaven than when
I saw you last, by the altitude of a chopine. Pray God, your voice, like a
piece of uncurrent gold, be not cracked within the ring. Masters, you are
all welcome. We'll e'en to't like French falconers, fly at any thing we see.
We'll have a speech straight. Come, give us a taste of your quality, come, 370
a passionate speech.

First Player
What speech, my lord?

HAMLET
I heard thee speak me a speech once, but it was never acted, or, if it was,
not above once; for the play, I remember, pleased not the million, 'twas
caviary to the general. But it was–as I received it, and others, whose 375
judgments in such matters cried in the top of mine–an excellent play, well
digested in the scenes, set down with as much modesty as cunning. I
remember, one said there were no sallets in the lines to make the matter
savory, nor no matter in the phrase that might indict the author of affec-
tation, but called it an honest method, as wholesome as sweet, and by 380
very much more handsome than fine. One speech in it I chiefly loved,
'twas Aeneas' tale to Dido, and thereabout of it especially, where he
speaks of Priam's slaughter. If it live in your memory, begin at this
line–let me see, let me see:
     The rugged Pyrrhus, like the Hyrcanian beast– 385
'Tis not so. It begins with Pyrrhus.
     The rugged Pyrrhus, he whose sable arms,
     Black as his purpose, did the night resemble
     When he lay couchèd in the ominous horse,
     Hath now this dread and black complexion smeared 390
     With heraldry more dismal. Head to foot
     Now is he total gules, horridly tricked
     With blood of fathers, mothers, daughters, sons,
     Baked and impasted with the parching streets,
     That lend a tyrannous and damnèd light 395
     To their vile murders. Roasted in wrath and fire,
     And thus o'er-sizèd with coagulate gore,
     With eyes like carbuncles, the hellish Pyrrhus
     Old grandsire Priam seeks.
So, proceed you. 400

POLONIUS
'Fore God, my lord, well spoken, with good accent and good discretion.

405: **Repugnant**: resistant

407: **fell**: fierce

408: **unnervèd**: without strength; **Ilium**: Troy's fortress

412: **declining**: descending; **milky**: white

414: **painted tyrant**: unmoving, as a portrait

415: **neutral to his will**: indifferent to the fighting

418: **rack**: cloud banks

421: **region**: sky

423: **Cyclops**: in Greco-Roman mythology, one-eyed monsters who were the Blacksmiths to the gods

424: **Mars his**: Mars'

429: **wheel**: Fortune had an ever-spinning wheel that was thought to control human lives.

430: **nave:** hub of the wheel; **heaven**: i.e., Mt. Olympus

433: **jig**: a silly verse or dance performed before or after a play

435: **moblèd**: ruffed

First Player
> Anon he finds him
> Striking too short at Greeks. His antique sword,
> Rebellious to his arm, lies where it falls,
> Repugnant to command. Unequal matched,   405
> Pyrrhus at Priam drives, in rage strikes wide;
> But with the whiff and wind of his fell sword
> The unnervèd father falls. Then senseless Ilium,
> Seeming to feel this blow, with flaming top
> Stoops to his base, and with a hideous crash   410
> Takes prisoner Pyrrhus' ear. For, lo, his sword,
> Which was declining on the milky head
> Of reverend Priam, seemed i' th' air to stick.
> So, as a painted tyrant, Pyrrhus stood,
> And like a neutral to his will and matter,   415
> Did nothing.
> But, as we often see against some storm,
> A silence in the heavens, the rack stand still,
> The bold winds speechless and the orb below
> As hush as death, anon the dreadful thunder   420
> Doth rend the region; so, after Pyrrhus' pause,
> Arousèd vengeance sets him new a-work;
> And never did the Cyclops' hammers fall
> On Mars his armor, forged for proof eterne
> With less remorse than Pyrrhus' bleeding sword   425
> Now falls on Priam.
> Out, out, thou strumpet, Fortune! All you gods,
> In general synod, take away her power,
> Break all the spokes and fellies from her wheel,
> And bowl the round nave down the hill of heaven,   430
> As low as to the fiends!

POLONIUS
This is too long.

HAMLET
It shall to the barber's, with your beard. Prithee, say on. He's for a jig or a tale of bawdry, or he sleeps. Say on, come to Hecuba.

First Player
> But who, O, who had seen the moblèd queen–   435

HAMLET
The moblèd queen?

POLONIUS
That's good, "moblèd queen" is good.

439: **bisson rheum**: blinding tears; **clout**: cloth

441: **o'er-teemèd loins**: worn out womb. According to Euripedes, Hecuba bore Priam fifty children.

444: **state**: rule

450: **milch**: milky, moist

451: **passion**: suffering

455: **bestowed**: lodged and fed; **well used**: treated well

459: **God's bodykins**: By God's good body

466: **ha't**; have it

Set rendering from the 1958 production at the Shakespeare Memorial Theatre directed by Glen Byam Shaw
Photo: Rare Book and Special Collections Library, University of Illinois at Urbana-Champaign

First Player

> Run barefoot up and down, threatening the flames
> With bisson rheum, a clout upon that head
> Where late the diadem stood, and for a robe,   440
> About her lank and all o'er-teemèd loins,
> A blanket, in the alarm of fear caught up,
> Who this had seen, with tongue in venom steeped,
> 'Gainst Fortune's state would treason have pronounced.
> But if the gods themselves did see her then   445
> When she saw Pyrrhus make malicious sport
> In mincing with his sword her husband's limbs,
> The instant burst of clamor that she made,
> Unless things mortal move them not at all,
> Would have made milch the burning eyes of heaven,   450
> And passion in the gods.

POLONIUS

Look, whether he has not turned his color and has tears in's eyes. Pray you, no more.

HAMLET

'Tis well. I'll have thee speak out the rest soon. Good my lord, will you see the players well bestowed? Do you hear, let them be well used, for   455
they are the abstract and brief chronicles of the time. After your death you were better have a bad epitaph than their ill report while you live.

POLONIUS

My lord, I will use them according to their desert.

HAMLET

God's bodykins, man, much better! Use every man after his desert, and who should 'scape whipping? Use them after your own honor and dignity.   460
The less they deserve, the more merit is in your bounty. Take them in.

POLONIUS

Come, sirs.

Exit POLONIUS

HAMLET

Follow him, friends. We'll hear a play tomorrow.
Dost thou hear me, old friend? Can you play "The Murder of Gonzago"?

First Player

Ay, my lord.   465

HAMLET

We'll ha't tomorrow night. You could, for a need, study a speech of some dozen or sixteen lines, which I would set down and insert in't, could you not?

tracks 13-16

473-529:
Richard Burton as Hamlet
Simon Russell Beale as Hamlet
Sir John Gielgud as Hamlet

476: **force...conceit**: make his feelings conform to an imagined situation

482-483: "What's Hecuba to him, or he to Hecuba, / That he should weep for her?":
Sara Bernhardt as Hamlet ca. 1899
Courtesy of Douglas Lanier

486: **general ear**: i.e., the ears of the audience

487: **free**: innocent

488: **amaze**: bewilder

490: **muddy-mettled**: dull-spirited; **peak**: mope

491: **John-a-dreams:** a daydreamer; **unpregnant of my cause**: not acting on my charge, unproductive

493: **property**: rightful title

495: **pate**: head

497: **gives me the lie**: i.e., calls me a liar

499: **'Swounds**: By God's wounds

500: **pigeon-livered**: It was thought that pigeon's livers did not produce gall (or bile), necessary to feel anger.

502: **kites**: birds of prey

First Player
Ay, my lord.

HAMLET
Very well. Follow that lord, and look you mock him not.
My good friends, I'll leave you till night. You are welcome to Elsinore.   470

ROSENCRANTZ
Good my lord!

Exit all but HAMLET

HAMLET
Ay, so, God be with you. Now I am alone.
O, what a rogue and peasant slave am I.
Is it not monstrous that this player here,
But in a fiction, in a dream of passion,   475
Could force his soul so to his own conceit
That from her working all his visage waned,
Tears in his eyes, distraction in his aspect,
A broken voice, and his whole function suiting
With forms to his conceit? And all for nothing?   480
For Hecuba?
What's Hecuba to him, or he to Hecuba,
That he should weep for her? What would he do,
Had he the motive and the cue for passion
That I have? He would drown the stage with tears   485
And cleave the general ear with horrid speech,
Make mad the guilty and appall the free,
Confound the ignorant, and amaze indeed
The very faculties of eyes and ears. Yet I,
A dull and muddy-mettled rascal, peak,   490
Like John-a-dreams, unpregnant of my cause,
And can say nothing–no, not for a king
Upon whose property and most dear life
A damned defeat was made. Am I a coward?
Who calls me villain? Breaks my pate across?   495
Plucks off my beard and blows it in my face?
Tweaks me by the nose, gives me the lie i' th' throat,
As deep as to the lungs? Who does me this?
Ha! 'Swounds, I should take it. For it cannot be
But I am pigeon-livered and lack gall   500
To make oppression bitter, or ere this
I should have fatted all the region kites
With this slave's offal. Bloody, bawdy villain!
Remorseless, treacherous, lecherous, kindless villain!

tracks 13-16

473-529:
Richard Burton as Hamlet
Simon Russell Beale as Hamlet
Sir John Gielgud as Hamlet

505: "O, vengeance!": Simon Russell Beale as Hamlet in the Brooklyn Academy of Music's 2002 production directed by John Caird
Photo: Richard Termine

510: **drab**: whore

511: **scullion**: kitchen maid

512: **About**: i.e., think

514: **cunning**: artfulness

515: **presently**: immediately

521: **tent**: probe (as a wound)

525: **melancholy**: Melancholia (one of the humours) caused inaction since it was a form of depression; it was believed to cause hallucinations as well.

526: **potent**: powerful

527: **Abuses**: deceives

528: **relative**: relevant

O, vengeance!   505
Why, what an ass am I! Ay, sure. This is most brave,
That I, the son of a dear father murdered,
Prompted to my revenge by heaven and hell,
Must, like a whore, unpack my heart with words,
And fall a-cursing, like a very drab,   510
A scullion! Fie upon't, foh!
About, my brain—I have heard
That guilty creatures sitting at a play
Have by the very cunning of the scene
Been struck so to the soul that presently   515
They have proclaimed their malefactions;
For murder, though it have no tongue, will speak
With most miraculous organ. I'll have these players
Play something like the murder of my father
Before mine uncle. I'll observe his looks,   520
I'll tent him to the quick. If he but blench,
I know my course. The spirit that I have seen
May be the devil, and the devil hath power
To assume a pleasing shape; yea, and perhaps
Out of my weakness and my melancholy,   525
As he is very potent with such spirits,
Abuses me to damn me. I'll have grounds
More relative than this. The play's the thing
Wherein I'll catch the conscience of the king.

                                                          Exit

[Hamlet

Act 3

0: Location: Castle chambers

0: Scene: In this scene is one of the most famous soliloquies in the Shakespearean canon, Hamlet's "To be or not to be." It is rarely ever cut in performance, surviving even the 800+ line cut made after the Restoration by Davenant and Betterton. A slightly different version of the soliloquy exists in the First Quarto, and William Poel upset audiences in his 1881 production by using that version: "To be or not to be, ay, there's the point."

Sir Derek Jacobi played Hamlet in an RSC (1977) production, and for the BBC (1980) series on television. His delivery of this soliloquy is said by some to be one of the finest in the twentieth century. Olivier delivers this soliloquy (following the nunnery scene) on a ledge of the castle overlooking the crashing waves of the sea beneath him. He seems to be contemplating suicide until he accidentally drops his "bodkin" over the edge, while he remains standing on the castle ledge.

2: **puts on this confusion**: i.e., acts in this distracted manner

5: **distracted**: uneasy, perturbed

7: **forward to be sounded**: very willing to be questioned

12: **disposition**: mood

13-14: **Niggard...reply**: Hamlet is reluctant to speak voluntarily, but he is willing to answer questions.

15: **assay**: tempt

17: **o'er-wrought**: passed (or overtook)

Act 3, Scene 1]

Enter CLAUDIUS, GERTRUDE, POLONIUS, OPHELIA,
ROSENCRANTZ, GUILDENSTERN, and Lords

CLAUDIUS
 And can you, by no drift of circumstance
 Get from him why he puts on this confusion,
 Grating so harshly all his days of quiet
 With turbulent and dangerous lunacy?

ROSENCRANTZ
 He does confess he feels himself distracted,   5
 But from what cause he will by no means speak.

GUILDENSTERN
 Nor do we find him forward to be sounded,
 But, with a crafty madness, keeps aloof
 When we would bring him on to some confession
 Of his true state.

GERTRUDE
                    Did he receive you well?   10

ROSENCRANTZ
 Most like a gentleman.

GUILDENSTERN
 But with much forcing of his disposition.

ROSENCRANTZ
 Niggard of question, but of our demands,
 Most free in his reply.

GERTRUDE
 Did you assay him to any pastime?   15

ROSENCRANTZ
 Madam, it so fell out that certain players
 We o'er-wrought on the way. Of these we told him;
 And there did seem in him a kind of joy
 To hear of it. They are about the court,
 And, as I think, they have already order   20
 This night to play before him.

26: **Give him further edge**: encourage his appetite or desire

31: **Affront**: confront; **espials**: spies

39: **wildness**: madness, insane behavior

43: **bestow**: hide

44-46: **That show...loneliness**: i.e., pretending to be reading a prayer book will be an excuse for being alone

POLONIUS
                    'Tis most true;
And he beseeched me to entreat your majesties
To hear and see the matter.

CLAUDIUS
    With all my heart; and it doth much content me
    To hear him so inclined. Good gentlemen,   25
    Give him a further edge, and drive his purpose on
    To these delights.

ROSENCRANTZ
    We shall, my lord.

                    Exeunt ROSENCRANTZ and GUILDENSTERN

CLAUDIUS
                    Sweet Gertrude, leave us too,
    For we have closely sent for Hamlet hither,
    That he, as 'twere by accident, may here   30
    Affront Ophelia. Her father and myself, lawful espials,
    Will so bestow ourselves that, seeing unseen,
    We may of their encounter frankly judge,
    And gather by him, as he is behaved,
    If 't be the affliction of his love or no   35
    That thus he suffers for.

GERTRUDE
                    I shall obey you.
    And for your part, Ophelia, I do wish
    That your good beauties be the happy cause
    Of Hamlet's wildness; so shall I hope your virtues
    Will bring him to his wonted way again,   40
    To both your honors.

OPHELIA
                    Madam, I wish it may.

                                        [Exit GERTRUDE]

POLONIUS
    Ophelia, walk you here.–Gracious, so please you,
    We will bestow ourselves. Read on this book,
    That show of such an exercise may color
    Your loneliness. We are oft to blame in this,   45
    'Tis too much proved, that with devotion's visage
    And pious action we do sugar o'er
    The devil himself.

50-52: **The harlot's...word**: i.e., the cosmetics that a whore uses to create an illusion are not as ugly as the true nature of Claudius's treachery

tracks 17-20

55-87:
John Barrymore as Hamlet
Sir Derek Jacobi as Hamlet
Simon Russell Beale as Hamlet

64: **rub**: an obstacle (from the game of bowls)

66: **shuffled off this mortal coil**: referring to the belief that when we die, we are literally cast off by our bodies

67: **respect**: consideration

68: **so long life**: a long-lived life

70: **contumely**: abuse, insolence

71: **disprized**: unvalued

74: **his quietus make**: as in the legal term, *quietus est*, meaning "to quit"

75: **bare bodkin**: mere dagger; **fardels**: troubles, burdens

78: **undiscovered**: unexplored; **bourn**: frontiers

79: **puzzles the will**: paralyzes us, keeps us from acting

82: **conscience**: knowledge

84: **cast**: shade

85: **pith and moment**: height and importance

86: **their currents turn awry**: i.e., our greatest enterprises fail. Like rivers, if they are diverted from their normal flow, they lose momentum and become stagnant.

CLAUDIUS
                  O, 'tis too true!
How smart a lash that speech doth give my conscience.
The harlot's cheek, beautied with plastering art,   50
Is not more ugly to the thing that helps it
Than is my deed to my most painted word,
O heavy burden.

POLONIUS
I hear him coming. Let's withdraw, my lord.
                    Exeunt CLAUDIUS and POLONIUS
                              Enter HAMLET

HAMLET
To be, or not to be. That is the question.   55
Whether 'tis nobler in the mind to suffer
The slings and arrows of outrageous fortune,
Or to take arms against a sea of troubles,
And by opposing end them. To die, to sleep
No more; and by a sleep to say we end   60
The heartache and the thousand natural shocks
That flesh is heir to, 'tis a consummation
Devoutly to be wished. To die, to sleep.
To sleep perchance to dream. Ay, there's the rub!
For in that sleep of death what dreams may come   65
When we have shuffled off this mortal coil,
Must give us pause. There's the respect
That makes calamity of so long life.
For who would bear the whips and scorns of time,
The oppressor's wrong, the proud man's contumely,   70
The pangs of disprized love, the law's delay,
The insolence of office and the spurns
That patient merit of the unworthy takes,
When he himself might his quietus make
With a bare bodkin? Who would these fardels bear,   75
To grunt and sweat under a weary life,
But that the dread of something after death,
The undiscovered country from whose bourn
No traveler returns, puzzles the will,
And makes us rather bear those ills we have   80
Than fly to others that we know not of?
Thus conscience does make cowards of us all;
And thus the native hue of resolution
Is sicklied o'er with the pale cast of thought,
And enterprises of great pith and moment   85
With this regard their currents turn awry,
And lose the name of action.–

tracks 17-20

55-87:
John Barrymore as Hamlet
Sir Derek Jacobi as Hamlet
Simon Russell Beale as Hamlet

87: **Soft you now**: a quiet interruption

102: **honest**: chaste, but can also mean "truthful"

106: **discourse to**: conversation with

106-107: "That if you be honest and fair, your honesty should admit no discourse to your beauty.": Wallace Acton as Hamlet and Nicole Lowrance as Ophelia in the Shakespeare Theatre Company's 2001 production directed by Gale Edwards
Photo: Carol Rosegg

                        Soft you now!
The fair Ophelia? Nymph, in thy orisons
Be all my sins remembered.

OPHELIA
                    Good my lord,
How does your honor for this many a day?   90

HAMLET
  I humbly thank you; well, well, well.

OPHELIA
  My lord, I have remembrances of yours,
  That I have longèd long to redeliver;
  I pray you now receive them.

HAMLET
  No, no, not I. I never gave you aught.   95

OPHELIA
  My honored lord, I know right well you did,
  And, with them, words of so sweet breath composed
  As made the things more rich. Their perfume lost,
  Take these again, for to the noble mind,
  Rich gifts wax poor when givers prove unkind.   100
  There, my lord.

HAMLET
  Ha, ha! Are you honest?

OPHELIA
  My lord?

HAMLET
  Are you fair?

OPHELIA
  What means your lordship?   105

HAMLET
  That if you be honest and fair, your honesty should admit no discourse to
  your beauty.

OPHELIA
  Could beauty, my lord, have better commerce than with honesty?

HAMLET
  Ay, truly. For the power of beauty will sooner transform honesty from
  what it is to a bawd than the force of honesty can translate beauty into   110

114-115: for virtue...relish of it: a metaphor comparing virtue to a hybrid plant. If a sweet bud is tied to a bitter one, the fruit of the new variety will have a slightly bitter taste.

117: nunnery: a convent, but it also implies a brothel

117: "Get thee to a nunnery!": Laurence Olivier as Hamlet and Jean Simmons as Ophelia in the 1948 film directed by Laurence Olivier
Courtesy of Douglas Lanier

118: indifferent honest: reasonably truthful and decent

120: beck: command

132: monsters: i.e., the horned beast, or the cuckold

135: paintings: cosmetics (as in illusions)

136-138: You jig...ignorance: You dance around the truth, using coyness, deceit, illusion, and tricks to disguise your knowledge. Then you use those same things to pretend innocence.

his likeness. This was sometime a paradox, but now the time gives it proof. I did love you once.

OPHELIA
Indeed, my lord, you made me believe so.

HAMLET
You should not have believed me, for virtue cannot so inoculate our old stock but we shall relish of it. I loved you not.   115

OPHELIA
I was the more deceived.

HAMLET
Get thee to a nunnery! Why wouldst thou be a breeder of sinners? I am myself indifferent honest, but yet I could accuse me of such things that it were better my mother had not borne me. I am very proud, revengeful, ambitious, with more offenses at my beck than I have thoughts to put   120 them in, imagination to give them shape, or time to act them in. What should such fellows as I do crawling between earth and heaven? We are arrant knaves all. Believe none of us. Go thy ways to a nunnery. Where's your father?

OPHELIA
At home, my lord.   125

HAMLET
Let the doors be shut upon him, that he may play the fool nowhere but in's own house. Farewell.

OPHELIA
O, help him, you sweet heavens!

HAMLET
If thou dost marry, I'll give thee this plague for thy dowry: be thou as chaste as ice, as pure as snow, thou shalt not escape calumny. Get thee to   130 a nunnery, go, farewell. Or, if thou wilt needs marry, marry a fool, for wise men know well enough what monsters you make of them. To a nunnery, go, and quickly too. Farewell.

OPHELIA
O heavenly powers restore him!

HAMLET
I have heard of your paintings too, well enough. God has given you one   135 face, and you make yourselves another. You jig, you amble, and you lisp, and nickname God's creatures, and make your wantonness your ignorance. Go to, I'll no more on't, it hath made me mad. I say, we will have no more marriages. Those that are married already, all but one, shall live. The rest shall keep as they are. To a nunnery, go.   140

                                                                   Exit

143: **The expectancy...state**: the hopes and the lovely prize and pride of the country

144: **The glass...form**: the model of perfection and the pattern of courtly behavior

147: **music**: lovely, lyrical

150: **blown**: blossoming

151: **Blasted with ecstasy**: cursed with madness

153: **affections**: feelings

156: **sits on brood**: Like a bird sitting on a nest about to hatch, Hamlet is brooding (or thinking) about what he will do.

157: **do doubt**: don't doubt; **hatch**: hatching (continuing the metaphor in the previous line of Hamlet nesting or brooding)

160: **set it down**: resolved on an action

164: **This something...heart**: i.e., the strange thoughts that he's keeping secret

166: **From fashion of himself**: makes him act uncharacteristically (unlike himself)

174: **round**: blunt

176: **find him not**: is not successful in discovering his secret

OPHELIA

O, what a noble mind is here o'erthrown!
The courtier's, soldier's, scholar's, eye, tongue, sword;
The expectancy and rose of the fair state,
The glass of fashion and the mould of form,
The observed of all observers—quite, quite down!   145
And I, of ladies most deject and wretched,
That sucked the honey of his music vows,
Now see that noble and most sovereign reason
Like sweet bells jangled, out of tune and harsh;
That unmatched form and feature of blown youth   150
Blasted with ecstasy. O, woe is me
To have seen what I have seen, see what I see!

Enter CLAUDIUS and POLONIUS

CLAUDIUS

Love? His affections do not that way tend;
Nor what he spake, though it lacked form a little,
Was not like madness. There's something in his soul   155
O'er which his melancholy sits on brood,
And I do doubt the hatch and the disclose
Will be some danger, which to prevent,
I have in quick determination
Thus set it down: he shall with speed to England   160
For the demand of our neglected tribute.
Haply the seas and countries different
With variable objects shall expel
This something-settled matter in his heart,
Whereon his brains still beating puts him thus   165
From fashion of himself. What think you on't?

POLONIUS

It shall do well. But yet do I believe
The origin and commencement of his grief
Sprung from neglected love. How now, Ophelia?
You need not tell us what Lord Hamlet said;   170
We heard it all. My lord, do as you please.
But, if you hold it fit, after the play
Let his queen mother all alone entreat him
To show his griefs. Let her be round with him,
And I'll be placed, so please you, in the ear   175
Of all their conference. If she find him not,
To England send him, or confine him where
Your wisdom best shall think.

CLAUDIUS

                    It shall be so.
Madness in great ones must not unwatched go.

Exeunt

0: Location: The castle

1-42: Scene: In Peter Hall's 1965 production, Hamlet (David Warner) seated the Player King and Player Queen in Claudius and Gertrude's usual chairs and then arranged the other actors around a table reminiscent of the Court. Claudius's chair symbolized the King himself and, at different points throughout the play, Hamlet sat on it, kicked it, and threw it across the stage.

2: **mouth it**: speak in an exaggerated manner; **as lief**: rather

7: **robustious:** bombastic; **periwig-pated**: wig-wearing

8-9: **groundlings**: In Elizabethan theaters, for less than a half-penny, the groundlings stood in the so-called "pit," an area in front of the stage where the audience could freely interact with the Players. Groundlings were usually apprentices or common laborers (unable to afford a seat in the Gallery) and known to enjoy the dances, songs, and common jokes of the prelude to performances.

9: **dumbshows**: mimed scenes that presented the argument or the plot of the play

10: **Termagant**: A termagant was a Muslim god usually portrayed as noisy and unrestrained; **out-Herod's Herod**: Herod was typically portrayed as a ranting and uncontrolled tyrant.

16: **from the purpose**: opposed to

19: **his form and pressure**: present state of things

20: **unskillful**: undiscriminating

20-21: **the censure of which one**: the judgment of one person

24: **Christians**: used generically to mean human beings

25: **nature's journeymen**: hired hands

28: **indifferently**: moderately well

31: **set on**: urge; **barren**: unthinking, without an original thought

Enter HAMLET, and two or three of the Players

HAMLET
Speak the speech, I pray you, as I pronounced it to you, trippingly on the tongue. But if you mouth it, as many of your players do, I had as lief the town-crier spoke my lines. Nor do not saw the air too much with your hand, thus, but use all gently; for in the very torrent, tempest, and, as I may say, the whirlwind of passion, you must acquire and beget a temperance that may give it smoothness. O, it offends me to the soul to hear a robustious periwig-pated fellow tear a passion to tatters, to very rags, to split the ears of the groundlings, who for the most part are capable of nothing but inexplicable dumbshows and noise. I would have such a fellow whipped for o'erdoing Termagant; it out-Herods Herod. Pray you, avoid it. 5 10

First Player
I warrant your honor.

HAMLET
Be not too tame neither, but let your own discretion be your tutor. Suit the action to the word, the word to the action, with this special observance, that you o'erstep not the modesty of nature. For anything so overdone is from the purpose of playing, whose end, both at the first and now, was and is, to hold, as 'twere, the mirror up to nature: to show virtue her own feature, scorn her own image, and the very age and body of the time his form and pressure. Now this overdone, or come tardy off, though it make the unskillful laugh, cannot but make the judicious grieve; the censure of the which one must in your allowance o'erweigh a whole theatre of others. O, there be players that I have seen play, and heard others praise, and that highly, not to speak it profanely, that, neither having the accent of Christians nor the gait of Christian, pagan, nor no man, have so strutted and bellowed that I have thought some of nature's journeymen had made men and not made them well, they imitated humanity so abominably. 15 20 25

First Player
I hope we have reformed that indifferently with us, sir.

HAMLET
O, reform it altogether. And let those that play your clowns speak no more than is set down for them; for there be of them that will themselves laugh to set on some quantity of barren spectators to laugh too, though, in the meantime, some necessary question of the play be then to be 30

34: "Go, make you ready.": Dion Flynn, George Morfogen, Marc Gwinn, Francis Jue as the players and Liev Schreiber as Hamlet in the 1999-2000 Public Theater production directed by Andrei Serban
Photo: Michal Daniel

36: **presently**: immediately

42: **just**: honest

43: **As e'er my conversation coped withal**: as I have ever encountered

45: **advancement**: political favors

48: **candied tongue**: insincere flatterer

49: **pregnant**: poised to bow

53: **sealed thee for herself**: marked you as her own

57: **blood**: passion

considered. That's villainous, and shows a most pitiful ambition in the
fool that uses it. Go, make you ready.

Exeunt Players
Enter POLONIUS, ROSENCRANTZ, and GUILDENSTERN
How now, my lord? Will the King hear this piece of work?   35

POLONIUS
And the Queen too, and that presently.

HAMLET
Bid the players make haste.

Exit POLONIUS

Will you two help to hasten them?

ROSENCRANTZ and GUILDENSTERN
We will, my lord.

Exeunt ROSENCRANTZ and GUILDENSTERN
Enter HORATIO

HAMLET
What ho, Horatio!   40

HORATIO
Here, sweet lord, at your service.

HAMLET
Horatio, thou art e'en as just a man
As e'er my conversation coped withal.

HORATIO
O, my dear lord–

HAMLET
                    Nay, do not think I flatter;
For what advancement may I hope from thee   45
That no revenue hast but thy good spirits,
To feed and clothe thee? Why should the poor be
flattered? No, let the candied tongue lick absurd pomp
And crook the pregnant hinges of the knee
Where thrift may follow fawning. Dost thou hear?   50
Since my dear soul was mistress of her choice
And could of men distinguish, her election
Hath sealed thee for herself. For thou hast been
As one in suffering all that suffers nothing,
A man that Fortune's buffets and rewards   55
Hath ta'en with equal thanks; and blest are those
Whose blood and judgment are so well commingled,
That they are not a pipe for Fortune's finger
To sound what stop she please. Give me that man
That is not passion's slave, and I will wear him   60

67: the very comment of thy soul: the most critical and discerning eye

68: occulted: hidden

75: seeming: outward appearance

80-282: Scene: There are many ways to present the play-within-the-play, as its theatrical and filmed history will attest. John Barton's 1980 production for the RSC set the players scene with only benches around a platform. Raised this way, the players dominated the scene—and then they played the play as Hamlet (Michael Pennington) advised them: quite seriously. The Brook 2005 production acted this scene with a troupe of Japanese actors, and the play-within-the-play has haiku-like overtones. Zeffirelli's film presents the scene in a traditional castle hall, lit by candles; the festive atmosphere contrasts with the darkness of the trap Hamlet has set for the King. Gibson's Hamlet runs around frenetically throughout the scene. Once the King reacts to the murder scene and departs, Hamlet literally dances out of his seat. He twirls the players around, grabs Horatio excitedly by the arm, and, spinning him slowly, asks, "Didst perceive?" He kisses Ophelia good-bye with a flippant, "To a nunnery go! And quickly too. Farewell."

80-81: Excellent...I eat the air: The chameleon was thought to feed on air, but this could also be a pun on "heir."

86: I did enact...Brutus killed me: Most scholars agree that this is an allusion to Shakespeare's play *Julius Caesar*, completed (1599) and staged shortly before *Hamlet* (1599-1601). It would have been fresh in the minds of regular playgoers, and the actor playing Polonius might have been the same actor who played Julius Caesar.

In my heart's core, ay, in my heart of heart,
As I do thee. Something too much of this.
There is a play tonight before the King.
One scene of it comes near the circumstance
Which I have told thee of my father's death. 65
I prithee, when thou seest that act afoot,
Even with the very comment of thy soul
Observe mine uncle. If his occulted guilt
Do not itself unkennel in one speech,
It is a damnèd ghost that we have seen, 70
And my imaginations are as foul
As Vulcan's stithy. Give him heedful note,
For I mine eyes will rivet to his face,
And after we will both our judgments join
In censure of his seeming.

HORATIO
                          Well, my lord. 75
If he steal aught the whilst this play is playing
And scape detecting, I will pay the theft.

HAMLET
They are coming to the play. I must be idle. Get you a place.
Danish march. A flourish of trumpets. Enter CLAUDIUS, GERTRUDE,
POLONIUS, OPHELIA, ROSENCRANTZ, GUILDENSTERN, Lords
and Attendants, and Guard carrying torches.

CLAUDIUS
How fares our cousin Hamlet?

HAMLET
Excellent, i'faith; of the chameleon's dish. I eat the air, promise- 80
crammed. You cannot feed capons so.

CLAUDIUS
I have nothing with this answer, Hamlet; these words are not mine.

HAMLET
No, nor mine now.–My lord, you played once i' th' university, you say?

POLONIUS
That I did, my lord, and was accounted a good actor.

HAMLET
What did you enact? 85

POLONIUS
I did enact Julius Caesar. I was killed i' th' Capitol. Brutus killed me.

87: **so capital a calf**: i.e., such a prize fool, and another example of word play on Capitol/capital

88: **stay**: wait

92: "Lady, shall I lie in your lap?": Ethan Hawke as Hamlet and Julia Stiles as Ophelia in the 2000 film directed by Michael Almereyda
Photo: Larry Riley © Miramax Films. Courtesy of Douglas Lanier

96: **country matters**: country pastimes involving sex; a vulgar reference to female genitalia

HAMLET
It was a brute part of him to kill so capital a calf there.–Be the players ready?

ROSENCRANTZ
Ay, my lord; they stay upon your patience.

GERTRUDE
Come hither, my good Hamlet, sit by me.

HAMLET
No, good mother, here's metal more attractive.   90

POLONIUS
O, ho! Do you mark that?

HAMLET
Lady, shall I lie in your lap?

OPHELIA
No, my lord.

HAMLET
I mean, my head upon your lap?

OPHELIA
Ay, my lord.   95

HAMLET
Do you think I meant country matters?

OPHELIA
I think nothing, my lord.

HAMLET
That's a fair thought to lie between maids' legs.

OPHELIA
What is, my lord?

HAMLET
Nothing.   100

OPHELIA
You are merry, my lord.

HAMLET
Who, I?

104: **jig-maker**: funny man. The leading comic actor often performed a farcical song-and-dance to open or close a performance.

108: **suit of sables**: suit made of expensive black fur, a reminder of Hamlet's continued mourning

112-113: **the hobby-horse**: a familiar object in May Day (fertility) celebrations and a common character in morris dances. A mock-horse was strapped to the body of a man and rocked back-and-forth in a motion reminiscent of sexual movements.

113: Stage Direction: *Hautboys*: an early version of the oboe

Roger Rees as Hamlet, Frances Barber as Ophelia, Dexter Fletcher as Player Queen, Brian Blessed as Claudius, Virginia McKenna as Gertrude, Bernard Horsfall as First Player, Stephen Simms as Player, and Frank Middlemass as Polonius in the Royal Shakespeare Company's 1984 production directed by Ron Daniels
Photo: Donald Cooper

115: **miching malicho**: sneaking mischief or trouble

OPHELIA
Ay, my lord.

HAMLET
O God, your only jig-maker. What should a man do but be merry? For,
look you, how cheerfully my mother looks, and my father died within   105
these two hours.

OPHELIA
Nay, 'tis twice two months, my lord.

HAMLET
So long? Nay then, let the devil wear black, for I'll have a suit of sables.
O heavens! Die two months ago, and not forgotten yet? Then there's
hope a great man's memory may outlive his life half a year. But, by'r   110
Lady, he must build churches, then, or else shall he suffer not thinking
on, with the hobby-horse, whose epitaph is "For O, for O, the hobby-
horse is forgot."

Hautboys play. The Dumb Show enters.

*Enter a King and a Queen very lovingly, the
Queen embracing him, and he her. She kneels, and
makes show of protestation unto him. He takes her
up, and declines his head upon her neck. He lays
him down upon a bank of flowers. She, seeing him
asleep, leaves him. Anon comes in a fellow, takes
off his crown, kisses it, and pours poison in the
King's ears, and exits. The Queen returns, finds
the King dead, and makes passionate action. The
Poisoner, with some two or three mutes, comes in
again, seeming to lament with her. The dead body
is carried away. The Poisoner woos the Queen
with gift. She seems loath and unwilling awhile,
but in the end accepts his love.*

Exeunt the Players

OPHELIA
What means this, my lord?

HAMLET
Marry, this is miching malicho. It means mischief.   115

OPHELIA
Belike this show imports the argument of the play.

Enter Prologue

122: **naught**: naughty, indecent

126: **posy of a ring**: the motto engraved within the circle of a ring

129: **Phoebus' cart**: Apollo's chariot, the sun

130: **Neptune's salt wash**: i.e., the ocean (Neptune was the Roman god of the sea); **Tellus' orbèd ground**: i.e., the earth (Tellus was the Roman goddess of the earth)

131: **borrowed sheen**: reflected light

140: **Discomfort**: sadden

143: **proof**: experience

Edward Gero as Player King, Jason Gilbert as Player Queen, and ensemble in the Shakespeare Theatre Company's 2001 production directed by Gale Edwards
Photo: Carol Rosegg

HAML1ET

We shall know by this fellow. The players cannot keep counsel; they'll
tell all.

OPHELIA

Will he tell us what this show meant?

HAMLET

Ay, or any show that you'll show him. Be not you ashamed to show, he'll   120
not shame to tell you what it means.

OPHELIA

You are naught, you are naught. I'll mark the play.

Prologue

> For us, and for our tragedy,
> Here stooping to your clemency,
> We beg your hearing patiently.   125

Exit Prologue

HAMLET

Is this a prologue, or the posy of a ring?

OPHELIA

'Tis brief, my lord.

HAMLET

As woman's love.

Enter Player King and Player Queen

Player King

> Full thirty times hath Phoebus' cart gone round
> Neptune's salt wash and Tellus'orbèd ground,   130
> And thirty dozen moons with borrowed sheen
> About the world have times twelve thirties been,
> Since love our hearts and Hymen did our hands
> Unite commutual in most sacred bands.

Player Queen

> So many journeys may the sun and moon   135
> Make us again count o'er ere love be done!
> But, woe is me, you are so sick of late,
> So far from cheer and from your former state,
> That I distrust you. Yet, though I distrust,
> Discomfort you, my lord, it nothing must;   140
> For women's fear and love holds quantity,
> In neither aught, or in extremity.
> Now what my love is, proof hath made you know,

145-146: Where love...grows there: Reminiscent of Hamlet's verse to Ophelia, this couplet from the Second Quarto completes the Player Queen's sentiment.

148: operant: vital; **leave:** cease

153: "Such love must needs be treason in my breast.": Joanne Pearce as Ophelia, Kenneth Branagh as Hamlet, John Shrapnel as Claudius, Jane Lapotaire as Gertrude, and David Bradley as Polonius in the Royal Shakespeare Company's 1992 production directed by Adrian Noble
Photo: Donald Cooper

156: Wormwood: a bitter herb (as in the old adage "A bitter pill to swallow")

157: instances...move: motives that prompted the second marriage

158: thrift: profit

164: validity: strength and vigor

167-168: we forget...we propose: we break promises we make to ourselves

171-172: violence...destroy: extreme grief or joy destroys themselves and the motive for action vanishes with them

180: advanced: promoted

And as my love is sized, my fear is so:
Where love is great, the littlest doubts are fear; 145
Where little fears grow great, great love grows there.

Player King

Faith, I must leave thee, love, and shortly too;
My operant powers their functions leave to do.
And thou shalt live in this fair world behind,
Honored, beloved; and haply one as kind 150
For husband shalt thou—

Player Queen

O, confound the rest!
Such love must needs be treason in my breast.
In second husband let me be accurst;
None wed the second but who killed the first. 155

HAMLET

Wormwood, wormwood.

Player Queen

The instances that second marriage move
Are base respects of thrift, but none of love.
A second time I kill my husband dead,
When second husband kisses me in bed. 160

Player King

I do believe you think what now you speak,
But what we do determine oft we break.
Purpose is but the slave to memory,
Of violent birth, but poor validity.
Which now, like fruit unripe, sticks on the tree, 165
But fall, unshaken, when they mellow be.
Most necessary 'tis that we forget
To pay ourselves what to ourselves is debt.
What to ourselves in passion we propose,
The passion ending, doth the purpose lose. 170
The violence of either grief or joy
Their own enactures with themselves destroy.
Where joy most revels, grief doth most lament;
Grief joys, joy grieves, on slender accident.
This world is not for aye, nor 'tis not strange 175
That even our loves should with our fortunes change;
For 'tis a question left us yet to prove,
Whether love lead fortune, or else fortune, love.
The great man down, you mark his favorite flies;
The poor advanced makes friends of enemies. 180

181: **hitherto**: in this extent

183: **try**: test

187: **still**: always

188: **ends**: results

193-194: **To desperation...face of joy**: from the Second Quarto

194: **anchor's:** anchorite's (hermit's); **cheer**: victuals

195: **opposite**: adversary; **blanks**: pales

201: **fain**: gladly

206: **doth**: From the Second Quarto, this word improves the meter of the line and turns it into the more familiar phrase.

208: **argument**: plot

Paul Freeman as Claudius and Diana Quick as Gertrude watch the players perform as a shadow play in the Royal Shakespeare Company's 1997 production directed by Matthew Warchus
Photo: Donald Cooper

And hitherto doth love on fortune tend,
For who not needs shall never lack a friend,
And who in want a hollow friend doth try,
Directly seasons him his enemy.
But, orderly to end where I begun,   185
Our wills and fates do so contrary run
That our devices still are overthrown;
Our thoughts are ours, their ends none of our own.
So think thou wilt no second husband wed,
But die thy thoughts when thy first lord is dead.   190

Player Queen
Nor earth to me give food, nor heaven light,
Sport and repose lock from me day and night,
To desperation turn my trust and hope,
An anchor's cheer in prison be my scope.
Each opposite that blanks the face of joy   195
Meet what I would have well and it destroy,
Both here and hence pursue me lasting strife,
If, once a widow, ever I be wife!

HAMLET
If she should break it now!

Player King
Tis deeply sworn. Sweet, leave me here awhile.   200
My spirits grow dull, and fain I would beguile
The tedious day with sleep.
[He sleeps]

Player Queen
Sleep rock thy brain,
And never come mischance between us twain.

Exit

HAMLET
Madam, how like you this play?   205

GERTRUDE
The lady doth protest too much, methinks.

HAMLET
O, but she'll keep her word.

CLAUDIUS
Have you heard the argument? Is there no offense in't?

211: **Tropically**: as a trope, or rhetorical figure (the First Quarto reads "trapically" as in "trap")

211-212: **This play...Vienna**: a popular Italian story about the alleged murder of the Duke of Urbino by Luigi Gonzaga in 1538

214: **free**: innocent; **galled jade**: horse with saddle sores

215: **withers**: the part of the horse between its shoulders; **unwrung**: not bruised or chafed

217: **chorus**: In Greek drama, the Chorus explained the upcoming action of the play.

220: **keen**: sharply satirical

221: **a groaning**: referring to groans during intercourse or in childbirth

222: **Still better and worse**: Hamlet is increasingly witty and increasingly obscene.

223: **mistake your husbands**: fool your husbands with false promises

226: **Confederate**: complicit

227: **rank**: foul

228: **Hecate's ban**: a curse from Hecate, the goddess of witchcraft

229: **dire property**: quality

HAMLET
No, no, they do but jest, poison in jest; no offense i' th' world.

CLAUDIUS
What do you call the play?   210

HAMLET
"The Mousetrap." Marry, how? Tropically. This play is the image of a
murder done in Vienna. Gonzago is the duke's name; his wife, Baptista.
You shall see anon. 'Tis a knavish piece of work. But what o' that? Your
majesty and we that have free souls, it touches us not. Let the galled jade
wince, our withers are unwrung.   215
                                          Enter Player LUCIANUS
This is one Lucianus, nephew to the King.

OPHELIA
You are a good chorus, my lord.

HAMLET
I could interpret between you and your love, if I could see the puppets
dallying.

OPHELIA
You are keen, my lord, you are keen.   220

HAMLET
It would cost you a groaning to take off my edge.

OPHELIA
Still better and worse.

HAMLET
So you mistake your husbands. Begin, murderer. Pox, leave thy damnable
faces and begin. Come–the croaking raven doth bellow for revenge.

LUCIANUS
    Thoughts black, hands apt, drugs fit, and time agreeing,   225
    Confederate season, else no creature seeing;
    Thou mixture rank, of midnight weeds collected,
    With Hecate's ban thrice blasted, thrice infected,
    Thy natural magic and dire property
    On wholesome life usurp immediately.   230
                          [He pours the poison into the Player's ear]

HAMLET
He poisons him i' th' garden for's estate. His name's Gonzago. The story
is extant, and writ in choice Italian. You shall see anon how the murderer
gets the love of Gonzago's wife.

Set rendering from the 1958 production at the Shakespeare Memorial Theatre directed by
Glen Byam Shaw
Photo: Rare Book and Special Collections Library, University of Illinois at Urbana-Champaign

235: **false fire**: from guns loaded with powder but no shot (or musket ball)

240: **let the...weep**: Deer were thought to weep when wounded.

243: **So...away**: i.e., that's the way of life

244: **feathers**: plumes worn as stage costumes

245: **turn Turk with me**: i.e., rebel against me (a Turk was a renegade); **razed shoes**: shoes decorated with slashes and rosettes

245-246: **a fellowship...players**: a share in a company of actors

249: **Damon**: In Roman mythology, Damon and Pythias exemplified the ideals of friendship.

252: **pajock**: a peacock and a symbol of pride

OPHELIA
The King rises.

HAMLET
What, frighted with false fire?   235

GERTRUDE
How fares my lord?

POLONIUS
Give o'er the play.

CLAUDIUS
Give me some light. Away!

COURTIERS
Lights, lights, lights!

Exeunt all but HAMLET and HORATIO

HAMLET
Why, let the stricken deer go weep,   240
The hart ungallèd play;
For some must watch, while some must sleep,
So runs the world away.
Would not this, sir, and a forest of feathers–if the rest of my fortunes turn
Turk with me–with two Provincial roses on my razed shoes, get me a   245
fellowship in a cry of players, sir?

HORATIO
Half a share.

HAMLET
A whole one, I.
For thou dost know, O Damon dear,
This realm dismantled was   250
Of Jove himself; and now reigns here
A very, very–pajock.

HORATIO
You might have rhymed.

HAMLET
O good Horatio, I'll take the ghost's word for a
thousand pound. Didst perceive?   255

HORATIO
Very well, my lord.

261: **pardie**: indeed

267: **distempered**: upset

269: **choler**: anger and indigestion, which were thought to result from an imbalance of yellow bile. Choler was one four so-called "humours" or elements. During the Early Modern Period, the "humours" were believed to control personality. One with a sanguine humour was optimistic, a person with choleric humour was short-tempered and ambitious, a phlegmatic was sluggish and lazy, and one with a melancholic humour (Hamlet) was introspective, sallow, and thin.

270: **richer**: resourceful

273: **frame**: order; **start**: jump

Angus Wright as Guildenstern, Kenneth Branagh as Hamlet, and Michael Gould as Rosencrantz in the Royal Shakespeare Company's 1992 production directed by Adrian Noble
Photo: Donald Cooper

HAMLET
Upon the talk of the poisoning?

HORATIO
I did very well note him.

Enter ROSENCRANTZ and GUILDENSTERN

HAMLET
Oh, ha? Come, some music. Come, the recorders!
For if the King like not the comedy,   260
Why then, belike, he likes it not, pardie.
Come, some music!

GUILDENSTERN
Good my lord, vouchsafe me a word with you.

HAMLET
Sir, a whole history.

GUILDENSTERN
The King, sir–   265

HAMLET
Ay, sir, what of him?

GUILDENSTERN
Is in his retirement marvelous distempered.

HAMLET
With drink, sir?

GUILDENSTERN
No, my lord, rather with choler.

HAMLET
Your wisdom should show itself more richer to signify this to his doctor;   270
for, for me to put him to his purgation would perhaps plunge him into far
more choler.

GUILDENSTERN
Good my lord, put your discourse into some frame, and start not so
wildly from my affair.

HAMLET
I am tame, sir. Pronounce.   275

GUILDENSTERN
The Queen, your mother, in most great affliction of spirit, hath sent me
to you.

279: **breed**: kind

280: **wholesome**: sane

281: **pardon**: permission to go

288: **admiration**: bewilderment

291: **closet**: private chamber

295: **pickers and stealers**: hands

296: **do freely**: voluntarily

HAMLET
You are welcome.

GUILDENSTERN
Nay, good my lord, this courtesy is not of the right breed. If it shall please
you to make me a wholesome answer, I will do your mother's command-   280
ment. If not, your pardon and my return shall be the end of my business.

HAMLET
Sir, I cannot.

GUILDENSTERN
What, my lord?

HAMLET
Make you a wholesome answer; my wit's diseased. But, sir, such answer
as I can make, you shall command; or, rather, as you say, my mother.   285
Therefore no more, but to the matter. My mother, you say—

ROSENCRANTZ
Then thus she says. Your behavior hath struck her into amazement and
admiration.

HAMLET
O wonderful son, that can so astonish a mother! But is there no sequel at
the heels of this mother's admiration? Impart.   290

ROSENCRANTZ
She desires to speak with you in her closet, ere you go to bed

HAMLET
We shall obey, were she ten times our mother. Have you any further trade
with us?

ROSENCRANTZ
My lord, you once did love me.

HAMLET
So I do still, by these pickers and stealers.   295

ROSENCRANTZ
Good my lord, what is your cause of distemper? You do freely bar the
door upon your own liberty if you deny your griefs to your friend.

HAMLET
Sir, I lack advancement.

301: **"while the grass grows"**: reference to the proverb, "while the grass grows, the horse starves."

301: **something**: somewhat

304: **my love is too unmannerly**: i.e., my love encourages me to act this way

311: **ventages**: finger holes of the recorder

313: **stops**: holes for notes

319: **compass**: range

322: **fret**: irritate, but also a play on the frets of a stringed instrument ("frets" are the raised ridges on the fingerboard of a stringed musical instrument)

ROSENCRANTZ
How can that be, when you have the voice of the himself for your succession in Denmark? 300

HAMLET
Ay, but sir, "while the grass grows"–the proverb is something musty.
Reenter Players with recorders
O, the recorders! Let me see. To withdraw with you. Why do you go
about to recover the wind of me, as if you would drive me into a toil?

GUILDENSTERN
O, my lord, if my duty be too bold, my love is too unmannerly.

HAMLET
I do not well understand that. Will you play upon this pipe? 305

GUILDENSTERN
My lord, I cannot.

HAMLET
I pray you.

GUILDENSTERN
Believe me, I cannot.

HAMLET
I do beseech you.

GUILDENSTERN
I know no touch of it, my lord. 310

HAMLET
'Tis as easy as lying. Govern these ventages with your fingers and thumb,
give it breath with your mouth, and it will discourse most excellent
music. Look you, these are the stops.

GUILDENSTERN
But these cannot I command to any utterance of harmony. I have not the
skill. 315

HAMLET
Why, look you now, how unworthy a thing you make of me. You would
play upon me, you would seem to know my stops, you would pluck out
the heart of my mystery, you would sound me from my lowest note to the
top of my compass; and there is much music, excellent voice, in this little
organ, yet cannot you make it speak. 'Sblood, do you think I am easier to 320
be played on than a pipe? Call me what instrument you will, though you
can fret me, yet you cannot play upon me.
Enter POLONIUS
God bless you, sir!

336-338: "'Tis now the very witching time of night, / When churchyards yawn and hell breathes out / Contagion to this world.": Martin Sheen as Hamlet in 1967-68 Public Theater production directed by Joseph Papp
Photo: George E. Joseph

341: **nature**: natural affection

336-347: **'Tis now...my soul, consent:** Although not as well known or as beautiful as "To be or not to be," this soliloquy defines an important point in Hamlet's development as an avenger. Mel Gibson's energetic and angry Hamlet is perfect for these lines. He stands, perched between his life that was and his life (and death) to come.

342: **Nero:** killer of his mother, Agrippina; **firm:** determined

345: **hypocrites:** I am not the aggressor that I will appear to be

346: **soever:** however; **shent:** rebuked

347: **seals:** confirmation based in deeds

POLONIUS
My lord, the Queen would speak with you, and presently.

HAMLET
Do you see that cloud? That's almost in shape like a camel?   325

POLONIUS
By the mass, and 'tis like a camel, indeed.

HAMLET
- Methinks it is like a weasel.

POLONIUS
It is backed like a weasel.

HAMLET
Or like a whale?

POLONIUS
Very like a whale.   330

HAMLET
Then I will come to my mother by and by. [*Aside*] They fool me to the top
of my bent.–I will come by and by.

POLONIUS
I will say so.

HAMLET
"By and by" is easily said.

Exit POLONIUS
Leave me, friends.   335
Exeunt all but HAMLET

'Tis now the very witching time of night,
When churchyards yawn and hell itself breathes out
Contagion to this world. Now could I drink hot blood,
And do such bitter business as the day
Would quake to look on. Soft, now to my mother.   340
O heart, lose not thy nature. Let not ever
The soul of Nero enter this firm bosom.
Let me be cruel, not unnatural.
I will speak daggers to her, but use none.
My tongue and soul in this be hypocrites,   345
How in my words soever she be shent,
To give them seals, never my soul consent!

[Exit]

0: Location: The castle

0: Scene: Claudius's closet scene is the only time we see the king truly alone with his thoughts. It is sometimes played sincerely, though directors also use this scene to comment on the nature of a political personality, making Claudius appear sanctimonious and hypocritical.

5: **estate**: reign

9: **fear**: care

12: **single and peculiar**: individual's private

14: **noyance**: harm

16: **cease**: death

17: **gulf**: whirlpool

18: **massy**: gigantic

21: **mortised**: affixed

25: **Arm**: prepare

Act 3, Scene 3]

CLAUDIUS
I like him not, nor stands it safe with us
To let his madness range. Therefore prepare you.
I your commission will forthwith dispatch,
And he to England shall along with you.
The terms of our estate may not endure   5
Hazard so dangerous as doth hourly grow
Out of his lunacies.

GUILDENSTERN
We will ourselves provide.
Most holy and religious fear it is
To keep those many many bodies safe   10
That live and feed upon your majesty.

ROSENCRANTZ
The single and peculiar life is bound
With all the strength and armor of the mind
To keep itself from noyance, but much more
That spirit upon whose weal depends and rests   15
The lives of many. The cease of majesty
Dies not alone, but, like a gulf, doth draw
What's near it with it. It is a massy wheel,
Fixed on the summit of the highest mount,
To whose huge spokes ten thousand lesser things   20
Are mortised and adjoined, which, when it falls,
Each small annexment, petty consequence,
Attends the boisterous ruin. Never alone
Did the king sigh, but with a general groan.

CLAUDIUS
Arm you, I pray you, to this speedy voyage;   25
For we will fetters put upon this fear,
Which now goes too free-footed.

ROSENCRANTZ
We will haste us.
Exeunt ROSENCRANTZ and GUILDENSTERN
Enter POLONIUS

29: **arras**: wall hanging

30: **process**: proceedings; **tax him home**: rebuke him thoroughly

32: **meet**: fitting

34: **of vantage**: from his hidden position

38: **primal eldest curse**: the first murder was committed by Cain against his brother Abel, and God cursed Cain to the life of "a fugitive and a vagabond": Genesis 4:10-12

48: **visage of offense**: face of sin

50: **forstallèd**: prevented or delayed

tracks 21-23

52-88:
Bob Peck as Claudius and Simon Russell Beale as Hamlet
Ian Thorne as Claudius and Sam Payne as Hamlet

58: **currents**: courses of events

59: **gilded**: golden (from bribery)

60: **wicked prize**: proceeds of the crime

61: **above**: i.e., heaven

62: **shuffling**: evasion

65: **rests**: remains

70: **engaged**: entangled; **assay**: effort

POLONIUS
My lord, he's going to his mother's closet.
Behind the arras I'll convey myself
To hear the process. I'll warrant she'll tax him home.   30
And, as you said, and wisely was it said,
'Tis meet that some more audience than a mother,
Since nature makes them partial, should o'erhear
The speech of vantage. Fare you well, my liege.
I'll call upon you ere you go to bed,   35
And tell you what I know.

CLAUDIUS
                    Thanks, dear my lord.

                                                    Exit POLONIUS

O, my offense is rank, it smells to heaven.
It hath the primal eldest curse upon't,
A brother's murder. Pray can I not.
Though inclination be as sharp as will,   40
My stronger guilt defeats my strong intent,
And, like a man to double business bound,
I stand in pause where I shall first begin
And both neglect. What if this cursèd hand
Were thicker than itself with brother's blood,   45
Is there not rain enough in the sweet heavens
To wash it white as snow? Whereto serves mercy
But to confront the visage of offense?
And what's in prayer but this twofold force,
To be forestallèd ere we come to fall,   50
Or pardoned being down? Then I'll look up.
My fault is past. But, O, what form of prayer
Can serve my turn? Forgive me my foul murder?
That cannot be, since I am still possessed
Of those effects for which I did the murder–   55
My crown, mine own ambition, and my queen.
May one be pardoned and retain the offense?
In the corrupted currents of this world
Offense's gilded hand may shove by justice;
And oft 'tis seen the wicked prize itself   60
Buys out the law. But 'tis not so above.
There is no shuffling, there the action lies
In his true nature, and we ourselves compelled
Even to the teeth and forehead of our faults
To give in evidence. What then? What rests?   65
Try what repentance can. What can it not?
Yet what can it when one can not repent?
O wretched state! O bosom black as death!
O limèd soul, that struggling to be free,
Art more engaged! Help, angels! Make assay.   70

52-88:
Bob Peck as Claudius and Simon Russell Beale as Hamlet
Ian Thorne as Claudius and Sam Payne as Hamlet

37-73: Scene: In Olivier's 1948 film, Basil Sydney (Claudius) delivered a Victorian era performance, emphasizing his speech and clutching at his chest as if he were having a heart attack. Alan Bates' interpretation in the Zeffirelli film is far more convincing, although equally as melodramatic with his arching brow. Patrick Stewart played Claudius in the BBC production with Sir Derek Jacobi. Stewart's Claudius is as powerful as his voice and he carries himself regally, not hiding the fact that he is strong, intelligent, and more than a match for his brother's throne. Still, there is a kind of humanity about Stewart's Claudius that makes him a sympathetic character. He tries, but ambition gets the better of him. All of this intensifies the effect of his near breakdown in the confession scene.

Wallace Acton as Hamlet and Ted van Griethuysen as Claudius in the Shakespeare Theatre Company's 2001 production directed by Gale Edwards
Photo: Carol Rosegg

Bow, stubborn knees; and, heart with strings of steel,
Be soft as sinews of the newborn babe.
All may be well.

Enter HAMLET

HAMLET
Now might I do it pat, now he is praying;
And now I'll do't.
                    And so he goes to heaven;   75
And so am I revenged? That would be scanned:
A villain kills my father; and for that
I, his sole son, do this same villain send
To heaven.
O, this is hire and salary, not revenge.   80
He took my father grossly, full of bread,
With all his crimes broad blown, as flush as May;
And how his audit stands who knows save heaven?
But in our circumstance and course of thought
'Tis heavy with him. And am I then revenged,   85
To take him in the purging of his soul,
When he is fit and seasoned for his passage?
No!
Up, sword, and know thou a more horrid hint.
When he is drunk asleep, or in his rage,   90
Or in the incestuous pleasure of his bed,
At gaming, swearing, or about some act
That has no relish of salvation in't–
Then trip him, that his heels may kick at heaven,
And that his soul may be as damned and black   95
As hell, whereto it goes. My mother stays.
This physic but prolongs thy sickly days.

Exit

CLAUDIUS
My words fly up, my thoughts remain below.
Words without thoughts never to heaven go.

Exit

0: Location: Gertrude's chambers

0: Scene: This scene has been the subject of much theatric and psychological evaluation. Freud labeled it as Oedipal, and actors and directors must examine how they want to act out the lines. John Barrymore, in 1922, was the first to use a Freudian, psycho-analytical approach to this scene, and there was a obvious and strong sexual undercurrent between Hamlet and his mother. Barrymore described his character as a "mother-loving pervert." The RSC 1948 production eschewed the Oedipal interpretation. Its Hamlet moved towards the queen with a determined anger rather than passion. Olivier's movie, released that same year, featured a bed on stage. Olivier's Hamlet crawled over the sensuously lovely Eileen Herlie as Gertrude, his knife point raised to her throat, his eyes wide with the excitement of attacking her. In 1964, Richard Burton's Hamlet and Herlie's Gertrude exchanged an over-long kiss on the lips, although there is no bed on stage and they are standing.

1. **lay home to him**: reprove him thoroughly

2: **broad**: outrageous

5: **round**: blunt

15: **rood**: Christ's cross

16: "You are the Queen, your husband's brother's wife; / And-would it were not so-you are my mother.": Glenn Close as Gertrude and Mel Gibson as Hamlet in the 1990 film directed by Franco Zeffirelli

Copyright © 1990 Icon Distribution, Inc. Courtesy of Douglas Lanier

Act 3, Scene 4]

Enter GERTRUDE and POLONIUS

POLONIUS
He will come straight. Look you lay home to him.
Tell him his pranks have been too broad to bear with,
And that your grace hath screened and stood between
Much heat and him. I'll silence me e'en here.
Pray you, be round with him.   5

HAMLET
[*Within*] Mother, mother, mother!

GERTRUDE
I'll warrant you. Fear me not. Withdraw, I hear him coming.
[POLONIUS hides behind the arras]
Enter HAMLET

HAMLET
Now, mother, what's the matter?

GERTRUDE
Hamlet, thou hast thy father much offended.

HAMLET
Mother, you have my father much offended.   10

GERTRUDE
Come, come, you answer with an idle tongue.

HAMLET
Go, go, you question with a wicked tongue.

GERTRUDE
Why, how now, Hamlet!

HAMLET
What's the matter now?

GERTRUDE
Have you forgot me?

HAMLET
                    No, by the rood, not so,   15
You are the Queen, your husband's brother's wife;
And—would it were not so—you are my mother.

18: **those to you that can speak**: i.e., those who can deal better with you

25: **for a ducat**: i.e., I'll bet a ducat

39: **damnèd custom**: sinful habits

40: **proof**: protective armor; **sense**: feeling

Laurence Olivier as Hamlet and Eileen Herlie as Gertrude in the 1948 film directed by
Laurence Olivier
Courtesy of Douglas Lanier

GERTRUDE
    Nay, then, I'll set those to you that can speak.

HAMLET
    Come, come, and sit you down. You shall not budge,
    You go not till I set you up a glass   20
    Where you may see the inmost part of you.

GERTRUDE
    What wilt thou do? Thou wilt not murder me?
    Help, help, ho!

POLONIUS
    [*From behind the arras*] What, ho! help, help, help!

HAMLET
    How now, a rat? Dead, for a ducat, dead!   25
                                                            Kills POLONIUS

POLONIUS
    O, I am slain!

GERTRUDE
                        O me, what hast thou done?

HAMLET
    Nay, I know not. Is it the King?

GERTRUDE
    O, what a rash and bloody deed is this!

HAMLET
    A bloody deed! Almost as bad, good mother,
    As kill a king and marry with his brother.   30

GERTRUDE
    As kill a king?

HAMLET
    Ay, lady, 'twas my word.
    Thou wretched, rash, intruding fool, farewell.
    I took thee for thy better. Take thy fortune;
    Thou find'st to be too busy is some danger–   35
    Leave wringing of your hands. Peace, sit you down,
    And let me wring your heart; for so I shall,
    If it be made of penetrable stuff,
    If damnèd custom have not brassed it so
    That it is proof and bulwark against sense.   40

46: **sets a blister there**: brands on the forehead (as a criminal)

47: **dicers' oaths**: gamblers' promises

51: **mass**: solid earth

52: **tristful**: sad; **doom**: Judgment Day

56: **counterfeit presentment**: painted image

58: **Hyperion's**: the sun god's; **front of Jove**: forehead of Jove, the father of the gods

59: **Mars**: the god of war

60: **Mercury**: the winged messenger of the gods

66: **a mildewed ear**: an ear of grain that has gone bad

67: **Blasting**: infesting

68: **leave**: cease

69: **batten on this moor**: glut yourself on something worthless; also, a pun on moor as "field" and moor as "blackamoor" or villain

71: **heyday in the blood**: excitement of sexual passion

72: **waits**: follows

74: **hoodman-blind**: blind-man's bluff (implying trickery)

tracks 24-26

75-122:
Simon Russell Beale as Hamlet and Jane Lapotaire as Gertrude
Peter Haworth as Hamlet and Joy Coghill as Gertrude

76: **mutine**: mutiny

79: **charge**: attack

81: **As reason panders will**: i.e., as reason should triumph over lust

GERTRUDE
What have I done, that thou dar'st wag thy tongue
In noise so rude against me?

HAMLET
                    Such an act
That blurs the grace and blush of modesty,
Calls virtue hypocrite, takes off the rose
From the fair forehead of an innocent love   45
And sets a blister there; makes marriage vows
As false as dicers' oaths. O, such a deed
As from the body of contraction plucks
The very soul, and sweet religion makes
A rhapsody of words. Heaven's face doth glow;   50
Yea, this solidity and compound mass
With tristful visage, as against the doom,
Is thought-sick at the act.

GERTRUDE
                    Ay me, what act,
That roars so loud, and thunders in the index?

HAMLET
Look here, upon this picture, and on this,   55
The counterfeit presentment of two brothers.
See what a grace was seated on this brow,
Hyperion's curls; the front of Jove himself,
An eye like Mars, to threaten or command;
A station like the herald Mercury,   60
New lighted on a heaven-kissing hill;
A combination and a form indeed
Where every god did seem to set his seal
To give the world assurance of a man.
This was your husband. Look you now, what follows.   65
Here is your husband, like a mildewed ear,
Blasting his wholesome brother. Have you eyes?
Could you on this fair mountain leave to feed
And batten on this moor? Ha? Have you eyes?
You cannot call it love, for at your age   70
The heyday in the blood is tame, it's humble,
And waits upon the judgment; and what judgment
Would step from this to this? What devil was it
That thus hath cozened you at hoodman-blind?
O shame, where is thy blush? Rebellious hell,   75
If thou canst mutine in a matron's bones,
To flaming youth let virtue be as wax
And melt in her own fire. Proclaim no shame
When the compulsive ardor gives the charge,
Since frost itself as actively doth burn,   80
As reason panders will.

tracks 24-26

75-122:
Simon Russell Beale as Hamlet and Jane Lapotaire as Gertrude
Peter Haworth as Hamlet and Joy Coghill as Gertrude

84: **grainèd**: indelible

85: **tinct**: color

86: **emseamèd**: greasy

94: **precedent**: previous; **vice**: clown or jester

95: **cutpurse**: pickpocket

99: **shreds and patches**: refers to the clothes of a fool

101: "What would you, gracious figure?": Robert Murch as the Ghost, Kevin Kline as Hamlet, and Dana Ivey as Gertrude in the 1989-90 Public Theater production directed by Kevin Kline
Photo: George E. Joseph

99: Stage Direction: *[Enter the Ghost in his nightgown]*: This stage direction is unique to the First Quarto. Unlike the Ghost on the battlements, this is a domestic scene, and the Ghost is presumably familiar with Gertrude's bedroom and their customary dress there. In light of that, this stage direction shows this scene to be intensely personal.

105: **important**: urging

110: **Conceit**: imagination

GERTRUDE
    O Hamlet, speak no more.
    Thou turn'st mine eyes into my very soul,
    And there I see such black and grainèd spots
    As will not leave their tinct.

HAMLET
                    Nay, but to live   85
    In the rank sweat of an enseamèd bed,
    Stewed in corruption, honeying and making love
    Over the nasty sty–

GERTRUDE
    O, speak to me no more.
    These words, like daggers, enter in mine ears;   90
    No more, sweet Hamlet.

HAMLET
    A murderer and a villain,
    A slave that is not twentieth part the tithe
    Of your precedent lord, a vice of kings,
    A cutpurse of the empire and the rule,   95
    That from a shelf the precious diadem stole
    And put it in his pocket–

GERTRUDE
    No more!

HAMLET
    A king of shreds and patches—

                              Enter the GHOST [in his nightgown]
    Save me, and hover o'er me with your wings,   100
    You heavenly guards! What would you, gracious figure?

GERTRUDE
    Alas, he's mad!

HAMLET
    Do you not come your tardy son to chide,
    That, lapsed in time and passion, lets go by
    The important acting of your dread command? O, say!   105

Ghost
    Do not forget. This visitation
    Is but to whet thy almost blunted purpose.
    But, look, amazement on thy mother sits.
    O, step between her and her fighting soul!
    Conceit in weakest bodies strongest works.   110
    Speak to her, Hamlet.

tracks 24-26

75-122:
Simon Russell Beale as Hamlet and Jane Lapotaire as Gertrude
Peter Haworth as Hamlet and Joy Coghill as Gertrude

115: **incorporal**: bodiless

117: **in the alarm**: called to arms

118: **like life in excrements**: like something living, yet only lifeless outgrowths (excrements)

120: **distemper**: unbalanced mind

126: **stern effects**: intended acts

127: **want**: lack

134: **in his habit as he lived**: dressed as he did in life

138: **very cunning in**: a typical hallucination of the insane

HAMLET
How is it with you, lady?

GERTRUDE
Alas, how is't with you,
That you do bend your eye on vacancy,
And with the incorporal air do hold discourse?   115
Forth at your eyes your spirits wildly peep,
And, as the sleeping soldiers in the alarm,
Your bedded hair, like life in excrements
Starts up, and stands on end. O gentle son,
Upon the heat and flame of thy distemper   120
Sprinkle cool patience. Whereon do you look?

HAMLET
On him, on him! Look you, how pale he glares!
His form and cause conjoined, preaching to stones,
Would make them capable.—Do not look upon me,
Lest with this piteous action you convert   125
My stern effects. Then what I have to do
Will want true color; tears perchance for blood.

GERTRUDE
To whom do you speak this?

HAMLET
Do you see nothing there?

GERTRUDE
Nothing at all; yet all that is I see.   130

HAMLET
Nor did you nothing hear?

GERTRUDE
No, nothing but ourselves.

HAMLET
Why, look you there! Look, how it steals away!
My father, in his habit as he lived!
Look, where he goes, even now out at the portal!   135
                                                    Exit GHOST

GERTRUDE
This the very coinage of your brain.
This bodiless creation ecstasy
Is very cunning in.

142: **reword**: repeat

143: **gambol**: move away

144: **unction**: relief

147: **mining**: undermining

151: **virtue**: virtuous exhortation

152: **fatness of these pursy times**: grossness of these gluttonous days

154: **curb**: bow

159: **Assume**: imitate

169: **minister**: agent of punishment

170: **bestow...answer well**: dispose of the body and accept responsibility for the murder

174: **One word more, good lady**: From the Second Quarto, this line completes the thought in the verse and anticipates the next.

HAMLET
                    Ecstasy?
My pulse as yours doth temperately keep time,
And makes as healthful music. It is not madness   140
That I have uttered. Bring me to the test,
And I the matter will reword, which madness
Would gambol from. Mother, for love of grace,
Lay not that flattering unction to your soul,
That not your trespass, but my madness speaks.   145
It will but skin and film the ulcerous place,
Whilst rank corruption, mining all within,
Infects unseen. Confess yourself to heaven;
Repent what's past; avoid what is to come;
And do not spread the compost on the weeds   150
To make them ranker. Forgive me this my virtue,
For in the fatness of these pursy times
Virtue itself of vice must pardon beg,
Yea, curb and woo for leave to do him good.

GERTRUDE
O Hamlet, thou hast cleft my heart in twain.   155

HAMLET
O, throw away the worser part of it,
And live the purer with the other half.
Good night, but go not to mine uncle's bed.
Assume a virtue, if you have it not.
Refrain tonight,   160
And that shall lend a kind of easiness
To the next abstinence, the next more easy.
Once more, good night,
And when you are desirous to be blessed,
I'll blessing beg of you.   165
For this same lord, I do repent.
But heaven hath pleased it so
To punish me with this and this with me,
That I must be their scourge and minister.
I will bestow him, and will answer well   170
The death I gave him. So, again, good night.
I must be cruel only to be kind.
Thus bad begins and worse remains behind.
One word more, good lady.

GERTRUDE
                    What shall I do?

178: **reechy**: filthy

179: **paddling**: fondly fingering

180: **ravel**: disclose

182: **in craft**: with cunning

184: **paddock:** toad; **gib:** tomcat

188: **famous ape**: from the story of an ape who tried to imitate birds and fell to his death

191-193: "Be thou assured, if words be made of breath, / And breath of life, I have no life to breathe / What thou hast said to me.": Kenneth Branagh as Hamlet and Julie Christie as Gertrude in the 1996 film directed by Kenneth Branagh
Photo: Peter Mountain © Columbia TriStar. Courtesy of Douglas Lanier

196-204: **There's letters...meet**: From the Second Quarto, these lines show the depth of Hamlet's understanding of Claudius' plan for him and his employ of Rosencrantz and Guildenstern.

199: **work**: proceed

200: **to have the engineer...petard**: to have the one who engineered the explosive device be blown skyward

202: **mines**: military tunnels

HAMLET

    Not this, by no means, that I bid you do: 175
    Let the bloat King tempt you again to bed,
    Pinch wanton on your cheek, call you his mouse,
    And let him, for a pair of reechy kisses,
    Or paddling in your neck with his damned fingers,
    Make you to ravel all this matter out, 180
    That I essentially am not in madness,
    But mad in craft. 'Twere good you let him know;
    For who, that's but a queen, fair, sober, wise,
    Would from a paddock, from a bat, a gib,
    Such dear concernings hide? Who would do so? 185
    No, in despite of sense and secrecy,
    Unpeg the basket on the house's top.
    Let the birds fly, and, like the famous ape,
    To try conclusions, in the basket creep
    And break your own neck down. 190

GERTRUDE

    Be thou assured, if words be made of breath,
    And breath of life, I have no life to breathe
    What thou hast said to me.

HAMLET

    I must to England. You know that?

GERTRUDE

             Alack,
    I had forgot. 'Tis so concluded on. 195

HAMLET

    There's letters sealed, and my two schoolfellows,
    Whom I will trust as I will adders fanged,
    They bear the mandate. They must sweep my way
    And marshal me to knavery. Let it work,
    For 'tis the sport to have the engineer 200
    Hoist with his own petard, and't shall go hard
    But I will delve one yard below their mines
    And blow them at the moon! O, 'tis most sweet,
    When in one line two crafts directly meet.
    This man shall set me packing. 205
    I'll lug the guts into the neighbor room.
    Mother, good night. Indeed this counselor
    Is now most still, most secret and most grave,
    Who was in life a foolish prating knave.
    Come, sir, to draw toward an end with you. 210
    Good night, mother.

               Exeunt HAMLET dragging POLONIUS

[Hamlet

Act 4

0: Location: the castle.

0: Scene: This scene is often shortened or included as part of 3.4.

In 1870, Fanny Morant delivered a voluptuous and sexual interpretation of Gertrude in *Hamlet* with Henry Irving. Her portrayal was imitated and developed by Margaret Leighton after 1884. Glenn Close, in Zeffirelli's *Hamlet*, sits on the floor after Hamlet leaves, staring disbelievingly at the medallion bearing the image of her dead husband that Hamlet left with her. She pockets it quickly as Claudius enters the room.

1: **matter**: significance

4: **Bestow...while**: From the Second Quarto, this line serves as a dismissal to Rosencrantz and Guildenstern, facilitating their exit.

11: **brainish apprehension**: brain-sick idea

13: **us**: me (the royal "we")

16: **answered**: accounted for

17: **laid to us**: blamed on us; **providence**: forethought and oversight

18: **short...out of haunt**: reined in, away from public gatherings

21: **owner**: victim

26: **mineral**: mine

Act 4, Scene 1]

Enter CLAUDIUS, GERTRUDE, ROSENCRANTZ,
and GUILDENSTERN

CLAUDIUS
There's matter in these sighs, these profound heaves.
You must translate. 'Tis fit we understand them.
Where is your son?

GERTRUDE
Bestow this place on us a little while.
Exeunt ROSENCRANTZ and GUILDENSTERN
Ah, my good lord, what have I seen tonight!   5

CLAUDIUS
What, Gertrude? How does Hamlet?

GERTRUDE
Mad as the sea and wind, when both contend
Which is the mightier. In his lawless fit,
Behind the arras hearing something stir,
He whips his rapier out and cries, "A rat, a rat!"   10
And, in this brainish apprehension, kills
The unseen good old man.

CLAUDIUS
                              O heavy deed!
It had been so with us, had we been there.
His liberty is full of threats to all,
To you yourself, to us, to everyone.   15
Alas, how shall this bloody deed be answered?
It will be laid to us, whose providence
Should have kept short, restrained and out of haunt
This mad young man. But so much was our love,
We would not understand what was most fit,   20
But, like the owner of a foul disease,
To keep it from divulging, lets it feed
Even on the pith of life. Where is he gone?

GERTRUDE
To draw apart the body he hath killed,
O'er whom, his very madness like some ore   25
Among a mineral of metals base,
Shows itself pure. He weeps for what is done.

32: **countenance**: condone

33: **join you with some further aid**: i.e., find others to help you

Costume rendering for Rosencrantz from the 1934 production at the New Theatre directed by Sir John Gielgud
Photo: Rare Book and Special Collections Library, University of Illinois at Urbana-Champaign

CLAUDIUS
    O Gertrude, come away!
    The sun no sooner shall the mountains touch
    But we will ship him hence, and this vile deed   30
    We must, with all our majesty and skill,
    Both countenance and excuse. Ho, Guildenstern!

Enter ROSENCRANTZ and GUILDENSTERN

    Friends both, go join you with some further aid.
    Hamlet in madness hath Polonius slain,
    And from his mother's closet hath he dragged him.   35
    Go seek him out, speak fair, and bring the body
    Into the chapel. I pray you, haste in this.

Exeunt ROSENCRANTZ and GUILDENSTERN

    Come, Gertrude, we'll call up our wisest friends
    And let them know, both what we mean to do
    And what's untimely done–   40
    O, come away!
    My soul is full of discord and dismay.

Exeunt

0: **Location**: the castle

0: **Scene**: Although frequently cut or included with 4.3, this scene has a comic element that leads nicely into 4.3. Rosencrantz and Guildenstern are usually played as a pathetic and bumbling twosome, outwitted and outclassed by Hamlet.

5: **Compounded...kin**: Mingled with dust

9: **That I can...own**: i.e., I can't grant your request and keep my secret

9-10: **demanded of a sponge**: questioned by those seeking royal favor

10: **replication**: reply

12: **countenance**: (the King's favorable) looks

14: **mouthed**: placed into the cheek so that the sweetness can be sucked out

Costume rendering for Guildenstern from the 1934 production at the New Theatre directed by Sir John Gielgud
Photo: Rare Book and Special Collections Library, University of Illinois at Urbana-Champaign

Act 4, Scene 2]

HAMLET
Safely stowed.

ROSENCRANTZ and GUILDENSTERN
Hamlet! Lord Hamlet!

HAMLET
What noise? Who calls on Hamlet? O, here they come.
[Enter ROSENCRANTZ and GUILDENSTERN]

ROSENCRANTZ
What have you done, my lord, with the dead body?

HAMLET
Compounded it with dust, whereto 'tis kin.   5

ROSENCRANTZ
Tell us where 'tis, that we may take it thence and bear it to the chapel.

HAMLET
Do not believe it.

ROSENCRANTZ
Believe what?

HAMLET
That I can keep your counsel and not mine own. Besides, to be demanded
of a sponge–what replication should be made by the son of a king?   10

ROSENCRANTZ
Take you me for a sponge, my lord?

HAMLET
Ay, sir, that soaks up the King's countenance, his rewards, his authorities.
But such officers do the King best service in the end. He keeps them, like
an apple in the corner of his jaw, first mouthed, to be last swallowed.
When he needs what you have gleaned, it is but squeezing you, and,   15
sponge, you shall be dry again.

ROSENCRANTZ
I understand you not, my lord.

18: **A knavish...ear**: A clever speech is never understood by a fool.

23: **Hide fox**: a game similar to hide-and-seek

Ben Aris as Rosencrantz and Clive Graham as Guildenstern in the 1969 film directed by Tony Richardson
Copyright © Columbia Pictures Industries, Inc. Courtesy of Douglas Lanier

HAMLET
I am glad of it. A knavish speech sleeps in a foolish ear.

ROSENCRANTZ
My lord, you must tell us where the body is, and go with us to the King.

HAMLET
The body is with the King, but the King is not with the body. The King   20
is a thing–

GUILDENSTERN
A thing, my lord!

HAMLET
Of nothing. Bring me to him. Hide fox, and all after.

Exeunt

0: Location: usually in a hall in the castle, but this scene has often been played on a staircase

0: Scene: In Branagh's film, Claudius (Derek Jacobi) gives Hamlet a stinging blow with the back of his hand, and in the Brook production, Kissooner seems to be holding back a strong desire to do the exact same thing. His frustrated anger is barely held in check. Mel Gibson's Hamlet plays this scene to the hilt, wearing the cap that Ian Holm (Polonius) has worn in every scene. He can barely hold back gleeful laughter as he dances around Claudius's questions.

4: **of the distracted multitude**: by the foolish and unsettled populace

5: **like not...their eyes**: choose not by reason but by outward appearance

6: **scourge**: punishment

7: **bear all smooth**: pass everything off

9: **pause**: careful planning

10: **appliance**: remedy

12: **bestowed**: hidden

Act 4, Scene 3]

Enter CLAUDIUS and Attendants

CLAUDIUS
  I have sent to seek him and to find the body.
  How dangerous is it that this man goes loose.
  Yet must not we put the strong law on him.
  He's loved of the distracted multitude,
  Who like not in their judgment, but their eyes;   5
  And where 'tis so, the offender's scourge is weighed,
  But never the offense. To bear all smooth and even,
  This sudden sending him away must seem
  Deliberate pause. Diseases desperate grown
  By desperate appliance are relieved,   10
  Or not at all.

Enter ROSENCRANTZ

                    How now! What hath befallen?

ROSENCRANTZ
  Where the dead body is bestowed, my lord,
  We cannot get from him.

CLAUDIUS
                    But where is he?

ROSENCRANTZ
  Without, my lord, guarded, to know your pleasure.

CLAUDIUS
  Bring him before us.   15

ROSENCRANTZ
  Ho, Guildenstern! Bring in my lord.

Enter HAMLET and GUILDENSTERN

CLAUDIUS
  Now, Hamlet, where's Polonius?

HAMLET
  At supper.

CLAUDIUS
  At supper? Where?

20-21: **convocation...diet**: a clever allusion to the Diet of Worms (1521), a convocation wherein Martin Luther explained his reform doctrine. He posted his treatise on the door of the cathedral in Wittenberg.

20: **politic**: From the Second Quarto, this supports Hamlet's pun.

23: **variable service**: different courses

35: **tender**: value

38: **at help**: favorable

39: **associates tend...bent**: companions wait and everything is ready

HAMLET
  Not where he eats, but where he is eaten. A certain convocation of politic   20
  worms are e'en at him. Your worm is your only emperor for diet. We fat
  all creatures else to fat us, and we fat ourselves for maggots. Your fat
  king and your lean beggar is but variable service, two dishes, but to one
  table. That's the end.

CLAUDIUS
  What dost you mean by this?   25

HAMLET
  Nothing but to show you how a king may go a progress through the guts
  of a beggar.

CLAUDIUS
  Where is Polonius?

HAMLET
  In heaven; send thither to see. If your messenger find him not there, seek
  him i' th' other place yourself. But indeed, if you find him not within this   30
  month, you shall nose him as you go up the stairs into the lobby.

CLAUDIUS
  [*To Attendants*] Go seek him there.

HAMLET
  He will stay till ye come.

                                                      Exeunt Attendants

CLAUDIUS
  Hamlet, this deed, for thine especial safety—
  Which we do tender as we dearly grieve   35
  For that which thou hast done—must send thee hence
  With fiery quickness. Therefore prepare thyself.
  The bark is ready, and the wind at help,
  The associates tend, and everything is bent
  For England.

HAMLET
                  For England?

CLAUDIUS
                  Ay, Hamlet.

HAMLET
                        Good.   40

42: **cherub**: Cherubs are angels who possessed the gift of knowledge.

47: **at foot**: closely, on his heels

50: **leans**: bears

51: **England**: the King of England

52: **give thee sense**: give you a reason to value my love

53: **cicatrice**: scar

54: **thy free awe**: your unconstrained show of respect

55: **not coldly set**: to set aside, disregard

58: **present**: immediate

59: **hectic**: fever

61: **Howe'er my haps**: whatever happens to me

CLAUDIUS
So is it, if thou knew'st our purposes.

HAMLET
I see a cherub that sees them. But, come; for England! Farewell, dear
mother.

CLAUDIUS
Thy loving father, Hamlet.

HAMLET
My mother. Father and mother is man and wife; man and wife is one   45
flesh; and so, my mother. Come, for England!

Exit

CLAUDIUS
Follow him at foot. Tempt him with speed aboard.
Delay it not. I'll have him hence tonight.
Away, for everything is sealed and done
That else leans on th' affair. Pray you, make haste.   50
Exeunt ROSENCRANTZ and GUILDENSTERN
And, England, if my love thou hold'st at aught,
As my great power thereof may give thee sense,
Since yet thy cicatrice looks raw and red
After the Danish sword, and thy free awe
Pays homage to us—thou mayst not coldly set   55
Our sovereign process, which imports at full,
By letters conjuring to that effect,
The present death of Hamlet. Do it, England,
For like the hectic in my blood he rages,
And thou must cure me. Till I know 'tis done,   60
Howe'er my haps, my joys were ne'er begun.

Exit

0: Location: the coast of Denmark

0: Scene: Branagh's *Hamlet* depicts a wintry scene: frozen tundra with a large army slowly moving across the land. The bleak, white terrain and the blackness of Hamlet's coat provide visual cues of Hamlet's chilly, dark mood.

2: **license**: permission (previously granted to Fortinbras by Claudius; Fortinbras is now seeking an escort through Denmark)

3: **conveyance of**: escort for

5: **would aught with us**: wishes anything of us

6: **in his eye**: in his presence

9: **powers**: forces

9-66: Scene: This scene from the Second Quarto, frequently cut, provides commentary on the events in Denmark and the possibility of invasion from Norway (even though Fortinbras has received safe passage through Denmark from Claudius). It also explains the arrival of Fortinbras in 5.2.

15: **the main**: the heart

Act 4, Scene 4]

Enter FORTINBRAS [with a Captain and soldiers]

FORTINBRAS
Go, captain, from me greet the Danish king;
Tell him that, by his license, Fortinbras
Claims the conveyance of a promised march
Over his kingdom. You know the rendezvous.
If that his majesty would aught with us,   5
We shall express our duty in his eye;
And let him know so.

Captain
I will do't, my lord.

FORTINBRAS
                    Go safely on.

Exeunt FORTINBRAS and soldiers
Enter HAMLET, ROSENCRANTZ, GUILDENSTERN, and others

HAMLET
Good sir, whose powers are these?

Captain
They are of Norway, sir.   10

HAMLET
How purposed, sir, I pray you?

Captain
Against some part of Poland.

HAMLET
Who commands them, sir?

Captain
The nephew to old Norway, Fortinbras.

HAMLET
Goes it against the main of Poland, sir,   15
Or for some frontier?

17: **addition**: exaggeration

20: **To pay...farm it**: i.e., it is not worth five ducats to rent

22: **ranker...fee**: a higher price, if it were sold outright

26: **straw**: i.e., trivial fight

27: **imposthume**: abscess

32: **inform against**: accuse

tracks 27-29

32-66:
Sir John Gielgud as Hamlet
Richard Burton as Hamlet

34: **market**: profit

36: **discourse**: capacity for reason

37: **before and after**: i.e., the past and the future

39: **fust**: become moldy

40: **Bestial oblivion**: mindlessness

46: **gross as earth**: as evident as the planet

47: **charge**: cast

Costume rendering for Fortinbras' Captain from the 1934 production at the New Theatre directed by Sir John Gielgud
Photo: Rare Book and Special Collections Library, University of Illinois at Urbana-Champaign

Captain
    Truly to speak, and with no addition,
    We go to gain a little patch of ground
    That hath in it no profit but the name.
    To pay five ducats, five, I would not farm it,   20
    Nor will it yield to Norway or the Pole
    A ranker rate, should it be sold in fee.

HAMLET
    Why, then the Polack never will defend it.

Captain
    Yes, it is already garrisoned.

HAMLET
    Two thousand souls and twenty thousand ducats   25
    Will not debate the question of this straw.
    This is the imposthume of much wealth and peace
    That inward breaks and shows no cause without
    Why the man dies. I humbly thank you, sir.

Captain
    God be wi' you, sir.

                                                    Exit

ROSENCRANTZ
                      Will't please you go, my lord?   30

HAMLET
    I'll be with you straight; go a little before.
                                Exeunt all except HAMLET

    How all occasions do inform against me,
    And spur my dull revenge! What is a man,
    If his chief good and market of his time
    Be but to sleep and feed? A beast, no more.   35
    Sure he that made us with such large discourse,
    Looking before and after, gave us not
    That capability and god-like reason
    To fust in us unused. Now, whether it be
    Bestial oblivion, or some craven scruple   40
    Of thinking too precisely on the event,
    A thought which, quartered, hath but one part wisdom
    And ever three parts coward, I do not know
    Why yet I live to say, "This thing's to do,"
    Since I have cause and will and strength and means   45
    To do't. Examples gross as earth exhort me.
    Witness this army of such mass and charge

tracks 27-29

32-66:
Sir John Gielgud as Hamlet
Richard Burton as Hamlet

48: **tender**: young

49: **puffed**: inspired

50: **Makes mouths**: makes faces

58: **Excitements**: urgings

61: **trick of fame**: illusion of honor

63: **the numbers cannot try the cause**: the armies don't have room for battle

65-66: "O, from this time forth, / My thoughts be bloody, or be nothing worth!": Kevin Kline
as Hamlet in the 1989-90 Public Theater production directed by Kevin Kline
Photo: George E. Joseph

Led by a delicate and tender prince,
Whose spirit with divine ambition puffed
Makes mouths at the invisible event,   50
Exposing what is mortal and unsure
To all that fortune, death and danger dare,
Even for an eggshell. Rightly to be great
Is not to stir without great argument,
But greatly to find quarrel in a straw   55
When honor's at the stake. How stand I then,
That have a father killed, a mother stained,
Excitements of my reason and my blood,
And let all sleep? While, to my shame, I see
The imminent death of twenty thousand men,   60
That, for a fantasy and trick of fame,
Go to their graves like beds; fight for a plot
Whereon the numbers cannot try the cause,
Which is not tomb enough and continent
To hide the slain? O, from this time forth,   65
My thoughts be bloody, or be nothing worth!

                                                                    Exit

0: Location: sometimes in the King's Chambers, sometimes in the courtyard

2: **importunate indeed distract**: insistent to the point of distraction

7: **Spurns...doubt**: stamps her foot in anger over anything and speaks uncertainly

9: **unshapèd use**: incoherent manner

9-10: **doth move...to collection**: makes people come to their own conclusion

10-11: **They aim...own thoughts**: i.e., people have to try to figure out what she's saying by patching the words together

17: **sin's true nature**: Sin was thought of as a sickness, its main symptoms being anxiety and depression.

18: **toy**: triviality; **amiss**: calamity

21: "Where is the beauteous majest of Denmark?": Anthony Hopkins as Claudius, Marianne Faithfull as Ophelia, and Judy Parfitt as Gertrude in the 1969 film directed by Tony Richardson
Copyright © Columbia Pictures Industries, Inc. Courtesy of Douglas Lanier

22: **How now**: i.e., what's this?

Act 4, Scene 5]

Enter GERTRUDE and HORATIO

GERTRUDE
I will not speak with her.

HORATIO
She is importunate, indeed distract.
Her mood will needs be pitied.

GERTRUDE
What would she have?

HORATIO
She speaks much of her father, says she hears   5
There's tricks i' th' world, and hems, and beats her heart,
Spurns enviously at straws, speaks things in doubt
That carry but half sense. Her speech is nothing,
Yet the unshapèd use of it doth move
The hearers to collection. They aim at it   10
And botch the words up fit to their own thoughts,
Which, as her winks, and nods, and gestures yield them,
Indeed would make one think there might be thought,
Though nothing sure, yet much unhappily.

GERTRUDE
'Twere good she were spoken with, for she may strew   15
Dangerous conjectures in ill-breeding minds. Let her come in.
To my sick soul—as sin's true nature is—
Each toy seems prologue to some great amiss.
So full of artless jealousy is guilt,
It spills itself in fearing to be spilt.   20

Enter OPHELIA distracted

OPHELIA
Where is the beauteous majesty of Denmark?

GERTRUDE
How now, Ophelia!

25: **cockle hat**: a hat with a cockleshell, originally a pilgrim's emblem

37: **Larded**: garnished

39: **true-love showers**: the tears of his true love

41: **They say...daughter**: a common folktale. Christ turned a baker's daughter into an owl because she was stingy with her bread.

42: "God be at your table!": Nicole Lowrance as Ophelia in the Shakespeare Theatre Company's 2001 production directed by Gale Edwards
Photo: Carol Rosegg

43: **Conceit upon**: she thinks of

OPHELIA
> *Sings*
> How should I your true love know
>> From another one?
> By his cockle hat and staff,   25
>> And his sandal shoon.

GERTRUDE
Alas, sweet lady, what imports this song?

OPHELIA
Say you? Nay, pray you, mark.
> *Sings*
> He is dead and gone, lady,
>> He is dead and gone;   30
> At his head a grass-green turf,
>> At his heels a stone.

Enter CLAUDIUS

GERTRUDE
Nay, but, Ophelia–

OPHELIA
Pray you, mark.
> *Sings*
> White his shroud as the mountain snow–   *35*

GERTRUDE
Alas, look here, my lord.

OPHELIA
> *Sings*
> Larded with sweet flowers
>> Which bewept to the grave did go
> With true-love showers.

CLAUDIUS
How do you, pretty lady?   40

OPHELIA
Well, God 'ild you! They say the owl was a baker's daughter. Lord, we
know what we are, but know not what we may be. God be at your table!

CLAUDIUS
Conceit upon her father.

46: **Saint Valentine's Day**: Legend had it that the first man seen by a maid on this day was destined to be her husband.

47: **morning betime**: early morning

51: **dupped**: opened, unlatched

55: **on't**: of it

56: **Gis**: Jesus

59: **cock**: euphemism for "god" and a play on "penis"

65-66: "But I cannot choose but weep, / to think they should lay him i' th' cold ground.": Leah Curney as Ophelia and Sally Wingert as a Gentlewoman in the Guthrie Theater's 2006 production directed by Joe Dowling
Photo: Michal Daniel

72: **spies**: scouts

75: **muddied**: confused

OPHELIA
Pray you, let's have no words of this. But when they ask you what it
means, say you this: 45
    Sings
    Tomorrow is Saint Valentine's day,
      All in the morning betime,
    And I a maid at your window,
      To be your Valentine."
    Then up he rose, and donn'd his clothes,   50
      And dupped the chamber door;
    Let in the maid, that out a maid
      Never departed more.

CLAUDIUS
Pretty Ophelia–

OPHELIA
Indeed, la! Without an oath, I'll make an end on't: 55
    Sings
    By Gis and by Saint Charity,
      Alack, and fie for shame!
    Young men will do't, if they come to't;
      By cock, they are to blame.
    Quoth she "Before you tumbled me,   60
      You promised me to wed."
    "So would I ha' done, by yonder sun,
      An thou hadst not come to my bed."

CLAUDIUS
[*To GERTRUDE*] How long hath she been thus?

OPHELIA
I hope all will be well. We must be patient. But I cannot choose but weep,   65
to think they should lay him i' th' cold ground. My brother shall know of
it. And so I thank you for your good counsel. Come, my coach! Good
night, ladies; good night, sweet ladies. Good night, good night.
                                        Exit

CLAUDIUS
Follow her close. Give her good watch, I pray you.
                                        Exit HORATIO
O, this is the poison of deep grief; it springs   70
All from her father's death. O Gertrude, Gertrude,
When sorrows come, they come not single spies
But in battalions. First, her father slain;
Next, your son gone; and he most violent author
Of his own just remove; the people muddied,   75

77: **greenly**: foolishly, without using mature judgment

78: **hugger-mugger**: secret haste

81: **and as much containing**: and as important

83: **keeps himself in clouds**: shrouds himself in gloomy aloofness

86: **of matter beggared**: i.e., without knowing the truth

87-88: **Will nothing... and ear**: i.e., will not hesitate to publicly accuse us

89: **murdering piece**: small cannon loaded with grapeshot

90: **superfluous**: redundant (one bullet would have been sufficient)

92: **Switzers**: Swiss mercenaries hired as royal guards

94: **overpeering of his list**: i.e., overflowing its boundary ("overpeer" literally means to look over a boundary or rim)

96: **a riotous head**: a force of rioters, a mob

98: **as the world were now but to begin**: if the world were to begin now

105: **counter**: i.e., treason

Thick and unwholesome in their thoughts and whispers,
For good Polonius' death; and we have done but greenly,
In hugger-mugger to inter him. Poor Ophelia
Divided from herself and her fair judgment,
Without the which we are pictures, or mere beasts;   80
Last, and as much containing as all these,
Her brother is in secret come from France,
Feeds on his wonder, keeps himself in clouds,
And wants not buzzers to infect his ear
With pestilent speeches of his father's death;   85
Wherein necessity, of matter beggared,
Will nothing stick our persons to arraign
In ear and ear. O my dear Gertrude, this,
Like to a murdering piece, in many places
Gives me superfluous death.   90

                                            A noise within
                                        Enter a Messenger

GERTRUDE
    Alack, what noise is this?

CLAUDIUS
    Where are my Switzers? Let them guard the door.
    What is the matter?

Messenger
                    Save yourself, my lord.
    The ocean, overpeering of his list,
    Eats not the flats with more impetuous haste   95
    Than young Laertes, in a riotous head,
    O'erbears your officers. The rabble call him lord,
    And, as the world were now but to begin,
    Antiquity forgot, custom not known,
    The ratifiers and props of every word,   100
    They cry, "Choose we! Laertes shall be king."
    Caps, hands, and tongues, applaud it to the clouds,
    "Laertes shall be king, Laertes king!"

GERTRUDE
    How cheerfully on the false trail they cry!
    O, this is counter, you false Danish dogs!   105

CLAUDIUS
    The doors are broke.

                                            A noise within
                            Enter LAERTES [with his followers]

113: **That...bastard**: i.e., I cannot remain calm and be a true son to my father

119: **fear**: fear for

120: **hedge**: i.e., protect (literally, surround by a hedge)

121: **That...peep**: treason can only peer through (continuing the imagery of the hedge)

Set rendering from the 1958 production at the Shakespeare Memorial Theatre directed by Glen Byam Shaw

Photo: Rare Book and Special Collections Library, University of Illinois at Urbana-Champaign

LAERTES
Where is this king? Sirs, stand you all without.

Followers
No, let's come in.

LAERTES
I pray you, give me leave.

Followers
We will, we will.   110

LAERTES
I thank you. Keep the door.

Exeunt followers

                    O thou vile king,
Give me my father!

GERTRUDE
                    Calmly, good Laertes.

LAERTES
That drop of blood that's calm proclaims me bastard,
Cries cuckold to my father, brands the harlot
Even here, between the chaste unsmirchèd brow   115
Of my true mother.

CLAUDIUS
What is the cause, Laertes,
That thy rebellion looks so giant-like?
Let him go, Gertrude. Do not fear our person.
There's such divinity doth hedge a king   120
That treason can but peep to what it would,
Acts little of his will. Tell me, Laertes,
Why thou art thus incensed. Let him go, Gertrude–
Speak, man.

LAERTES
Where is my father?

CLAUDIUS
                    Dead.

GERTRUDE
                    But not by him.   125

CLAUDIUS
Let him demand his fill.

127: **juggled with**: deceived

130: **I stand**: I am resolved

133: **stay**: prevent

135: **husband them**: use them thriftily

139: **sweepstake**: in a clean sweep; **draw**: take from

143: **life-rendering pelican**: The pelican was supposed to feed its young from its own blood.

147: **sensibly**: sympathetically

LAERTES
   How came he dead? I'll not be juggled with.
   To hell, allegiance! Vows, to the blackest devil!
   Conscience and grace, to the profoundest pit!
   I dare damnation. To this point I stand,   130
   That both the worlds I give to negligence,
   Let come what comes, only I'll be revenged
   Most thoroughly for my father.

CLAUDIUS
                Who shall stay you?

LAERTES
   My will, not all the world;
   And for my means, I'll husband them so well   135
   They shall go far with little.

CLAUDIUS
              Good Laertes,
   If you desire to know the certainty
   Of your dear father's death, is't writ in your revenge,
   That, sweepstake, you will draw both friend and foe,
   Winner and loser?

LAERTES
            None but his enemies.   140

CLAUDIUS
   Will you know them then?

LAERTES
   To his good friends thus wide I'll ope my arms,
   And like the kind life-rendering pelican,
   Repast them with my blood.

CLAUDIUS
            Why, now you speak
   Like a good child and a true gentleman.   145
   That I am guiltless of your father's death,
   And am most sensibly in grief for it,
   It shall as level to your judgment pierce
   As day does to your eye.

                    A noise within: Let her come in
                                Enter OPHELIA

LAERTES
   How now! What noise is that?   150

152: **virtue**: natural power

tracks 30-32

154-189:
Ellen Terry as Ophelia
Emma Fielding as Ophelia

164: "Fare you well, my dove.": Jean Simmons as Ophelia, Terence Morgan as Laertes, Eileen Herlie as Gertrude, and Basil Sydney as Claudius in the 1948 film directed by Laurence Olivier
Courtesy of Douglas Lanier

165: **persuade**: argue for

169: Scene: David Garrick began the tradition of a mad Ophelia carrying a "neatly arranged" handful of straws instead of flowers, which continued into the nineteenth and twentieth centuries. Garrick's most admired Ophelia was Mrs. Cibber who, according to Dover Wilson, "preserved favor and prettiness through all her grief and terror." Ellen Terry, Sir John Gielgud's grandmother, played Ophelia to Henry Irving's Hamlet. Terry gave her Ophelia a distracted and disturbing madness, eliminating any call for delicacy or "prettiness." In Zeffirelli's production, Helena Bonham-Carter ran through the castle barefoot and loosely robed, in an overtly sexual and powerful portrayal of an insane and lost Ophelia.

172-175: **There's fennel...father died**: The distribution of herbs and flowers was an old funeral custom, and Ophelia imagines herself giving her father a proper burial. Each flower carries it own particular significance. Ophelia is compared to violets throughout the play.

178: **favor**: beauty

O heat, dry up my brains! Tears seven times salt,
Burn out the sense and virtue of mine eye!
By heaven, thy madness shall be paid by weight,
Till our scale turn the beam. O rose of May!
Dear maid, kind sister, sweet Ophelia!   155
O heavens! Is't possible, a young maid's wits
Should be as mortal as an old man's life?
Nature is fine in love, and where 'tis fine,
It sends some precious instance of itself
After the thing it loves.   160

OPHELIA
     Sings
     They bore him barefaced on the bier;
     Hey non nony, nony, hey nony;
     And in his grave rained many a tear—
Fare you well, my dove.

LAERTES
Hadst thou thy wits, and didst persuade revenge, It could not move thus.   165

OPHELIA
You must sing "A-down a-down"; and you "Call him a-down-a". O, how the
wheel becomes it! It is the false steward that stole his master's daughter.

LAERTES
This nothing's more than matter.

OPHELIA
There's rosemary, that's for remembrance. Pray, love, remember. And
there is pansies, that's for thoughts.   170

LAERTES
A document in madness—thoughts and remembrance fitted.

OPHELIA
There's fennel for you, and columbines. There's rue for you, and here's
some for me. We may call it herb-grace o' Sundays. O you must wear your
rue with a difference. There's a daisy. I would give you some violets, but
they withered all when my father died. They say he made a good end.   175
     Sings
     For bonny sweet Robin is all my joy.

LAERTES
Thought and affliction, passion, hell itself
She turns to favor and to prettiness.

154-189:
Ellen Terry as Ophelia
Emma Fielding as Ophelia

185: **flaxen**: white; **poll**: head

190: "Do you see this, you Gods?": Poppy Miller as Ophelia and Michael Shaeffer Laertes in the 2005 Northampton production directed by Rupert Goold
Photo: Donald Cooper

193: **of whom**: whichever of

195: **collateral**: an agent's

196: **touched**: implicated (touched by guilt)

198: **satisfaction**: recompense

203: **hatchment**: coat-of-arms carried in a funeral and placed on the grave as a marker

OPHELIA
>*Sings*
>And will he not come again?
>>And will he not come again?   180
>No, no, he is dead,
>>Go to thy death-bed,
>He never will come again.
>>His beard was as white as snow,
>All flaxen was his poll.   185
>>He is gone, he is gone,
>And we cast away moan.
>>God ha' mercy on his soul.
>And of all Christian souls, I pray God. God be wi' ye.

>> *Exit*

LAERTES
>Do you see this, you Gods?   190

CLAUDIUS
>Laertes, I must commune with your grief,
>Or you deny me right. Go but apart,
>Make choice of whom your wisest friends you will.
>And they shall hear and judge 'twixt you and me.
>If by direct or by collateral hand   195
>They find us touched, we will our kingdom give,
>Our crown, our life, and all that we call ours,
>To you in satisfaction. But if not,
>Be you content to lend your patience to us,
>And we shall jointly labor with your soul   200
>To give it due content.

LAERTES
>>Let this be so.
>His means of death, his obscure burial–
>No trophy, sword, nor hatchment o'er his bones,
>No noble rite nor formal ostentation–
>Cry to be heard, as 'twere from heaven to earth,   205
>That I must call't in question.

CLAUDIUS
>>So you shall.
>And where th' offense is, let the great axe fall.
>I pray you, go with me.

>> *Exeunt*

0: Location: The castle

0: Scene: There is a scene in the First Quarto of *Hamlet*, scene 14, that does not appear in either the second quarto or the First Folio. In this brief scene, Horatio brings a letter from Hamlet to the queen, telling her his story of being captured by the pirates and his arrival home to face Claudius. She and Horatio then collaborate on making sure that Hamlet is informed and prepared for the likely dangers he will face. Thus, Gertrude is shown to be a strong woman, more than capable of facing the king. With this scene, Gertrude's insistence on drinking the poisoned wine can be seen as a purposeful act to protect her son, instead of purely accidental.

8: **an't**: if it

12: **overlooked**: read

13: **means**: access

14: **appointment**: equipment

15: **compelled valor**: necessary bravery

17-18: **They have...they did**: i.e., they were merciful, but they expect something in return

19: **repair**: come

21: **bore**: caliber, size

Act 4, Scene 6]

Enter HORATIO and a Servant

HORATIO
What are they that would speak with me?

Servant
Sailors, sir. They say they have letters for you.

HORATIO
Let them come in.

Exit Servant

I do not know from what part of the world
I should be greeted, if not from Lord Hamlet.   5

Enter Sailors

First Sailor
God bless you, sir.

HORATIO
Let him bless thee too.

First Sailor
He shall, sir, an't please him. There's a letter for
you, sir. It comes from th' ambassador that was
bound for England—if your name be Horatio, as I am   10
let to know it is.

HORATIO

Reads the letter

*Horatio, when thou shalt have overlooked this, give these fellows some
means to the King. They have letters for him. Ere we were two days old
at sea, a pirate of very warlike appointment gave us chase. Finding ourselves too slow of sail, we put on a compelled valor, and in the grapple I*   15
*boarded them. On the instant they got clear of our ship, so I alone became
their prisoner. They have dealt with me like thieves of mercy, but they
knew what they did; I am to do a good turn for them. Let the King have
the letters I have sent and repair thou to me with as much speed as thou
wouldst fly death. I have words to speak in thine ear will make thee*   20
*dumb, yet are they much too light for the bore of the matter. These good
fellows will bring thee where I am. Rosencrantz and Guildenstern hold
their course for England. Of them I have much to tell thee. Farewell.*
He that thou knowest thine,
Hamlet.   25

26: **way:** means

Costume rendering for Horatio from the 1958 production at the Shakespeare Memorial
Theatre directed by Glen Byam Shaw
Photo: Rare Book and Special Collections Library, University of Illinois at Urbana-Champaign

Come, I will give you way for these your letters,
And do't the speedier, that you may direct me
To him from whom you brought them.

Exeunt

0: Location: Chamber rooms in the castle

1: **my acquaintance seal**: affirm my innocence

6: **feats**: acts

7: **capital**: deserving death

9: **mainly**: strongly

10: **unsinewed**: weak

14: **conjunctive**: closely united

15: **in his sphere**: in his orbit. In the Ptolemaic system, stars and planets moved within specific spheres.

17: **count**: accounting, trial

20: **like the...stone**: a reference to mineral springs that petrify wood

21: **convert his gyves to graces**: i.e., make him a martyr (gyves are shackles)

22: **slightly timbered**: i.e., light

27: **if praises...again**: i.e., if one may praise her for what she once was

28: **Stood challenger...age**: stood out in perfection among all other women

Act 4, Scene 7]

CLAUDIUS
  Now must your conscience my acquaintance seal,
  And you must put me in your heart for friend,
  Sith you have heard, and with a knowing ear,
  That he which hath your noble father slain
  Pursued my life.

LAERTES
                  It well appears. But tell me   5
  Why you proceeded not against these feats,
  So crimeful and so capital in nature,
  As by your safety, wisdom, all things else,
  You mainly were stirred up.

CLAUDIUS
                  O, for two special reasons,
  Which may to you, perhaps seem much unsinewed,   10
  But yet to me they are strong. The queen his mother
  Lives almost by his looks; and for myself–
  My virtue or my plague, be it either which–
  She's so conjunctive to my life and soul,
  That, as the star moves not but in his sphere,   15
  I could not but by her. The other motive,
  Why to a public count I might not go,
  Is the great love the general gender bear him,
  Who, dipping all his faults in their affection,
  Would, like the spring that turneth wood to stone,   20
  Convert his gyves to graces, so that my arrows,
  Too slightly timbered for so loud a wind,
  Would have reverted to my bow again,
  And not where I had aimed them.

LAERTES
  And so have I a noble father lost,   25
  A sister driven into desperate terms,
  Whose worth, if praises may go back again,
  Stood challenger on mount of all the age
  For her perfections. But my revenge will come.

43: **set naked on:** destitute in

45: **pardon:** permission

49: **abuse:** deception

51: **character:** handwriting

Clyde Berning as Laertes and John Kani as Claudius in the 2006 Baxter Theatre Centre in South
Africa production directed by Janet Suzman as part of the RSC's Complete Works Festival
Photo: Donald Cooper

CLAUDIUS
    Break not your sleeps for that. You must not think   30
    That we are made of stuff so flat and dull
    That we can let our beard be shook with danger
    And think it pastime. You shortly shall hear more.
    I loved your father, and we love ourself;
    And that, I hope, will teach you to imagine–   35

Enter a Messenger

    How now! What news?

Messenger
                Letters, my lord, from Hamlet.
    This to your majesty; this to the queen.

CLAUDIUS
    From Hamlet? Who brought them?

Messenger
    Sailors, my lord, they say; I saw them not.
    They were given me by Claudio; he received them   40
    Of him that brought them.

CLAUDIUS
    Laertes, you shall hear them. Leave us.

Exit Messenger

    [*Reads*]
    High and mighty, you shall know I am set naked on your kingdom.
    Tomorrow shall I beg leave to see your kingly eyes, when I shall, first
    asking your pardon thereunto, recount the occasion of my sudden and   45
    more strange return.
                    Hamlet.

    What should this mean? Are all the rest come back?
    Or is it some abuse, and no such thing?

LAERTES
    Know you the hand?   50

CLAUDIUS
    'Tis Hamlet's character. "Naked"?
    And in a postscript here, he says "alone".
    Can you advise me?

LAERTES
    I'm lost in it, my lord. But let him come.
    It warms the very sickness in my heart,   55
    That I shall live and tell him to his teeth,
    Thus didest thou!

60: **So**: provided that

62: **checking**: (term from falconry) swerving away from

64: **device**: plans

67: **uncharge the practice**: acquit us of plotting

68-82: **My lord...and graveness**: From the Second Quarto, these lines illustrate Claudius' Machiavellian nature: getting people to do what he wants through flattery.

70: **organ**: instrument

73: **sum of parts**: abilities

76: **unworthiest siege**: lowest rank

79: **becomes**: is suited by

80: **livery**: dress

81: **sables and his weeds**: dignified robes

82: **Importing health**: denoting well-being

85: **can well**: are skilled

88: **as he had...demi-natured**: i.e., as if he became part of the horse

CLAUDIUS
                    If it be so, Laertes–
As how should it be so? How otherwise?
Will you be ruled by me?

LAERTES
                    Ay, my lord,
So you will not o'errule me to a peace.   60

CLAUDIUS
To thine own peace. If he be now returned,
As checking at his voyage, and that he means
No more to undertake it, I will work him
To an exploit, now ripe in my device,
Under the which he shall not choose but fall,   65
And for his death no wind of blame shall breathe,
But even his mother shall uncharge the practice
And call it accident.

LAERTES
                    My lord, I will be ruled;
The rather, if you could devise it so
That I might be the organ.

CLAUDIUS
                    It falls right.   70
You have been talked of since your travel much,
And that in Hamlet's hearing, for a quality
Wherein, they say you shine. Your sum of parts
Did not together pluck such envy from him
As did that one, and that, in my regard,   75
Of the unworthiest siege.

LAERTES
What part is that, my lord?

CLAUDIUS
A very ribbon in the cap of youth,
Yet needful too, for youth no less becomes
The light and careless livery that it wears   80
Than settled age his sables and his weeds,
Importing health and graveness. Two months since,
Here was a gentleman of Normandy.
I have seen myself, and served against, the French,
And they can well on horseback, but this gallant   85
Had witchcraft in't. He grew unto his seat,
And to such wondrous doing brought his horse
As he had been incorpsed and demi-natured

90: **forgery**: construction, invention

94: **brooch**: ornament, jewel

96: **confession**: he spoke of you

101-103: **The scrimers...opposed them**: from the Second Quarto, more intrigue from Claudius

101: **scrimers**: fencers

104: **envenom**: poison

With the brave beast. So far he topped my thought,
That I, in forgery of shapes and tricks,   90
Come short of what he did.

LAERTES
                    A Norman was't?

CLAUDIUS
    A Norman.

LAERTES
    Upon my life, Lamord.

CLAUDIUS
                    The very same.

LAERTES
    I know him well. He is the brooch indeed
    And gem of all the nation.   95

CLAUDIUS
    He made confession of you,
    And gave you such a masterly report
    For art and exercise in your defense
    And for your rapier most especially,
    That he cried out, 'twould be a sight indeed,   100
    If one could match you, sir. The scrimers of their nation,
    He swore, had had neither motion, guard, nor eye,
    If you opposed them. Sir, this report of his
    Did Hamlet so envenom with his envy
    That he could nothing do but wish and beg   105
    Your sudden coming o'er, to play with him.
    Now, out of this—

LAERTES
                    What out of this, my lord?

CLAUDIUS
    Laertes, was your father dear to you?
    Or are you like the painting of a sorrow,
    A face without a heart?

LAERTES
                    Why ask you this?   110

114: **qualifies:** moderates

115-124: **There lives...o' th' ulcer:** From the second quarto, these lines show Claudius continuing to draw Laertes into his plan.

116: **snuff:** accumulation of smoldering wick that caused the candle to smoke and burn less brightly

117: **a like:** an equal; **still:** always

118: **a pleurisy:** an excess

119: **too much:** overabundance

123: **spendthrift sigh:** wasteful sigh. It was believed that sighing was bad for the blood.

124: **quick o' th' ulcer:** heart of the matter

128: **murder sanctuarize:** give sanctuary to a murderer

134: **in fine:** in conclusion

135: **remiss:** unwary

136: **generous:** noble

142: **unction:** ointment; **mountebank:** quack alchemist

145: **simples:** herbs or medicinal plants; **virtue:** potency

CLAUDIUS
  Not that I think you did not love your father,
  But that I know love is begun by time,
  And that I see, in passages of proof,
  Time qualifies the spark and fire of it.
  There lives within the very flame of love   115
  A kind of wick or snuff that will abate it,
  And nothing is at a like goodness still,
  For goodness, growing to a pleurisy,
  Dies in his own too much. That we would do
  We should do when we would, for this "would" changes   120
  And hath abatements and delays as many
  As there are tongues, are hands, are accidents;
  And then this "should" is like a spendthrift sigh
  That hurts by easing. But, to the quick o' th' ulcer–
  Hamlet comes back; what would you undertake,   125
  To show yourself your father's son in deed
  More than in words?

LAERTES
               To cut his throat i' th' church.

CLAUDIUS
  No place indeed should murder sanctuarize;
  Revenge should have no bounds. But, good Laertes,
  Will you do this? Keep close within your chamber.   130
  Hamlet, returned, shall know you are come home.
  We'll put on those shall praise your excellence
  And set a double varnish on the fame
  The Frenchman gave you; bring you, in fine, together
  And wager on your heads. He, being remiss,   135
  Most generous and free from all contriving,
  Will not peruse the foils, so that with ease,
  Or with a little shuffling, you may choose
  A sword unbated, and in a pass of practice
  Requite him for your father.

LAERTES
             I will do't,   140
  And, for that purpose I'll anoint my sword.
  I bought an unction of a mountebank,
  So mortal that but dip a knife in it,
  Where it draws blood, no cataplasm so rare,
  Collected from all simples that have virtue   145
  Under the moon, can save the thing from death
  That is but scratched withal. I'll touch my point
  With this contagion, that, if I gall him slightly,
  It may be death.

152: **our drift look**: i.e., our intention revealed itself

158: **motion**: exercise

161: **nonce**: occasion

162: **stuck**: thrust

168: **willow**: For a long time, the willow tree was a symbol of mourning and forbidden love (thus, the "weeping" willow).

169: **hoar**: frosty white. The underside of the willow leaf is gray-white.

175: **envious sliver**: malicious twig

180: **incapable**: uncomprehending

CLAUDIUS
                    Let's further think of this;
Weigh what convenience both of time and means   150
May fit us to our shape. If this should fail,
And that our drift look through our bad performance,
'Twere better not assayed. Therefore this project
Should have a back or second, that might hold
If this should blast in proof. Soft, let me see.   155
We'll make a solemn wager on your cunnings—
I ha't.
When in your motion you are hot and dry,
As make your bouts more violent to that end,
And that he calls for drink, I'll have prepared him   160
A chalice for the nonce, whereon but sipping,
If he by chance escape your venomed stuck,
Our purpose may hold there. But stay, what noise?

                                        Enter GERTRUDE

How now, sweet queen?

GERTRUDE
One woe doth tread upon another's heel,   165
So fast they follow. Your sister's drowned, Laertes.

LAERTES
Drowned! O, where?

GERTRUDE
There is a willow grows aslant a brook
That shows his hoar leaves in the glassy stream.
There with fantastic garlands did she make   170
Of crow-flowers, nettles, daisies, and long purples
That liberal shepherds give a grosser name,
But our cold maids do dead men's fingers call them.
There, on the pendant boughs her coronet weeds
Clambering to hang, an envious sliver broke,   175
When down her weedy trophies and herself
Fell in the weeping brook. Her clothes spread wide
And, mermaid-like, awhile they bore her up,
Which time she chanted snatches of old tunes
As one incapable of her own distress,   180
Or like a creature native and endued
Unto that element. But long it could not be
Till that her garments, heavy with their drink,
Pulled the poor wretch from her melodious lay
To muddy death.

LAERTES
                    Alas, then, she is drowned?   185

187: Scene: Glenda Jackson played a hard and unsympathetic Ophelia in Peter Hall's 1980 RSC production. The reviewer for the *Birmingham Mail* called her "frigidly spinsterish" and *The Observer* wrote that she was "full of rancor...the only Ophelia I have ever seen that has in it the real shriveled roots of madness." Her cynical bitterness, increasingly exaggerated as madness enveloped her, created a unique Ophelia, but one that the audience ultimately could not accept. Jean Simmons played Ophelia in the Olivier production as an ingénue who was not able to accept the change in Hamlet or the death of her father. Simmons' performance in this film won her a nomination for Best Supporting Actress at that year's Oscars. Her drowning scene was purposefully set up as a perfect recreation of the Millais nineteenth century painting.

John Everett Millais's 1852 painting of Ophelia's drowing

189: **trick**: characteristic way

192: **fain**: gladly

193: **douts**: extinguishes

GERTRUDE
Drowned, drowned.

LAERTES
Too much of water hast thou, poor Ophelia,
And therefore I forbid my tears. But yet
It is our trick; nature her custom holds,
Let shame say what it will. When these are gone,   190
The woman will be out. Adieu, my lord.
I have a speech of fire that fain would blaze,
But that this folly douts it.

Exit LAERTES

CLAUDIUS
                    Let's follow, Gertrude.
How much I had to do to calm his rage!
Now fear I this will give it start again;   195
Therefore let's follow.

Exeunt

[*Hamlet*

Act 5

0: Location: a graveyard on the fringes of Elsinore

0: Stage Direction: **Enter two Clowns**: This stage direction indicates that these characters, more commonly referred to in modern editions as "gravediggers," were played by comic actors.

1: **Christian burial**: consecrated ground

2: **straight**: right away; **crowner**: coroner

3. **sat**: held an inquest

4: **How...in her own defense**: The cause of Ophelia's death is deemed to be questionable. If her death was a suicide, then by Canon Law, she cannot be blessed in a church ceremony and buried in a church cemetery.

6: *se offendendo*: The gravedigger means *se defendendo*, a killing in self-defense.

7: **wittingly**: knowingly

8: **Argal**: The gravedigger means *ergo*, Latin for "therefore."

10: **Goodman Delver**: Master Digger

12: **will he nill he**: (willy-nilly) whether he wishes to or not

13-14: "But if the water come to him and drown him, he drowns / not himself.": Derek Crewe as Second Gravedigger and Sebastian Shaw as First Gravedigger in the Royal Shakespeare Company's 1984 production directed by Ron Daniels
Photo: Donald Cooper

17: **crowner's quest law**: coroner's inquest

Act 5, Scene 1]

Enter two Clowns carrying a spade and a pickaxe

First Clown
Is she to be buried in Christian burial that wilfully seeks her own salvation?

Second Clown
I tell thee she is; and therefore make her grave straight. The crowner hath sat on her, and finds it Christian burial.

First Clown
How can that be, unless she drowned herself in her own defense?

Second Clown
Why, 'tis found so.   5

First Clown
It must be *se offendendo,* it cannot be else. For here lies the point: if I drown myself wittingly, it argues an act, and an act hath three branches–it is to act, to do, and to perform. Argal, she drowned herself wittingly.

Second Clown
Nay, but hear you, Goodman Delver–   10

First Clown
Give me leave. Here lies the water–good. Here stands the man–good. If the man go to this water and drown himself, it is, will he nill he, he goes. Mark you that. But if the water come to him and drown him, he drowns not himself. Argal, he that is not guilty of his own death shortens not his own life.   15

Second Clown
But is this law?

First Clown
Ay, marry, is't–crowner's quest law.

Second Clown
Will you ha' the truth on't? If this had not been a gentlewoman, she should have been buried out o' Christian burial.

20: **there thou say'st**: i.e., how right you are

21: **countenance**: permission

22: **even**: fellow

23: **hold up**: carry on

25: **arms**: a coat of arms (as a gentleman)

29: **Confess thyself**: the beginning of an old proverb that continues, "and be hanged"

31-32: "What is he that builds stronger than either the mason, the shipwright, or the carpenter?": Jason Gilbert as a Gravedigger's companion and Floyd King as a Gravedigger in the Shakespeare Theatre Company's 2001 production directed by Gale Edwards
Photo: Carol Rosegg

33: **frame**: structure

34: **does**: works

39: **unyoke**: i.e., your work is finished for the day

First Clown
Why, there thou say'st, and the more pity that great folk should have   20
countenance in this world to drown or hang themselves more than their
even Christian. Come, my spade. There is no ancient gentleman but gar-
deners, ditchers, and grave-makers. They hold up Adam's profession.

Second Clown
Was he a gentleman?

First Clown
He was the first that ever bore arms.   25

Second Clown
Why, he had none.

First Clown
What, art a heathen? How dost thou understand the Scripture? The
Scripture says Adam digged. Could he dig without arms? I'll put another
question to thee. If thou answerest me not to the purpose, confess thyself–

Second Clown
Go to.   30

First Clown
What is he that builds stronger than either the mason, the shipwright, or
the carpenter?

Second Clown
The gallows-maker, for that frame outlives a thousand tenants.

First Clown
I like thy wit well, in good faith. The gallows does well. But how does it
well? It does well to those that do ill. Now thou dost ill to say the gallows   35
is built stronger than the church. Argal, the gallows may do well to thee.
To't again, come.

Second Clown
Who builds stronger than a mason, a shipwright, or a carpenter?

First Clown
Ay, tell me that, and unyoke.

Second Clown
Marry, now I can tell.   40

First Clown
To't.

42: **Mass**: short for "by the mass"

43: **mend**: improve

46: **Yaughan**: Johann (probably a local tavern-keeper); **stoup**: flagon

49: **contract**: shorten; **behove**: advantage

50: **meet**: suitable

52: **Custom...property of easiness**: i.e., habit has made him indifferent to the grimness of his occupation

56: **intil**: into

58: **knave**: rude fellow; **jowls**: throws

60: **pate of a politician**: the skull of a schemer; **o'er-offices:** lords his rank over others

Norman Wooland as Horatio, Laurence Olivier as Hamlet, and Stanley Holloway as Gravedigger in the 1948 film directed by Laurence Olivier
Courtesy of Douglas Lanier

Second Clown
Mass, I cannot tell.

Enter HAMLET and HORATIO at a distance

First Clown
Cudgel thy brains no more about it, for your dull ass will not mend his
pace with beating. And, when you are asked this question next, say "a
grave-maker". The houses that he makes last till doomsday. Go, get thee   45
to Yaughan. Fetch me a stoup of liquor.

Exit Second Clown

Sings
In youth, when I did love, did love,
    Methought it was very sweet,
To contract O–the time, for-ah-my behove,
    O–methought there-a-was nothing meet.   50

HAMLET
Has this fellow no feeling of his business that he sings at grave-making?

HORATIO
Custom hath made it in him a property of easiness.

HAMLET
'Tis e'en so; the hand of little employment hath the daintier sense.

First Clown
Sings
But age, with his stealing steps
    Hath caught me in his clutch,   55
And hath shipped me intil the land,
    As if I had never been such.

[Throws up a skull]

HAMLET
That skull had a tongue in it and could sing once. How the knave jowls
it to th' ground, as if it were Cain's jawbone, that did the first murder. It
might be the pate of a politician, which this ass now o'er-offices; one that   60
would circumvent God, might it not?

HORATIO
It might, my lord.

HAMLET
Or of a courtier, which could say "Good morrow, sweet lord! How dost
thou, good lord?" This might be my lord such-a-one, that praised my lord
such-a-one's horse, when he meant to beg it, might it not?   65

67: **chapless**: jawless

68: **mazzard**: head

69: **trick**: ability

70: **loggats**: a game played by throwing small wooden clubs at a stake

76: **quiddits:** subtle distinctions; **quillets:** arguments; **tenures:** property titles

77: **sconce**: head

80: **fines**: lawsuits

81: **fine**: end; **recoveries**: profit; **fine**: subtle

82: **fine dirt**: small grains of dirt (like sand)

84: **box**: chest of deeds (like a coffin)

89: **sheep and calves**: simpletons and fools; **assurance**: security

HORATIO
Ay, my lord.

HAMLET
Why, e'en so, and now my Lady Worm's, chapless, and knocked about
the mazzard with a sexton's spade. Here's fine revolution, if we had the
trick to see't. Did these bones cost no more the breeding, but to play at
loggats with 'em? Mine ache to think on't.   70

FIRST CLOWN
        Sings
        A pickaxe, and a spade, a spade,
            For and a shrouding sheet:
        O, a pit of clay for to be made
            For such a guest is meet.

                                    [Throws up another skull]

HAMLET
There's another. Why may not that be the skull of a lawyer? Where be   75
his quiddits now, his quillets, his cases, his tenures, and his tricks? Why
does he suffer this rude knave now to knock him about the sconce with a
dirty shovel, and will not tell him of his action of battery? Hum! This
fellow might be in 's time a great buyer of land, with his statutes, his
recognizances, his fines, his double vouchers, his recoveries. Is this the   80
fine of his fines, and the recovery of his recoveries, to have his fine pate
full of fine dirt? Will his vouchers vouch him no more of his purchases,
and double ones too, than the length and breadth of a pair of indentures?
The very conveyances of his lands will hardly lie in this box; and must
the inheritor himself have no more, ha?   85

HORATIO
Not a jot more, my lord.

HAMLET
Is not parchment made of sheepskins?

HORATIO
Ay, my lord, and of calfskins too.

HAMLET
They are sheep and calves which seek out assurance in that. I will speak
to this fellow.–Whose grave's this, sirrah?   90

First Clown
    Mine, sir.
        Singing
        O, a pit of clay for to be made
        For such a guest is meet.

95-96: "You lie out on't, sir, and therefore is not yours.": Billy Crystal as the Gravedigger in the 1996 film directed by Kenneth Branagh
Photo: Rolf Konow © Columbia TriStar. Courtesy of Douglas Lanier

97-98: **the quick**: the living

106: **absolute**: precise; **speak by the card**: define our meanings; **equivocation**: double meaning or ambiguous speech

108: **picked**: refined

109: **galls his kibe**: chafes his heel

HAMLET
I think it be thine, indeed, for thou liest in't.

First Clown
You lie out on't, sir, and therefore it is not yours. For my part, I do not lie   95
in't, and yet it is mine.

HAMLET
Thou dost lie in't, to be in't and say 'tis thine. 'Tis for the dead, not for
the quick; therefore thou liest.

First Clown
'Tis a quick lie, sir; 'twill away 'gain, from me to you.

HAMLET
What man dost thou dig it for?   100

First Clown
For no man, sir.

HAMLET
What woman, then?

First Clown
For none, neither.

HAMLET
Who is to be buried in't?

First Clown
One that was a woman, sir; but, rest her soul, she's dead.   105

HAMLET
How absolute the knave is! We must speak by the card, or equivocation
will undo us. By the Lord, Horatio, these three years I have taken a note
of it; the age is grown so picked that the toe of the peasant comes so near
the heel of the courtier, he galls his kibe.–How long hast thou been a
grave-maker?   110

First Clown
Of all the days i' th' year, I came to't that day that our last King Hamlet
overcame Fortinbras.

HAMLET
How long is that since?

First Clown
Cannot you tell that? Every fool can tell that. It was the very day that
young Hamlet was born–he that is mad, and sent into England.   115

125: **Upon what ground**: Hamlet asks, "Upon what ground?" meaning, "Upon what cause?" but the Clown understands him to mean "On what country?"

129: **pocky**: diseased with venereal infections

130: **laying in**: the wake and funeral ceremony

134: **your water is a sore decayer**: water causes quick decay; **whoreson**: vile, diseased

Alan David as First Gravedigger, Samuel West as Hamlet, and Conor Moloney as Second Gravedigger in the Royal Shakespeare Company's 2001 production directed by Steven Pimlott
Photo: Donald Cooper

HAMLET
Ay, marry. Why was he sent into England?

First Clown
Why, because he was mad. He shall recover his wits there. Or, if he do
not, 'tis no great matter there.

HAMLET
Why?

First Clown
'Twill, a not be seen in him there. There the men are as mad as he.   120

HAMLET
How came he mad?

First Clown
Very strangely, they say.

HAMLET
How strangely?

First Clown
Faith, e'en with losing his wits.

HAMLET
Upon what ground?   125

First Clown
Why, here in Denmark. I have been sexton here, man and boy, thirty
years.

HAMLET
How long will a man lie i' th' earth ere he rot?

First Clown
I'faith, if he be not rotten before he die–as we have many pocky corpses
nowadays that will scarce hold the laying in–he will last you some eight   130
year or nine year. A tanner will last you nine year.

HAMLET
Why he more than another?

First Clown
Why, sir, his hide is so tanned with his trade, that he will keep out water
a great while, and your water is a sore decayer of your whoreson dead
body. Here's a skull now. This skull has lain in the earth three and twenty   135
years.

140: **Rhenish**: Rhine wine

tracks 33-36

145-153:
Sir John Gielgud as Hamlet
Richard Burton as Hamlet
Sir Derek Jacobi as Hamlet

145: Scene: In Zeffirelli's film, Hamlet and Horatio enter on horseback, encounter the gravedigger, and dismount when the man, still working in the grave, begins to intrigue Hamlet with his wit. Instead of holding the skull (as in most classic images), Gibson's Hamlet sets it firmly on a mound of earth, lies in front of it, and converses with it. Sarah Bernhardt is said to have tapped Yorick's teeth with her finger. "She handled the skull as easily," writes Elizabeth Robins, "and as lightly as a lap-dog."

145: "Alas, poor Yorick": Stacy Keach as Hamlet in the 1971-72 Public Theater production directed by Gerald Freedman
Photo: George E. Joseph

147: **gorge**: stomach contents

149: **gibes**: jests

151: **chop-fallen**: dejected (literally, a skull whose lower jaw has fallen out)

152: **favor**: appearance

155: **Alexander**: referring to Alexander the Great (336-323 BCE), regarded as one of the greatest military strategists who ever lived

HAMLET
Whose was it?

First Clown
A whoreson mad fellow's it was. Whose do you think it was?

HAMLET
Nay, I know not.

First Clown
A pestilence on him for a mad rogue! A' poured a flagon of Rhenish on   140
my head once. This same skull, sir, was Yorick's skull, the King's jester.

HAMLET
This?

First Clown
E'en that.

HAMLET
Let me see.

[Takes the skull]

Alas, poor Yorick! I knew him, Horatio, a fellow of infinite jest, of most   145
excellent fancy. He hath borne me on his back a thousand times, and
now, how abhorred in my imagination it is! My gorge rises at it. Here
hung those lips that I have kissed I know not how oft. Where be your
gibes now? Your gambols? Your songs? Your flashes of merriment that
were wont to set the table on a roar? Not one now, to mock your own   150
grinning? Quite chop-fallen? Now get you to my lady's chamber, and tell
her, let her paint an inch thick, to this favor she must come. Make her
laugh at that. Prithee, Horatio, tell me one thing.

HORATIO
What's that, my lord?

HAMLET
Dost thou think Alexander looked o' this fashion i' th' earth?   155

HORATIO
E'en so.

HAMLET
And smelt so? Pah!

HORATIO
E'en so, my lord.

160: **a bunghole**: a hole for filling and emptying a cask

162: **follow...modesty enough**: simply to face the reality of death

164: **loam**: a mix of clay and straw

169: **earth**: i.e., Caesar

170: **winter flaw**: fiercely cold winds

173: **maimèd**: shortened (because of the questionable circumstances of Ophelia's death)

175: **Fordo its own life**: destroyed itself; **estate**: noble rank

176: **Couch**: hide

181: **warranties**: authority; **Her death was doubtful**: i.e., her death might not have been natural

182: **But...o'ersways th order**: Claudius used his rank to overrule the Church.

187: **maiden strewments**: flowers for the grave of an unmarried girl/woman (a virgin) and later hung in the church in tribute to her innocence

188: **bell and burial**: the ritual funeral bells and funeral ceremony

Costume rendering for the Priest from the 1934 production at the New Theatre directed by Sir John Gielgud

Photo: Rare Book and Special Collections Library, University of Illinois at Urbana-Champaign

HAMLET
> To what base uses we may return, Horatio! Why may not imagination
> trace the noble dust of Alexander till he find it stopping a bunghole?   160

HORATIO
> 'Twere to consider too curiously to consider so.

HAMLET
> No, faith, not a jot, but to follow him thither with modesty enough, and
> likelihood to lead it, as thus: Alexander died, Alexander was buried,
> Alexander returneth into dust. The dust is earth, of earth we make loam,
> and why of that loam whereto he was converted might they not stop a   165
> beer-barrel?
>> Imperious Caesar, dead and turned to clay,
>> Might stop a hole to keep the wind away.
>> O, that that earth, which kept the world in awe,
>> Should patch a wall to expel the winter flaw.   170
> But soft. But soft. Aside. Here comes the king.

>> *Enter [a Priest], CLAUDIUS, GERTRUDE, LAERTES,*
>> *and a coffin, with Lords Attendant*

> The Queen, the courtiers. Who is that they follow?
> And with such maimèd rites? This doth betoken
> The corse they follow did with desperate hand
> Fordo its own life. 'Twas of some estate.   175
> Couch we awhile and mark.

LAERTES
> What ceremony else?

HAMLET
> That is Laertes. A very noble youth. Mark.

LAERTES
> What ceremony else?

Priest
> Her obsequies have been as far enlarged   180
> As we have warranties. Her death was doubtful;
> And but that great command o'ersways the order,
> She should in ground unsanctified have lodged
> Till the last trumpet. For charitable prayers,
> Shards, flints, and pebbles should be thrown on her.   185
> Yet here she is allowed her virgin rites,
> Her maiden strewments and the bringing home
> Of bell and burial.

189: "No more be done.": Emery Battis as a Priest and Bo Foxworth as Laertes in the Shakespeare Theatre Company's 2001 production directed by Gale Edwards
Photo: Carol Rosegg

191: **sage**: solemn

192: **peace-parted souls**: Those who died after confessing and receiving Last Rites were said to die peacefully.

192: Scene: **Lay her i' th' earth**: At the Globe, the trap door (through which the Ghost descended to the cellarage below) was probably used for Ophelia's grave as well. If straps are placed under the body, then it can be carefully lowered into the cellarage. Of course, using a dummy for Ophelia's body was (and is) considered to be a good idea.

194: **churlish**: rude

196: **liest howling**: as in hell

202: **most ingenious sense**: intelligence and good sense

207: **Pelion**: a mountain in Greece. In Greek mythology, two giants piled Mount Pelion on Ossa, another mountain in Greece, in order to scale Mount Olympus.

208: **Olympus**: the famous mountain home of Zeus and the Greek gods

210: **an emphasis**: a violent expression

211: **wand'ring stars**: planets

212: **wonder-wounded**: awestruck

213: **Hamlet the Dane**: Hamlet identifies himself as the King of Denmark (for the only time)

LAERTES
   Must there no more be done?

Priest
                  No more be done.
   We should profane the service of the dead   190
   To sing sage requiem and such rest to her
   As to peace-parted souls.

LAERTES
                  Lay her i' th' earth,
   And from her fair and unpolluted flesh
   May violets spring! I tell thee, churlish priest,
   A ministering angel shall my sister be   195
   When thou liest howling.

HAMLET
                  What, the fair Ophelia!

GERTRUDE
   Sweets to the sweet. Farewell!
   I hoped thou shouldst have been my Hamlet's wife.
   I thought thy bride-bed to have decked, sweet maid,
   And not t'have strewed thy grave.

LAERTES
                  O, treble woe   200
   Fall ten times treble on that cursèd head,
   Whose wicked deed thy most ingenious sense
   Deprived thee of! Hold off the earth awhile,
   Till I have caught her once more in mine arms.

                                          He leaps into the grave
   Now pile your dust upon the quick and dead,   205
   Till of this flat a mountain you have made
   To o'ertop old Pelion or the skyish head
   Of blue Olympus.

HAMLET
   What is he whose grief
   Bears such an emphasis? Whose phrase of sorrow   210
   Conjures the wand'ring stars, and makes them stand
   Like wonder-wounded hearers? This is I,
   Hamlet the Dane.

LAERTES
                  The devil take thy soul!

216: **splenative**: hot-tempered

222: **no longer wag**: stop blinking

228: **forbear him**: make allowances for his grief

Costume rendering for the Queen from the 1958 production at the Shakespeare Memorial
Theatre directed by Glen Byam Shaw
Photo: Rare Book and Special Collections Library, University of Illinois at Urbana-Champaign

HAMLET
  Thou pray'st not well.
  I prithee, take thy fingers from my throat,   215
  For, though I am not splenative and rash,
  Yet have I something in me dangerous,
  Which let thy wiseness fear. Hold off thy hand.

CLAUDIUS
  Pluck them asunder.

GERTRUDE
              Hamlet, Hamlet!

All
                Gentlemen!

HORATIO
  Good my lord, be quiet.   220

HAMLET
  Why, I will fight with him upon this theme
  Until my eyelids will no longer wag.

GERTRUDE
  O my son, what theme?

HAMLET
  I loved Ophelia. Forty thousand brothers
  Could not–with all their quantity of love–   225
  Make up my sum! What wilt thou do for her?

CLAUDIUS
  O, he is mad, Laertes.

GERTRUDE
  For love of God, forbear him.

Set rendering from the 1958 production at the Shakespeare Memorial Theatre directed by
Glen Byam Shaw
Photo: Rare Book and Special Collections Library, University of Illinois at Urbana-Champaign

229: **'Swounds**: By Christ's wounds

233: **outface**: outdo

237: **Singeing...zone**: i.e., burning his head in the sun

238: **Make Ossa like a wart**: make this famous Greek mountain as small and as insignificant
as a wart

239: **mere**: utter

241: **Anon**: soon

242: **her golden couplets are disclosed**: i.e., her twin chicks are hatched

250: **the present push**: immediate action

252: **This grave...living monument**: a warning that Hamlet might soon join Ophelia in death

HAMLET
 'Swounds, show me what thou'lt do.
 Woo't weep? Woo't fight? Woo't fast? Woo't tear thyself?   230
 Woo't drink up eisel? Eat a crocodile?
 I'll do't! Dost thou come here to whine?
 To outface me with leaping in her grave?
 Be buried quick with her, and so will I.
 And, if thou prate of mountains, let them throw   235
 Millions of acres on us, till our ground,
 Singeing his pate against the burning zone,
 Make Ossa like a wart! Nay, an thou'lt mouth,
 I'll rant as well as thou.

CLAUDIUS
     This is mere madness;
 And thus awhile the fit will work on him.   240
 Anon, as patient as the female dove
 When that her golden couplets are disclosed,
 His silence will sit drooping.

HAMLET
     Hear you, sir.
 What is the reason that you use me thus?
 I loved you ever. But it is no matter;   245
 Let Hercules himself do what he may,
 The cat will mew, and dog will have his day.

CLAUDIUS
 I pray you, good Horatio, wait upon him.
            [Exit HORATIO]

 [To LAERTES] Strengthen your patience in our last night's speech.
 We'll put the matter to the present push.   250
 Good Gertrude, set some watch over your son.–
 This grave shall have a living monument.
 An hour of quiet shortly shall we see,
 Till then, in patience our proceeding be.
              Exeunt

0: Location: the castle

6: **mutines in the bilboes**: mutineers in fetters (chains)

7: **know**: acknowledge

8: **Our indiscretion...well**: Hamlet acknowledges that it is sometimes good to act on the spur of the moment, without delay.

9: **deep plots**: plots that have been much considered; **pall**: lose strength

13: **sea-gown:** a skirted garment worn by sailors

14: **them**: i.e., Rosencrantz and Guildenstern

15: **Fingered**: stole

20: **Larded:** fattened

21: **Importing**: concerning

22: **bugs and goblins**: i.e., terrors

23: **on the supervise**: upon reading the letter; **bated:** allowed

Act 5, Scene 2]

HAMLET
  So much for this, sir. Now shall you see the other,
  You do remember all the circumstance?

HORATIO
  Remember it, my lord?

HAMLET
  Sir, in my heart there was a kind of fighting
  That would not let me sleep. Methought I lay 5
  Worse than the mutines in the bilboes. Rashly,
  And praised be rashness for it, let us know,
  Our indiscretion sometimes serves us well
  When our deep plots do pall; and that should teach us
  There's a divinity that shapes our ends, 10
  Rough-hew them how we will–

HORATIO
          That is most certain.

HAMLET
  Up from my cabin,
  My sea-gown scarfed about me, in the dark
  Groped I to find out them, had my desire,
  Fingered their packet, and in fine withdrew 15
  To mine own room again, making so bold,
  My fears forgetting manners, to unseal
  Their grand commission; where I found, Horatio–
  O royal knavery!–an exact command,
  Larded with many several sorts of reason, 20
  Importing Denmark's health and England's too,
  With, ho! Such bugs and goblins in my life,
  That, on the supervise, no leisure bated,
  No, not to stay the grinding of the axe,
  My head should be struck off.

HORATIO
          Is't possible? 25

HAMLET
  Here's the commission; read it at more leisure.
  But wilt thou hear me how I did proceed?

29: **benetted round**: surrounded

30: **a prologue**: an introductory speech

33: **hold**: consider; **statists**: statesmen

34: **baseness**: lowly skill

36: **yeoman's service**: Yeoman were known as reliable soldiers.

41: **wheaten garland**: wreath of wheat, a symbol of prosperity

42: **stand...amities**: provide a further connection between them

43: **charge**: import

45: **debatement**: arguing

47: **Not shriving time**: no time for Confession

48: **ordinant**: provident

50: **model**: copy

52: **Subscribed...impression**: signed and sealed it

53: **changeling**: i.e., switch (a changeling was a fairy child switched with a human child with no one the wiser)

56: **go to't**: have had it

57: **did make love to this employment**: embraced this assignment with their eyes open

58: **They...conscience:** i.e., I don't feel guilt for taking just action

59: **insinuation**: meddling

HORATIO
  I beseech you.

HAMLET
  Being thus benetted round with villains,
  Ere I could make a prologue to my brains,   30
  They had begun the play. I sat me down,
  Devised a new commission, wrote it fair.
  I once did hold it, as our statists do,
  A baseness to write fair and labored much
  How to forget that learning; but, sir, now   35
  It did me yeoman's service. Wilt thou know
  The effect of what I wrote?

HORATIO
                        Ay, good my lord.

HAMLET
  An earnest conjuration from the King,
  As England was his faithful tributary,
  As love between them like the palm should flourish,   40
  As peace should still her wheaten garland wear
  And stand a comma 'tween their amities,
  And many such-like 'as'es of great charge,
  That on the view and knowing of these contents,
  Without debatement further more or less,   45
  He should the bearers put to sudden death,
  Not shriving time allowed.

HORATIO
                        How was this sealed?

HAMLET
  Why, even in that was heaven ordinant.
  I had my father's signet in my purse,
  Which was the model of that Danish seal;   50
  Folded the writ up in form of th' other,
  Subscribed it, gave't th' impression, placed it safely,
  The changeling never known. Now the next day
  Was our sea-fight; and what to this was sequent
  Thou know'st already.   55

HORATIO
  So Guildenstern and Rosencrantz go to't.

HAMLET
  Why, man, they did make love to this employment.
  They are not near my conscience. Their defeat
  Does by their own insinuation grow.

60-62: **'Tis...opposites**: it is dangerous for inferiors to come between two mighty opponents

61: **pass**: (fencing term) thrust; **fell**: deadly; **incensed points**: angry swords

63: **Does...upon**: i.e., do you not agree that this is my duty

65: **Popped in between the election and my hopes**: i.e., maneuvered himself onto the throne by blocking my rightful election

66: **angle**: fishing tackle

67: **cozenage**: treachery

68: **To quit him**: to pay him back

68-70: **And...evil?**: And won't I be further damned if I allow this evil to continue?

74: **"one"**: one second

77-78: **by the image...portraiture of his:** i.e., my situation and Laertes' are similar

83: **water-fly**: insignificant insect

85: **more gracious**: better off

86: **lord of beasts**: a rich man

86-87: **the king's mess**: the king's table

'Tis dangerous when the baser nature comes   60
Between the pass and fell incensèd points
Of mighty opposites.

HORATIO
                          Why, what a king is this!

HAMLET
  Does it not, think'st thee, stand me now upon–
  He that hath killed my king and whored my mother,
  Popped in between the election and my hopes,   65
  Thrown out his angle for my proper life,
  And with such cozenage – is't not perfect conscience,
  To quit him with this arm? And is't not to be damned,
  To let this canker of our nature come
  In further evil?   70

HORATIO
  It must be shortly known to him from England
  What is the issue of the business there.

HAMLET
  It will be short. The interim is mine;
  And a man's life's no more than to say "one."
  But I am very sorry, good Horatio,   75
  That to Laertes I forgot myself,
  For, by the image of my cause, I see
  The portraiture of his. I'll court his favors.
  But, sure, the bravery of his grief did put me
  Into a tow'ring passion.   80

HORATIO
  Peace! Who comes here?

                                                          Enter young OSRIC

OSRIC
  Your lordship is right welcome back to Denmark.

HAMLET
  I humbly thank you, sir. Dost know this water-fly?

HORATIO
  No, my good lord.

HAMLET
  Thy state is the more gracious, for 'tis a vice to know him. He hath much   85
  land, and fertile. Let a beast be lord of beasts, and his crib shall stand at the
  king's mess. 'Tis a chough, but, as I say, spacious in the possession of dirt.

94: **indifferent**: rather

95: **complexion**: temperament

99: **remember**: remember your manners (put your hat back on)

100-123: **Sir, here is newly come...sir**: In these lines from the Second Quarto, Hamlet further toys with Osric and displays his and Horatio's quick wits.

102-103: **feelingly**: appreciatively

103: **the card or calendar of gentry**: a model gentleman

105-110: **Sir, his definement...nothing more**: Hamlet mocks Osric by using excessively florid language, one that Osric does not always understand.

105: **definement:** picture; **perdition:** detraction

107: **extolment**: truthful phrase

108: **infusion:** essence; **dearth:** value

109: **semblable**: likeness

OSRIC
  Sweet lord, if your lordship were at leisure, I should impart a thing to you
  from his majesty.

HAMLET
  I will receive it, sir, with all diligence of spirit. Put your bonnet to his   90
  right use; 'tis for the head.

OSRIC
  I thank your lordship, 'tis very hot.

HAMLET
  No, believe me, 'tis very cold. The wind is northerly.

OSRIC
  It is indifferent cold, my lord, indeed.

HAMLET
  But yet methinks it is very sultry and hot for my complexion.   95

OSRIC
  Exceedingly, my lord. It is very sultry, as 'twere–I cannot tell how. But,
  my lord, his majesty bade me signify to you that he has laid a great wager
  on your head. Sir, this is the matter–

HAMLET
  I beseech you remember.

OSRIC
  Nay, good my lord, for mine ease, in good faith. Sir, here is newly come   100
  to court Laertes; believe me, an absolute gentleman, full of most excellent
  differences, of very soft society and great showing; indeed, to speak feelingly of him, he is the card or calendar of gentry, for you shall find in him
  the continent of what part a gentleman would see.

HAMLET
  Sir, his definement suffers no perdition in you; though, I know, to divide   105
  him inventorially would dizzy the arithmetic of memory, and yet but yaw
  neither, in respect of his quick sail. But, in the verity of extolment, I take
  him to be a soul of great article, and his infusion of such dearth and
  rareness, as, to make true diction of him, his semblable is his mirror, and
  who else would trace him, his umbrage, nothing more.   110

OSRIC
  Your lordship speaks most infallibly of him.

112: **concernancy**: relevance

117: **nomination**: mention

122: **approve**: commend

125-128: **I dare not...unfellowed**: These lines from the second quarto continue and complete the previous thought.

128: **meed:** merit; **unfellowed:** unmatched

Costume rendering for Osric from the 1958 production at the Shakespeare Memorial Theatre directed by Glen Byam Shaw
Photo: Rare Book and Special Collections Library, University of Illinois at Urbana-Champaign

HAMLET
The concernancy, sir? Why do we wrap the gentleman in our more rawer
breath?

OSRIC
Sir?

HORATIO
[*Aside to HAMLET*] Is't not possible to understand in another tongue?   115
You will do't, sir, really.

HAMLET
[*To OSRIC*] What imports the nomination of this gentleman?

OSRIC
Of Laertes?

HORATIO
His purse is empty already; all's golden words are spent.

HAMLET
Of him, sir.   120

OSRIC
I know you are not ignorant–

HAMLET
I would you did, sir; yet, in faith, if you did, it would not much approve
me. Well, sir?

OSRIC
You are not ignorant of what excellence Laertes is–

HAMLET
I dare not confess that, lest I should compare with him in excellence. But   125
to know a man well were to know himself.

OSRIC
I mean, sir, for his weapon; but in the imputation laid on him by them, in
his meed he's unfellowed.

HAMLET
What's his weapon?

OSRIC
Rapier and dagger.   130

133: **imponed**: staked; **poniards**: daggers

134: **assigns**: accessories; **girdle**: belt; **hangers**: knife holder

136: **liberal conceit**: fanciful design

144: **hath laid**: placed his bid

145: **three hits**: Laertes must score three more hits (out of twelve) than Hamlet to win the wager.

146-147: **vouchsafe the answer**: accept the challenge

150-151: **breathing time of day**: time for exercising

155: **flourish**: fancy speech

HAMLET
That's two of his weapons. But, well.

OSRIC
The King, sir, hath wagered with him six Barbary horses, against the
which he has imponed, as I take it, six French rapiers and poniards, with
their assigns, as girdle, hangers, and so. Three of the carriages, in faith,
are very dear to fancy, very responsive to the hilts, most delicate   135
carriages, and of very liberal conceit.

HAMLET
What call you the carriages?

OSRIC
The carriages, sir, are the hangers.

HAMLET
The phrase would be more germane to the matter, if we could carry
cannon by our sides. I would it might be hangers till then. But, on. Six   140
Barbary horses against six French swords, their assigns, and three
liberal-conceited carriages; that's the French bet against the Danish.
Why is this "imponed," as you call it?

OSRIC
The King, sir, hath laid, sir, that in a dozen passes between yourself and
him, he shall not exceed you three hits. He hath laid on twelve for nine,   145
and it would come to immediate trial if your lordship would vouchsafe
the answer.

HAMLET
How if I answer no?

OSRIC
I mean, my lord, the opposition of your person in trial.

HAMLET
Sir, I will walk here in the hall. If it please his majesty, 'tis the breathing   150
time of day with me. Let the foils be brought, the gentleman willing, and
the King hold his purpose, I will win for him an I can. If not, I will gain
nothing but my shame and the odd hits.

OSRIC
Shall I redeliver you e'en so?

HAMLET
To this effect, sir, after what flourish your nature will.   155

156: **commend my duty**: dedicate my service

157: **Yours, yours**: i.e., at your service; **turn**: purpose

158: **with...head**: like a new-hatched chick carrying its shell on its head

160: **did comply...sucked it**: i.e., first made polite conversation with the breast from which he was about to nurse

161: **drossy**: worthless

162: **outward habit of encounter**: fashionable turn of speech

162-163: **yeasty collection**: frothy repertoire

163-164: **most fond and winnowed opinions**: i.e., most polite and elite society

164: **do but blow them...are out**: i.e., dissipate like bubbles when tested

170: **gain-giving**: misgivings

172: **repair**: coming

174: **augury**: omens, an attempt to understand signs of what the future will bring; **a special providence**: Divine care (referring to Matthew 10:29-31)

176: **it**: i.e., death

176-177: **Since...betimes**: i.e., since humans can take nothing earthly with them at death, what does it matter if one dies young or old

Costume rendering for Hamlet from the 1958 production at the Shakespeare Memorial Theatre directed by Glen Byam Shaw

Photo: Rare Book and Special Collections Library, University of Illinois at Urbana-Champaign

OSRIC
I commend my duty to your lordship.

HAMLET
Yours, yours.

Exit OSRIC

He does well to commend it himself; there are no tongues else for 's turn.

HORATIO
This lapwing runs away with the shell on his head.

HAMLET
He did comply with his dug before he sucked it. Thus has he–and many   160
more of the same bevy that I know the drossy age dotes on–only got the
tune of the time and outward habit of encounter, a kind of yeasty collection, which carries them through and through the most fond and winnowed opinions; and do but blow them to their trials, the bubbles are out.

HORATIO
You will lose this wager, my lord.   165

HAMLET
I do not think so. Since he went into France, I have been in continual
practice. I shall win at the odds. But thou wouldst not think how ill all's
here about my heart. But it is no matter.

HORATIO
Nay, good my lord–

HAMLET
It is but foolery. But it is such a kind of gain-giving as would perhaps   170
trouble a woman.

HORATIO
If your mind dislike any thing, obey it. I will forestall their repair hither,
and say you are not fit.

HAMLET
Not a whit, we defy augury. There's a special providence in the fall of a
sparrow. If it be now, 'tis not to come. If it be not to come, it will be now.   175
If it be not now, yet it will come. The readiness is all. Since no man has
aught of what he leaves, what is't to leave betimes? Let be.

Enter CLAUDIUS, GERTRUDE, LAERTES, and Lords
with other Attendants with foils and gauntlets,
a table and flagons of wine on it

CLAUDIUS
Come, Hamlet, come, and take this hand from me.

181: **this presence**: the assembled court

184: **exception**: resentment

194: **purposed evil**: intentional wrong

203: **name ungored**: reputation intact

206: **frankly**: freely

207: **foils**: fencing weapons

210: **Stick fiery off**: stand out brilliantly

Ethan Hawke and Live Schreiber in the 2000 film directed by Michael Almereyda
Photo: Larry Riley © Miramax Films. Courtesy of Douglas Lanier

HAMLET
Give me your pardon, sir. I've done you wrong;
But pardon't, as you are a gentleman.   180
This presence knows,
And you must needs have heard how I am punished
With sore distraction. What I have done
That might your nature, honor, and exception
Roughly awake, I here proclaim was madness.   185
Was't Hamlet wronged Laertes? Never Hamlet
If Hamlet from himself be ta'en away,
And when he's not himself does wrong Laertes,
Then Hamlet does it not, Hamlet denies it.
Who does it, then? His madness. If't be so,   190
Hamlet is of the faction that is wronged;
His madness is poor Hamlet's enemy.
Sir, in this audience,
Let my disclaiming from a purposed evil
Free me so far in your most generous thoughts   195
That I have shot mine arrow o'er the house
And hurt my brother.

LAERTES
                    I am satisfied in nature,
Whose motive in this case should stir me most
To my revenge. But in my terms of honor
I stand aloof, and will no reconcilement,   200
Till by some elder masters of known honor,
I have a voice and precedent of peace
To keep my name ungored. But till that time
I do receive your offered love like love,
And will not wrong it.

HAMLET
                    I embrace it freely,   205
And will this brother's wager frankly play.
Give us the foils. Come on.

LAERTES
                    Come, one for me.

HAMLET
I'll be your foil, Laertes. In mine ignorance
Your skill shall, like a star i' th' darkest night,
Stick fiery off indeed.

LAERTES
                    You mock me, sir.   210

216: **bettered:** favored; **odds:** given a handicap

218: **likes me well:** pleases me

220: **stoops:** flagons

222: **quit...third exchange:** score a return hit in the third exchange

224: **breath:** energy

225: **union:** exquisite pearl

228: **kettle:** kettledrum

234: Scene: ***They play***: Hamlet (David Warner), in Hall's 1965 production, fended off Laertes' blows with barely a move of his sword or body. Laertes (Charles Thomas), on the other hand, danced around attacking him from every possible angle, sweating and puffing his way around a seemingly uncaring opponent.

Pierre Wilkner as Laertes and Peter Stormare as Hamlet in the 1987 Royal Dramatic Theatre of Stockholm production at the National Theatre in London directed by Ingmar Bergman
Photo: Donald Cooper

HAMLET
  No, by this hand.

CLAUDIUS
  Give them the foils, young Osric. Cousin Hamlet,
  You know the wager?

HAMLET
                      Very well, my lord.
  Your grace hath laid the odds o' th' weaker side.

CLAUDIUS
  I do not fear it; I have seen you both.   215
  But since he is bettered, we have therefore odds.

LAERTES
  This is too heavy, let me see another.

HAMLET
  This likes me well. These foils have all a length?

                                            They prepare to play

OSRIC
  Ay, my good lord.

CLAUDIUS
  Set me the stoops of wine upon that table.   220
  If Hamlet give the first or second hit,
  Or quit in answer of the third exchange,
  Let all the battlements their ordnance fire.
  The King shall drink to Hamlet's better breath,
  And in the cup an union shall he throw   225
  Richer than that which four successive kings
  In Denmark's crown have worn. Give me the cups,
  And let the kettle to the trumpet speak,
  The trumpet to the cannoneer without,
  The cannons to the heavens, the heavens to earth,   230
  'Now the King drinks to Hamlet.' Come, begin–
  And you, the judges, bear a wary eye.

HAMLET
  Come on, sir.

LAERTES
  Come on, sir.

                                                  They play

238: **palpable**: evident

240: **Stay**: Stop

245: **fat**: sweaty; **scant of breath**: out of breath

246: **napkin**: handkerchief

247: **carouses**: toasts

250: "I will, my lord; I pray you, pardon me.": Diane Fletcher as Gertrude in the 2003 Birmingham Repertory Theatre & Edinburgh International Festival production directed by Calixto Bieito at the Royal Lyceum Theatre in Edinburgh
Photo: Donald Cooper

251: Scene: **It is...too late**: Perhaps of all the filmed versions of the play, Zeffirelli's sword fight stands out as one of the best. Gibson (filled with a righteous and frenetic energy) plays to the court spectators, making a joke of what he knows to be deadly serious. Alan Bates plays Claudius with his own kind of nervousness: an anxiety born of guilt. When Glenn Close's Gertrude drinks the poisoned wine, Claudius seems to realize that this is the end. No matter what the outcome, for him it is finished.

HAMLET
　One.   235

LAERTES
　No.

HAMLET
　Judgment.

OSRIC
　A hit, a very palpable hit.

LAERTES
　Well, again.

CLAUDIUS
　Stay. Give me drink. Hamlet, this pearl is thine.   240
　Here's to thy health. Give him the cup.

Trumpets sound, and shot goes off

HAMLET
　I'll play this bout first. Set it by awhile.
　Come.

They play

　　　　Another hit. What say you?

LAERTES
　A touch, a touch, I do confess.

CLAUDIUS
　Our son shall win.

GERTRUDE
　　　　　　He's fat, and scant of breath.   245
　Here, Hamlet, take my napkin, rub thy brows.
　The Queen carouses to thy fortune, Hamlet.

HAMLET
　Good madam.

CLAUDIUS
　Gertrude, do not drink.

GERTRUDE
　I will, my lord; I pray you, pardon me.   250

CLAUDIUS
　It is the poisoned cup. It is too late.

257: **pass**: thrust

258: **wanton**: spoiled child

267: **woodcock**: proverbially stupid bird; **mine own springe**: my own trap (recalling Polonius' line to Ophelia in 1.3.18)

Roger Rees as Hamlet, Nicholas Farrell as Horatio, Brian Blessed as Claudius, and Kenneth Branagh as Laertes in the Royal Shakespeare Company's 1984 production directed by Ron Daniels
Photo: Donald Cooper

HAMLET
I dare not drink yet, madam; by and by.

GERTRUDE
Come, let me wipe thy face.

LAERTES
My lord, I'll hit him now.

CLAUDIUS
                    I do not think't.

LAERTES
And yet 'tis almost 'gainst my conscience.   255

HAMLET
Come, for the third, Laertes. You but dally.
I pray you, pass with your best violence,
I am afeard you make a wanton of me.

LAERTES
Say you so? Come on.

They play

OSRIC
Nothing, neither way.   260

LAERTES
Have at you now!

In scuffling, they change rapiers

CLAUDIUS
Part them. They are incensed.

HAMLET
Nay, come, again.

OSRIC
Look to the Queen there. Ho!

HORATIO
They bleed on both sides. How is't, my lord?   265

OSRIC
How is't, Laertes?

LAERTES
Why, as a woodcock to mine own springe, Osric.
I am justly killed with mine own treachery.

278: **Unbated and envenomed**: sharp and poisoned; **foul practice:** evil deed

286-287: "Here, thou incestuous, murd'rous, damnèd Dane, / Drink off this potion.": Santino Fontana as Hamlet and Matthew Greer as Claudius in the Guthrie Theater's 2006 production directed by Joe Dowling
Photo: Michal Daniel

287: **union**: referring to the poison pearl and also to his incestuous marriage

HAMLET
How does the queen?

CLAUDIUS
                    She swoons to see them bleed.

GERTRUDE
No, no, the drink, the drink–O my dear Hamlet!   270
The drink, the drink! I am poisoned.

                                        [She dies]

HAMLET
O villainy! Ho! Let the door be locked.
Treachery! Seek it out.

                                        [Exit OSRIC]

LAERTES
It is here, Hamlet. Hamlet, thou art slain.
No med'cine in the world can do thee good.   275
In thee there is not half an hour of life.
The treacherous instrument is in thy hand,
Unbated and envenomed. The foul practice
Hath turned itself on me. Lo, here I lie,
Never to rise again. Thy mother's poisoned.   280
I can no more. The King, the King's to blame.

HAMLET
The point envenomed too?
Then, venom, to thy work.

                                        [He stabs CLAUDIUS]

All
Treason! Treason!

CLAUDIUS
O, yet defend me, friends. I am but hurt.   285

HAMLET
Here, thou incestuous, murd'rous, damnèd Dane,
Drink off this potion. Is thy union here?
Follow my mother.

                                        CLAUDIUS dies

293: **make thee free**: acquit you

297: **fell sergeant**: cruel officer

301: **the unsatisfied**: the uninformed

302: **antique Roman**: Romans regarded suicide as more honorable then defeat.

305: **wounded name**: tarnished reputation

314: **warlike volley**: i.e., the firing of cannons in a military salute

Set rendering from the 1958 production at the Shakespeare Memorial Theatre directed by Glen Byam Shaw

Photo: Rare Book and Special Collections Library, University of Illinois at Urbana-Champaign

LAERTES
He is justly served;
It is a poison tempered by himself.
Exchange forgiveness with me, noble Hamlet.   290
Mine and my father's death come not upon thee,
Nor thine on me.

LAERTES dies

HAMLET
Heaven make thee free of it! I follow thee.
I am dead, Horatio. Wretched Queen, adieu!
You that look pale and tremble at this chance,   295
That are but mutes or audience to this act,
Had I but time–as this fell sergeant, Death,
Is strict in his arrest–O, I could tell you–
But let it be. Horatio, I am dead;
Thou liv'st; report me and my cause aright   300
To the unsatisfied.

HORATIO
Never believe it.
I am more an antique Roman than a Dane.
Here's yet some liquor left.

HAMLET
As thou'rt a man,
Give me the cup. Let go by heaven, I'll have't.
O good Horatio, what a wounded name,   305
Things standing thus unknown, shall live behind me!
If thou didst ever hold me in thy heart,
Absent thee from felicity awhile
And in this harsh world draw thy breath in pain,
To tell my story.   310
March afar off, and shout within
What warlike noise is this?

Enter OSRIC

OSRIC
Young Fortinbras, with conquest come from Poland,
To th' ambassadors of England gives
This warlike volley.

tracks 37-38

314-320:
Sir John Gielgud as Hamlet

315: **o'ercrows**: triumphs over (like a victorious rooster in a cockfight)

318: **He has my dying voice**: Hamlet voices his preference for Fortinbras to succeed to the Danish throne.

320: **solicited**: happened

320: Scene: *[HAMLET] dies*: Richard Burbage is reported to have been so convincing in playing Hamlet's death that the audience wasn't sure if he had actually died or just pretended to, using his great talent at "personation," a newly coined word in the seventeenth century.

321-322: Scene: **Good night...thy rest**: In Zeffirelli's film, Fortinbras was cut. The performance ends with Hamlet (Gibson) falling bit by painful bit to the stage. He looks to an unbelieving Horatio for comfort and says, "I am dead, Horatio," and then, "Horatio, I am dead." Horatio cradles the prince as he dies, and the film ends with the Horatio's line as the camera moves up and up and away from Hamlet, revealing the bodies of Laertes, Gertrude, and Claudius, a stunned court, and two empty thrones.

323: Scene: *Enter FORTINBRAS*: In 1999, Andrei Serban directed Liev Schrieber as Hamlet at the Joseph Papp Public Theatre. At the death scene, Fortinbras arrives as two warriors: a woman in armor and her twin brother, with whom she shares the final lines of the play. When asked about this choice, Serban replied, "Hamlet's death is a kind of sacrifice, He wants to give an example of what will give other people a chance to get things right. Fortinbras appears, like the Archangel Gabriel, in the outfit of a warrior. But they are warriors in a spiritual army, bringing peace, a caressing kind of hope."

326: **quarry**: pile of bodies (in hunting, "quarry" refers to the heap of dead animals after a hunt)

327: **toward**: prepared

332: **him**: i.e., Claudius

337: **so jump upon this bloody question**: i.e., to jump immediately to the matter

HAMLET
>   O, I die, Horatio.
> The potent poison quite o'ercrows my spirit.   315
> I cannot live to hear the news from England,
> But I do prophesy the election lights
> On Fortinbras. He has my dying voice.
> So tell him, with the occurrents, more and less,
> Which have solicited. The rest is silence.   320
>   *[HAMLET] dies*

HORATIO
> Now cracks a noble heart. Good night sweet prince,
> And flights of angels sing thee to thy rest.
> Why does the drum come hither?
>   *Enter FORTINBRAS and English Ambassador*
>   *with Drums, Colors, and Attendants*

FORTINBRAS
> Where is this sight?

HORATIO
>   What is it you would see?
> If aught of woe or wonder, cease your search.   325

FORTINBRAS
> This quarry cries on havoc. O proud Death,
> What feast is toward in thine eternal cell,
> That thou so many princes at a shot
> So bloodily hast struck?

English Ambassador
>   The sight is dismal;
> And our affairs from England come too late.   330
> The ears are senseless that should give us hearing
> To tell him his commandment is fulfilled,
> That Rosencrantz and Guildenstern are dead.
> Where should we have our thanks?

HORATIO
>   Not from his mouth,
> Had it th' ability of life to thank you.   335
> He never gave commandment for their death.
> But since, so jump upon this bloody question,
> You from the Polack wars, and you from England,
> Are here arrived give order that these bodies
> High on a stage be placed to the view,   340
> And let me speak to the yet unknowing world

343: **carnal**: lustful

344: **accidental judgments:** mistaken motives; **casual slaughters:** unthinking retributions

345: **put on**: instigated

351: **rights of memory**: remembered rights

354: **on more**: affirming votes

356: **mischance**: unfortunate mistakes

359: **put on**: i.e., crowned king

360: **proved**: acted

363-364: **Such a sight...much amiss**: i.e., this kind of butchery is expected on the battlefield, but in the palace chambers of a royal family, it indicates a calamitous event

Costume rendering for Fortinbras from the 1934 production at the New Theatre directed by Sir John Gielgud
Photo: Rare Book and Special Collections Library, University of Illinois at Urbana-Champaign

How these things came about. So shall you hear
Of carnal, bloody, and unnatural acts,
Of accidental judgments, casual slaughters,
Of deaths put on by cunning and forced cause,   345
And, in this upshot, purposes mistook
Fallen on the inventors' heads. All this can I
Truly deliver.

FORTINBRAS
              Let us haste to hear it,
And call the noblest to the audience.
For me, with sorrow I embrace my fortune.   350
I have some rights of memory in this kingdom,
Which now to claim my vantage doth invite me.

HORATIO
Of that I shall have also cause to speak,
And from his mouth whose voice will draw on more.
But let this same be presently performed,   355
Even while men's minds are wild, lest more mischance
On plots and errors happen.

FORTINBRAS
              Let four captains
Bear Hamlet like a soldier to the stage,
For he was likely, had he been put on,
To have proved most royally; and, for his passage,   360
The soldiers' music and the rites of war
Speak loudly for him.
Take up the bodies. Such a sight as this
Becomes the field, but here shows much amiss.
Go, bid the soldiers shoot.   365

                      Exeunt marching, after which,
                      a peal of ordinance is shot off

The Cast Speaks

Marie Macaisa

In the text of the play, directors, actors, and other interpreters of Shakespeare's work find a wealth of information. Similarly, readers of his plays find many questions to ponder. A hallmark of Shakespeare's writing is to tell us more than we need to know about a particular character, more than is needed to understand the plot. For example, through his soliloquies, we know quite a bit about what Hamlet is thinking. Yet we are left with much uncertainty: Is Hamlet mad or just pretending to be? Is he a coward for not acting, or is he being careful and thoughtful? What about his relationship with Ophelia? How serious was it, and was he aware that Polonius and Claudius were eavesdropping on their conversation? Is the Ghost real or in his imagination? How much can it be blamed for Hamlet's behavior?

While providing extra information, Shakespeare (like all playwrights and unlike novelists) also leaves gaps. We are thus coaxed to fill in the missing information ourselves, either through reasonable surmises (we can guess that Gertrude and Claudius were attracted to each other before Old Hamlet died) or through back stories we supply on our own (perhaps Hamlet had trouble living up to the expectations of the king). This mix, simultaneously knowing too much and not enough about the characters, enables us to paint vivid, varied interpretations of the same play.

In staging a play, directors create a vision for their production starting from the text but also moving beyond that, by making decisions on what *isn't* in the text. In collaboration with actors, they flesh out the characters: they discuss what they might be like, they create stories that explain their actions, they determine motivations, and they speculate on the nature of their relationships. In Shakespeare they have a rich text to draw on and hundreds of years of performances for inspiration. Thus we, the audience, can experience a play anew each time we see a different production: perhaps it is in an unfamiliar setting, perhaps it is in a scene or characterization we hadn't noticed in the past, perhaps it is in the realization that we have somehow grown to sympathize with different characters (for example, the parent, Gertrude or Polonius, instead of the child, Hamlet or Laertes). Whatever the case, a closer look into one cast's interpretation creates an opportunity for us to make up our own minds about their stories and in the process, gain new insights not just into a play hundreds of years old but quite possibly, ourselves.

ACTORS FROM THE LONDON STAGE, 2006

Now in its thirtieth year, Actors From The London Stage (AFTLS) is one of the oldest established touring Shakespeare theater companies in the world. Their approach to performance is a unique one. In each tour five classically trained actors, working without a director and guided only by the text, work through the staging of the play by themselves. Each actor plays multiple roles, using only their voice and bearing, along with simple props and costumes, to delineate the characters from each other. The sets are minimal. Through it all, their emphasis is on Shakespeare's words. According to Prof. Peter Holland, their current academic director, "The aim is to make Shakespeare's words exert their magic and their power in performance. The actors ask the audience to perform that same kind of imaginative engagement that Shakespeare was thinking about when, in the Prologue to Henry V, he instructed his spectators:

> Think, when we speak of horses, that you see them,
> Printing their proud hoofs i'th' receiving earth
> For 'tis your thoughts that now must deck our kings."

The following actors were interviewed in September, 2006, at the University of Notre Dame in South Bend, Indiana, in the beginning of their tour of *Hamlet*:

AFTLS Cast

Geoffrey Beevers	Polonius, Osric, 4th Player, 1st Gravedigger, Norwegian Captain, Marcellus, Priest
Anna Northam	Gertrude, Ophelia, 2nd Player, Sailor
Robert Mountford	Horatio, Laertes, Rosencrantz, Guildenstern, 3rd Player
Richard Stacey	Hamlet, Bernardo, Fortinbras
Terence Wilton	Claudius, Ghost, 1st Player, Francisco, Reynaldo, 2nd Gravedigger

We held a group discussion and the actors were asked about their own characters as well as the approach of the group to the play. In many cases, because the group had worked on the scenes together, actors had a lot to say about the portrayal of each others' characters. Keep in mind that their thoughts and ideas represent but one interpretation of the play. You may be

Geoffrey Beevers, Anna Northam, Richard Stacey, Terence Wilton, and Robert Mountford
Photo: Patrick Ryan

surprised, and you may agree or disagree strongly with some of their choices. That is exactly the point.

> *"The country is in a warlike situation,"* the group surmised, *"and the sol-diers are looking out over the battlements, at the threat from Norway."* *"How-ever, that's not where the threat lies,"* Terence Wilton (Claudius) explains. *"It's in the lobbies and corridors, behind arrases, in the bedroom. That's where you find the heart of the play. A focus on the domestic seemed to us the right way to approach it."*

Geoffrey Beevers: Polonius

We thought it was important to set up a loving family. Polonius is a loving father who cares for his children (or thinks he does). His children seem to care for him in return, judging by their reaction when he is killed. One goes mad and the other returns from school perfectly intent on revenge and ready to commit murder.

In the scene where he is giving Laertes advice before Laertes goes back to Paris (1.3), you realize in listening to him that he's very controlling. After his talk with his son, he goes on to ask about his daughter's relationship with Hamlet. He wants to know all the time what's going on—with his children, Hamlet, with the state—and to be in control of the information. That's the key to Polonius. In the beginning court scene, I give the king some vital papers (the country is at war, after all), and he gives it right back to me. It's clear the king doesn't involve himself in the day-to-day activities of the government; he leaves it to me and I like that.

There is another scene that supports our understanding of the character of Polonius and that's 2.1, his meeting with Reynaldo. It's a light, funny scene, but there is also something serious going on. He's arranging for Rey-naldo to spy on his son and report back to him. He's careful to warn Rey-naldo not to go overboard with accusations: "none so rank / As may dishonor him," and tells him to lay "slight sullies" on him. He goes so far as to name acceptable offenses: "drinking, fencing, swearing" and even "drabbing" (deal-ing with prostitutes). He doesn't mind giving Laertes some rein as long as he knows what's going on with him. With Ophelia, he's still treating her like a baby, and he doesn't realize that she's a grown woman.

I don't think Polonius thinks of himself as a control freak. Instead, he believes he is a loving, caring parent who wants to do the best for his family and for his country.

Anna Northam as Gertrude, Geoffrey Beevers as Polonius, and Terence Wilton as Claudius
Photo: Patrick Ryan

Anna Northam: Ophelia

Ophelia has a loving relationship with her father. We all get on with each other. Some parents are very strict and the children are scared of them, and that's not us. We put in a bit of teasing during our scene together (1.3).

Ophelia is her father's daughter. If you look at her words and how she speaks, it's very similar to him. She talks in lists, and her sentences are very structured. Polonius does the same thing. He lists, and then he qualifies. He finds it impossible to say something without further qualifying it. From her speech, you can tell she's his daughter.

She's a woman of her time and of her circumstance. She's obedient and will not go against her father's wishes. She simply would not do that. She respects him enormously. My thinking is that my mother has been gone for a while and my father brought me up from a very early age. I miss the female presence in my life. He has tried to bridge that gap but not very successfully.

Robert Mountford: Laertes

The first time we read through the play, our family naturally came out as a warm, giggly, happy family, which led to the discussion of what we think each of our characters is like. Laertes, I think, has special privileges because of his dad's position in court. Here he is, in front of the assembled court, addressing the new king, and asking for permission to go back to Paris. All because of his dad. Laertes is tremendously proud of that. Because of his affection for his father, he feels additional responsibility for taking care of Ophelia, his baby sister, and presumes to offer her advice (just like his father) on her relationship with Hamlet. I think Laertes quite enjoys the company of women but he wants to protect Ophelia from being on the receiving end of such attention. He playfully sets her up before he leaves by warning her in front of their father, "Remember well / What I have told you." He knows she's going to be questioned about it. It's a bit of sibling cheek.

In contrast to the warm images presented by Polonius' family, the relations in Hamlet's broken family are uneasy at best. When we first meet Hamlet, in front of the assembled court, he is mourning his father's death, his mother has married his uncle (within a month of the death, we find out), and his uncle has also taken over the throne.

Terence Wilton: Claudius

I prepare for my role by writing down anything that anybody says about your character and also what your character says about everyone else. Out of this, you find out where a character's obsession resides. It's what's repeated, repeated, repeated.

With Claudius, it's clearly Hamlet. When political issues are brought to him in the beginning of 1.2, he dismisses them very, very quickly, in just a few sentences. After that his attention is on Hamlet: cousin, son, my son, cousin, our son, your son. How he talks about Hamlet parallels the decay of his relationship with Gertrude. By the time he says of Gertrude (in 4.7.14), "She's so conjunctive to my life and soul," you're not sure anymore whether he means it or is just playing politics. At the beginning of the play though, it was probably heartfelt.

In terms of what's said about him, you have: villain; bloody, bawdy, villain; incestuous, damned villain, smile and smile and be a villain. And you have to pick what to play. Yes, he turned out to be a villain, but you don't know that for sure until the middle of the play in the prayer scene (3.3.36) that he committed the murder. So I thought, "smile and smile and be a villain" was the way to go.

When he says in 1.2.47-49,

> The head is not more native to the heart,
> The hand more instrumental to the mouth,
> Than is the throne of Denmark to thy father.

…he is talking to Laertes about Polonius, but he could just as easily been talking about himself.

Claudius talks about the "King's rouse" (boozing) and drinking in the battlements; he's obsessed with alcohol. He's a boozer, sensualist, lust-driven coward who turns into a most extraordinarily clever operator. He has his own journey into self-discovery, and the prayer scene (3.3.36) is at the end of that. He really does try to pray for redemption. But when he realizes "My words fly up, my thoughts remain below" (3.3.98), he decides that this is the world he must live in, and he resolves to do whatever he needs to in order to cover his tracks.

Anna Northam: Gertrude

I don't think she's a weak woman. That's not why she married so soon after her husband's death. I've been asked whether she was in on his death, and I couldn't find any evidence for it at all. My thinking about it is that it doesn't matter how Old Hamlet died; he's dead. Whether or not she wants to remain queen, I absolutely believe that she wants Hamlet to be king someday. With Claudius taking over, that's not a certainty, and there is the possibility that Claudius will appoint someone other than my son to succeed him. So I play her being motivated by that. She adores Hamlet and loves him to death.

I also think she quite fancies this old bloke, for selfish reasons and not-so-selfish reasons. They might have a great sexual relationship. They possibly had an affair while the other king was alive (Old Hamlet did sleep in the garden). There are possibilities. I do like to think that they had fun.

In the court scene, 1.2, when Claudius announces that Hamlet is now next in line ("let the world take note, / You are the most immediate to our throne" 1.2.108-109), that's a triumph for her. That's all she wanted, and now they can have a boozy, fun night. It's not such a bad life and she likes being queen.

Robert Mountford as Rosencrantz and Guildenstern, Terence Wilton as Claudius, and Anna Northam as Gertrude
Photo: Patrick Ryan

Terence Wilton: Claudius
With the country under threat from Norway, it's good for the king to demonstrate continuity and for the king and queen to show a stable family.

Anna Northam: Gertrude
Hamlet isn't stable. I'm desperately worried that he's going off the rails. His father just died, and he's not reacting well to my marriage. But his life is a political one, and he should be used to what that means. She's trying to protect him, and she watches him all the time. When Polonius tells her that he

knows why Hamlet is mad, though she doesn't like Polonius calling him that, she's extremely relieved that there could be simple explanation.

When that turns out not to be the case, she doesn't give up on him. No matter what he's done, even killing Polonius, she will stand by him. One of her last thoughts when she is dying is of him. "O my dear Hamlet!" she says as she lays poisoned (5.2.270).

Richard Stacey: Hamlet

To Hamlet, his father is like a god. He thought his mother was the perfect consort for him in that relationship, and now he feels that she has let him down, and very badly.

I think he has other issues—he's at university at Wittenburg doing liberal arts and trying to write poetry. He wants to be a poet and he's got this father who's the captain of the football team and runs a successful business—a man's man who wants his son to be like him. But Hamlet isn't. And before he has time to deal with that issue, his father dies and his mother marries his uncle, of whom he doesn't think too highly:

> Here is your husband, like a mildewed ear,
> Blasting his wholesome brother.
>
> (3.4.66-67)

One of his problems is that Hamlet's view of sex is a very immature one. He's not experienced like Laertes (judging from Ophelia's description of Laertes as a "puffed and reckless libertine" who treads "the primrose path of dalliance" and from Polonius' implicit acceptance of his "drabbing" i.e., consorting with prostitutes). Hamlet sits at home and holds Ophelia's hands and writes dreadful love poetry.

He's viewed his mother as "the queen," and suddenly he has to confront the reality that his mother has sex. Though this happens to him when he's older, I think he has a teenager's point of view in this respect. He dares go to her bedroom and give her advice about her sex life:

> go not to mine uncle's bed.
> Assume a virtue, if you have it not.

> Refrain tonight,
> And that shall lend a kind of easiness
> To the next abstinence, the next more easy.
>
> (3.4.158-162)

It's the height of arrogance, really, but that sums up Hamlet in terms of other people.

The nature of Hamlet's relationship with his mother and with Ophelia has been handled by various productions in different ways (see the notes at the beginning of 3.4). In this one, Hamlet does get into sexually charged situations with Gertrude and Ophelia. However, Stacey believes the energy is about sex only generally, not specifically with Ophelia or something Oedipal with his mother.

Richard Stacey: Hamlet

He gets into situations with both of them where he bullies them physically. In some respects, I think he enjoys the power. But it's a misogyny born of youth.

No, I don't think he's had sex with Ophelia. For him to have done that doesn't jibe with the other parts of the play where he's so morally absolute about people's bad behavior. When he views something as being immoral, he gets on his high horse and gets very cross about it.

Yet, he also shows himself to be a moral relativist, at least when it comes to very serious offenses. For example, he has no compunction at all about having murdered Polonius, because Polonius shouldn't have been where he was. He's a wretched, rash, intruding fool and he shouldn't have been eavesdropping. He also doesn't feel any remorse for what he did to Rosencrantz and Guildenstern:

> Why, man, they did make love to this employment.
> They are not near my conscience.
>
> (5.2.57-58)

The only person for whom he feels any kind of regret is Laertes. He believes that Laertes is the only person who can empathize with him, having lost his

Richard Stacey as Hamlet and Anna Northam as Ophelia
Photo: Patrick Ryan

father too. He conveniently leaves out the part where he's responsible. And Laertes has lost his sister in the same way he's lost his mother (again ignoring that he had something to do with that). But that's his moral elasticity.

He sees in Laertes what he sees in Fortinbras. They both make decisions. They would make much better kings than he would.

Robert Mountford: Laertes

Would Laertes make a good king? Yes, he makes decisions. But what I've found is that although he makes up his mind easily and firmly, he doesn't have the experience to recognize when he's gone down the wrong path. He's determined to stay on the path he's on, even if he has doubts. Hamlet, at some point, realizes he has to let go and let things turn out the way they will, but Laertes just drives through single-mindedly. When he gets to where he wants to be, which is mortally wounding Hamlet and thus avenging his father, it's unfortunately the first time he realizes he got it wrong.

Laertes is not the smartest person and he's easily manipulated. It's obvious that everything is about revenge for him and it doesn't take many words for Claudius to convince him to go along with his plan. I don't think he's entirely happy about it, but he very quickly agrees. It's important to note that Laertes is a proper revenger, with proper motive. His father was murdered and he has the right to seek revenge. Claudius, instead of acknowledging that and leaving him to it, offers to stack the odds by poisoning the sword:

> you may choose
> A sword unbated, and in a pass of practice
> Requite him for your father.
>
> (4.7.138-140)

As soon as he hears that, he goes along with it, and that's when he goes wrong. It's the "poison in the air."

Terence Wilton: Claudius

The king and Polonius have a lot to do with that atmosphere. They're running around the court, hiding behind arrases, and spying on people. Since they practice and enjoy it, you can imagine how that attitude must permeate the court.

We use that metaphor of "poison in the air" quite a lot throughout the play. Before each scene, we pick up the language of the previous scene and whisper it repeatedly under our breaths. There's something in the air.

The presence of Hamlet's dead father is also inescapable, and the origins of the apparition are not made clear. The ghost could be imagined; it could be a diabolical presence; or perhaps it is Old Hamlet back from the dead.

Terence Wilton: Claudius

We take the position that the ordinary soldiers have seen the ghost. Horatio, the skeptic, has confirmed it. So we think the ghost does exist. And then the poison that was put into his ear, the hebenon, is put into Hamlet's ear as well, and he leaps like a salmon to it.

Richard Stacey: Hamlet

When Hamlet first meets the ghost, he is quite emotional, saying, "Alas, poor ghost!" But his father cuts him off, shuts him up:

> Pity me not, but lend thy serious hearing
> To what I shall unfold.

(1.5.5-6)

His father urges him to revenges; he keeps saying "revenge."

> So art thou to revenge, when thou shalt hear. (1.5.8)
> Revenge his foul and most unnatural murder. (1.5.26)

And then his father challenges him with this speech, appealing to his intelligence and questioning his loyalty as his son. What kind of son would he be if he didn't do this?

> I find thee apt;
> And duller shouldst thou be than the fat weed
> That roots itself in ease on Lethe wharf,
> Wouldst thou not stir in this.

(1.5.33-36)

Terence Wilton: Claudius

What fathers do to their children in this play, the damage they cause, is horrendous. Yet Hamlet has an idealized view of his father, the king. Horatio says, "I saw him once; he was a goodly king," and Hamlet responds with, "I shall not look upon his like again." That's it. I don't think he knows the man. It's winter; he's been off to boarding school. He doesn't know his father, but he has lots of pictures of him. Then his dead hand comes out and claws Hamlet's life away, saying that the only way in which he can continue to exist is if he commits murder. That's a terrible, terrible legacy.

Richard Stacey: Hamlet

"Something is rotten in the state of Denmark," and we focus on that. Elsinore is a strange and isolated place; the castle is oddly on its own. We play that quite strongly. People come in from the outside, trying to be agents of change, like Horatio from Wittenburg, Rosencrantz and Guildenstern arriving, Laertes coming back from Paris, Hamlet returning from England. They try to affect the action in the play. Being inside too long taints Horatio, and he tries to kill himself in the end, before Hamlet stops him.

Terence Wilton: Claudius

We try to show the discoloration of relationships, of friendships, and the isolation of Hamlet. The line before "O, what a rogue and peasant slave am I" is "Now I am alone." Becoming a revenger is a solitary thing.

The decisions must come from the text. That's the AFTLS way. There are only five of you, you can't buy that many props that you have to carry around, and all of you just end up figuring out how to tell the story clearly. You try and work out a version that's true and fully realized. You look to the text to explain why people act the way they do.

Richard Stacey as Hamlet
Photo: Patrick Ryan

A Voice Coach's Perspective on Speaking Shakespeare

KEEPING SHAKESPEARE PRACTICAL

Andrew Wade

Why, you might be wondering, is it so important to keep Shakespeare practical? What do I mean by practical? Why is this the way to discover how to speak the text and understand it?

Plays themselves are not simply literary events—they demand interpreters in the deepest sense of the word, and the language of Shakespeare requires, therefore, not a vocal demonstration of writing techniques but an imaginative response to that writing. The key word here is imagination. The task of the voice coach is to offer relevant choices to the actor so that the actor's imagination is titillated, excited by the language, which he or she can then share with an audience, playing on that audience's imagination. Take the word "IF"—it is only composed of two letters when written, but if you say it aloud and listen to what it implies, then your reaction, the way the word plays through you, can change the perception of meaning. "Iffffffff"... you might hear and feel it implying "possibilities," "choices," "questioning," "trying to work something out." The saying of this word provokes active investigation of thought. What an apt word to launch a play: "If music be the food of love, play on" (Act 1, Scene 1 in *Twelfth Night, or What You Will*). How this word engages the listener and immediately sets up an involvement is about more than audibility. How we verbalize sounds has a direct link to meaning and understanding. In the words of Touchstone in *As You Like It*, "Much virtue in if."

I was working with a company in Vancouver on *Macbeth,* and at the end of the first week's rehearsal—after having explored our voices and opening out different pieces of text to hear the possibilities of the rhythm, feeling how the meter affects the thinking and feeling, looking at structure and form— one of the actors admitted he was also a writer of soap operas and that I had completely changed his way of writing. Specifically, in saying a line like, "The multitudinous seas incarnadine / Making the green one red" he heard the complexity of meaning revealed in the use of polysyllabic words becoming monosyllabic, layered upon the words' individual dictionary definitions. The writer was reminded that merely reproducing the speech of everyday life was nowhere near as powerful and effective as language that is shaped.

Do you think soap operas would benefit from rhyming couplets? Somehow this is difficult to imagine! But, the writer's comments set me thinking. As I am constantly trying to find ways of exploring the acting process, of opening out actors' connection with language that isn't their own, I thought it would be a good idea to involve writers and actors in some practical work on language. After talking to Cicely Berry (Voice Director, the Royal Shakespeare Company) and Colin Chambers (the then RSC Production Adviser), we put together a group of writers and actors who were interested in taking part. It was a fascinating experience all round, and it broke down barriers and misconceptions.

The actors discovered, for instance, that a writer is not coming from a very different place as they are in their creative search; that an idea or an image may result from a struggle to define a gut feeling and not from some crafted, well-formed idea in the head. The physical connection of language to the body was reaffirmed. After working with a group on Yeats' poem *Easter 1916*, Ann Devlin changed the title of the play she was writing for the Royal Shakespeare Company to *After Easter*. She had experienced the poem read aloud by a circle of participants, each voice becoming a realization of the shape of the writing. Thus it made a much fuller impact on her and caused her thinking to shift. Such practical exchanges, through language work and voice, feed and stimulate my work to go beyond making sure the actors' voices are technically sound.

It is, of course, no different when we work on a Shakespeare play. A similar connection with the language is crucial. Playing Shakespeare, in many ways, is crafted instinct. The task is thus to find the best way to tap into someone's imagination. As Peter Brook put it: "People forget that a text is dumb. To make it speak, one must create a communication machine. A living network, like a nervous system, must be made if a text which comes from far away is to touch the sensibility of the present."

This journey is never to be taken for granted. It is the process that every text must undergo every time it is staged. There is no definitive rehearsal that would solve problems or indicate ways of staging a given play. Again, this is where creative, practical work on voice can help forge new meaning by offering areas of exploration and challenge. The central idea behind my work comes back to posing the question, "How does meaning change by speaking out aloud?" It would be unwise to jump hastily to the end process for, as Peter Brook says, "Shakespeare's words are records of the words that he wanted spoken, words issuing from people's mouths, with pitch, pause and rhythm and gesture as part of their meaning. A word does not start as a word—it is the end product which begins as an impulse, stimulated by attitude and behavior which dictates the need for expression." (1)

PRACTICALLY SPEAKING

Something happens when we vocalize, when we isolate sounds, when we start to speak words aloud, when we put them to the test of our physicality, of our anatomy. We expose ourselves in a way that makes taking the language back more difficult. Our body begins a debate with itself, becomes alive with the vibrations of sound produced in the mouth or rooted deep in the muscles that aim at defining sound. In fact, the spoken words bring into play all the senses, before sense and another level of meaning are reached.

"How do I know what I think, until I see what I say," Oscar Wilde once said. A concrete illustration of this phrase was reported to me when I was leading a workshop recently. A grandmother said the work we had done that day reminded her of what her six-year-old grandson had said to his mother while they were driving through Wales: "Look, mummy, sheep! Sheep! Sheep!" "You don't have to keep telling us," the mother replied, but the boy said, "How do I know they're there, if I don't tell you?!"

Therefore, when we speak of ideas, of sense, we slightly take for granted those physical processes which affect and change their meaning. We tend to separate something that is an organic whole. In doing so, we become blind to the fact that it is precisely this physical connection to the words that enables the actors to make the language theirs.

The struggle for meaning is not just impressionistic theater mystique; it is an indispensable aspect of the rehearsal process and carries on during the life of every production. In this struggle, practical work on Shakespeare is vital and may help spark creativity and shed some light on the way meaning is born into language. After a performance of *More Words*, a show devised and directed by Cicely Berry and myself, Katie Mitchell (a former artistic director of The Other Place in Stratford-upon-Avon) gave me an essay by Ted Hughes that echoes with the piece. In it, Ted Hughes compares the writing of a poem—the coming into existence of words—to the capture of a wild animal. You will notice that in the following passage Hughes talks of "spirit" or "living parts" but never of "thought" or "sense." With great care and precaution, he advises, "It is better to call [the poem] an assembly of living parts moved by a single spirit. The living parts are the words, the images, the rhythms. The spirit is the life which inhabits them when they all work together. It is impossible to say which comes first, parts or spirit."

This is also true of life in words, as many are connected directly to one or several of our senses. Here Hughes talks revealingly of "the five senses," of "word," "action," and "muscle," all things which a practical approach to language is more likely to allow one to perceive and do justice to.

Words that live are those which we hear, like "click" or "chuckle," or which we see, like "freckled" or "veined," or which we taste, like "vinegar" or "sugar," or touch, like "prickle" or "oily," or smell, like "tar" or "onion," words which belong to one of the five senses. Or words that act and seem to use their muscles, like "flick" or "balance." (2)

In this way, practically working on Shakespeare to arrive at understanding lends itself rather well, I think, to what Adrian Noble (former artistic director of the RSC) calls "a theater of poetry," a form of art that, rooted deeply in its classical origins, would seek to awaken the imagination of its audiences through love and respect for words while satisfying our eternal craving for myths and twice-told tales.

This can only be achieved at some cost. There is indeed a difficult battle to fight and hopefully win "the battle of the word to survive." This phrase was coined by Michael Redgrave at the beginning of the 1950s, a period when theater began to be deeply influenced by more physical forms, such as mime. (3) Although the context is obviously different, the fight today is of the same nature.

LISTENING TO SHAKESPEARE

Because of the influence of television, our way of speaking as well as listening has changed. It is crucial to be aware of this. We can get fairly close to the way *Henry V* or *Hamlet* was staged in Shakespeare's time; we can try also to reconstruct the way English was spoken. But somehow, all these fall short of the real and most important goal: the Elizabethan ear. How did one "hear" a Shakespeare play? This is hardest to know. My personal view is that we will probably never know for sure. We are, even when we hear a Shakespeare play or a recording from the past, bound irrevocably to modernity. The Elizabethan ear was no doubt different from our own, as people were not spoken to or entertained in the same way. A modern voice has to engage us in a different way in order to make us truly listen in a society that seems to rely solely on the belief that image is truth, that it is more important to show than to tell.

Sometimes, we say that a speech in Shakespeare, or even an entire production, is not well-spoken, not up to standard. What do we mean by that? Evidently, there are a certain number of "guidelines" that any actor now has to know when working on a classical text. Yet, even when these are known, actors still have to make choices when they speak. A sound is not a sound without somebody to lend an ear to it: rhetoric is nothing without an audience.

There are a certain number of factors that affect the receiver's ear. These can be cultural factors such as the transition between different acting styles or the level of training that our contemporary ear has had. There are also personal and emotional factors. Often we feel the performance was not well-spoken because, somehow, it did not live up to our expectations of how we think it should have been performed. Is it that many of us have a self-conscious model, perhaps our own first experience of Shakespeare, that meant something to us and became our reference point for the future (some treasured performance kept under glass)? Nothing from then on can quite compare with that experience.

Most of the time, however, it is more complex than nostalgia. Take, for example, the thorny area of accent. I remind myself constantly that audibility is not embedded in Received Pronunciation or Standard American. The familiarity that those in power have with speech and the articulate confidence gained from coming from the right quarters can lead us all to hear certain types of voices as outshining others. But, to my mind, the role of theater is at least to question these assumptions so that we do not perpetuate those givens but work towards a broader tolerance.

In Canada on a production of *Twelfth Night*, I was working with an actor who was from Newfoundland. His own natural rhythms in speaking seemed completely at home with Shakespeare's. Is this because his root voice has direct links back to the voice of Shakespeare's time? It does seem that compared to British dialects, which are predominantly about pitch, many North American dialects have a wonderful respect and vibrancy in their use of vowels. Shakespeare's language seems to me very vowel-aware. How useful it is for an actor to isolate the vowels in the spoken words to hear the music they produce, the rich patterns, their direct connection to feelings. North Americans more easily respond to this and allow it to feed their speaking. I can only assume it is closer to how the Elizabethans spoke.

In *Othello* the very names of the characters have a direct connection to one vowel in particular. All the male names, except the Duke, end in the sound OH: Othello, Cassio, Iago, Brabantio, etc. Furthermore, the sound OH ripples through the play both consciously and unconsciously. "Oh" occurs repeatedly and, more interestingly, is contained within other words: "so," "soul," and "know." These words resonate throughout the play, reinforcing another level of meaning. The repeating of the same sounds affects us beyond what we can quite say.

Vowels come from deep within us, from our very core. We speak vowels before we speak consonants. They seem to reveal the feelings that require the consonants to give the shape to what we perceive as making sense.

Working with actors who are bilingual (or ones for whom English is not the native language) is fascinating because of the way it allows the actor to have an awareness of the cadence in Shakespeare. There seems to be an objective perception to the musical patterns in the text, and the use of alliteration and assonance are often more easily heard not just as literary devices, but also as means by which meaning is formed and revealed to an audience.

Every speech pattern (i.e., accent, rhythm) is capable of audibility. Each has its own music, each can become an accent when juxtaposed against another. The point at which a speech pattern becomes audible is in the dynamic of the physical making of those sounds. The speaker must have the desire to get through to a listener and must be confident that every speech pattern has a right to be heard.

Speaking Shakespeare

So, the way to speak Shakespeare is not intrinsically tied to a particular sound; rather, it is how a speaker energetically connects to that language. Central to this is how we relate to the form of Shakespeare. Shakespeare employs verse, prose, and rhetorical devices to communicate meaning. For example, in *Romeo and Juliet*, the use of contrasts helps us to quantify Juliet's feelings: "And learn me how to lose a winning match," "Whiter than new snow upon a raven's back." These extreme opposites, "lose" and "winning," "new snow" and "raven's back," are her means to express and make sense of her feelings.

On a more personal note, I am often reminded how much, as an individual, I owe to Shakespeare's spoken word. The rather quiet and inarticulate schoolboy I once was found in the speaking and the acting of those words a means to quench his thirst for expression.

Notes:

(1) Peter Brook, *The Empty Space* (Harmondsworth: Penguin, 1972)

(2) Ted Hughes, *Winter Pollen* (London: Faber and Faber, 1995)

(3) Michael Redgrave, *The Actor's Ways and Means*
    (London: Heinemann, 1951)

In the Age of Shakespeare

Thomas Garvey

One of the earliest published pictures of Shakespeare's birthplace, from an original watercolor by Phoebe Dighton (1834)

The works of William Shakespeare have won the love of millions since he first set pen to paper some four hundred years ago, but at first blush, his plays can seem difficult to understand, even willfully obscure. There are so many strange words: not fancy, exactly, but often only half-familiar. And the very fabric of the language seems to spring from a world of forgotten assumptions, a vast network of beliefs and superstitions that have long been dispelled from the modern mind.

In fact, when "Gulielmus filius Johannes Shakespeare" (Latin for "William, son of John Shakespeare") was baptized in Stratford-on-Avon in 1564, English itself was only just settling into its current form; no dictionary had yet been written, and Shakespeare coined hundreds of words himself. Astronomy and medicine were entangled with astrology and the occult arts; democracy was waiting to be reborn; and even educated people believed in witches and fairies, and that the sun revolved around the Earth. Yet somehow Shakespeare still speaks to us today, in a voice as fresh and direct as the day his lines were first spoken, and to better understand both their artistic depth and enduring power, we must first understand something of his age.

REVOLUTION AND RELIGION

Shakespeare was born into a nation on the verge of global power, yet torn by religious strife. Henry VIII, the much-married father of Elizabeth I, had

From *The Book of Martyrs* (1563), this woodcut shows the Archbishop of Canterbury being burned at the stake in March 1556

Map of London ca. 1625

defied the Pope by proclaiming a new national church, with himself as its head. After Henry's death, however, his daughter Mary reinstituted Catholicism via a murderous nationwide campaign, going so far as to burn the Archbishop of Canterbury at the stake. But after a mere five years, the childless Mary also died, and when her half-sister Elizabeth was crowned, she declared the Church of England again triumphant.

In the wake of so many religious reversals, it is impossible to know which form of faith lay closest to the English heart, and at first, Elizabeth was content with mere outward deference to the Anglican Church. Once the Pope hinted her assassination would not be a mortal sin, however, the suppression of Catholicism grew more savage, and many Catholics—including some known in Stratford—were hunted down and executed, which meant being hanged, disemboweled, and carved into quarters. Many scholars suspect that Shakespeare himself was raised a Catholic (his father's testament of faith was found hidden in his childhood home). We can speculate about the impact this religious tumult may have had on his plays. Indeed, while explicit Catholic themes, such as the description of Purgatory in *Hamlet*, are rare, the larger themes of disguise and double allegiance are prominent across the canon. Prince Hal offers false friendship to Falstaff in the histories, the heroines of the comedies are forced to disguise themselves as men, and the action of the tragedies is driven by double-dealing villains. "I am not what I am," Iago tells us (and himself) in *Othello*, summing up in a single stroke what may have been Shakespeare's formative social and spiritual experience.

If religious conflict rippled beneath the body politic like some ominous undertow, on its surface the tide of English power was clearly on the rise. The defeat of the Spanish Armada in 1588 had established Britain as a global power; by 1595 Sir Walter Raleigh had founded the colony of Virginia (named for the Virgin Queen), and discovered a new crop, tobacco, which would inspire a burgeoning international trade. After decades of strife and the threat of invasion, England enjoyed a welcome stability. As the national coffers grew, so did London; over the course of Elizabeth's reign, the city would nearly double in size to a population of some 200,000.

Hornbook from Shakespeare's lifetime

A 1639 engraving of a scene from a royal state visit of Marie de Medici depicts London's packed, closely crowded half-timbered houses.

FROM COUNTRY TO COURT

The urban boom brought a new dimension to British life—the mentality of the metropolis. By contrast, in Stratford-on-Avon, the rhythms of the rural world still held sway. Educated in the local grammar school, Shakespeare was taught to read and write by a schoolmaster called an "abecedarian", and as he grew older, he was introduced to logic, rhetoric, and Latin. Like most schoolboys of his time, he was familiar with Roman mythology and may have learned a little Greek, perhaps by translating passages of the New Testament. Thus while he never attended a university, Shakespeare could confidently refer in his plays to myths and legends that today we associate with the highly educated.

Beyond the classroom, however, he was immersed in the life of the countryside, and his writing all but revels in its flora and fauna, from the wounded deer of *As You Like It* to the herbs and flowers which Ophelia scatters in *Hamlet*. Pagan rituals abounded in the rural villages of Shakespeare's day, where residents danced around maypoles in spring, performed "mummers' plays" in winter, and recited rhymes year-round to ward off witches and fairies.

The custom most pertinent to Shakespeare's art was the medieval "mystery play," in which moral allegories were enacted in country homes and village squares by troupes of traveling actors. These strolling players—usually four men and two boys who played the women's roles—often lightened the moralizing with bawdy interludes in a mix of high and low feeling, which would become a defining feature of Shakespeare's art. Occasionally even a professional troupe, such as Lord Strange's Men, or the Queen's Men, would arrive in town, perhaps coming straight to Shakespeare's door (his father was the town's bailiff) for permission to perform.

Rarely, however, did such troupes stray far from their base in London, the nation's rapidly expanding capital and cultural center. The city itself had existed since the time of the Romans (who built the original London Bridge), but it was not until the Renaissance that its population spilled beyond its ancient walls and began to grow along (and across) the Thames, by whose banks the Tudors had built their glorious palaces. It was these two contradictory worlds—a modern metropolis cheek-by-jowl with a medieval court—that provided the two very different audiences who applauded Shakespeare's plays.

Londoners both high and low craved distraction. Elizabeth's court constantly celebrated her reign with dazzling pageants and performances that required a local pool of professional actors and musicians. Beyond the graceful landscape of the royal parks, however, the general populace was packed into little more than a square mile of cramped and crooked streets where theatrical entertainment was frowned upon as compromising public morals.

Just outside the jurisdiction of the city fathers, however, across the twenty arches of London Bridge on the south bank of the Thames, lay the wilder district of "Southwark." A grim reminder of royal power lay at the end of the bridge—the decapitated heads of traitors stared down from pikes at passersby. Once beyond their baleful gaze, people found the amusements they desired, and their growing numbers meant a market suddenly existed for daily entertainment. Bear-baiting and cockfighting flourished, along with taverns, brothels, and even the new institution of the theater.

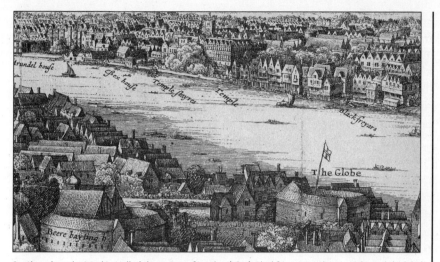

Southwark, as depicted in Hollar's long view of London (1647). Blackfriars is on the top right and the labels of Bear-baiting and the Globe were inadvertently reversed.

THE ADVENT OF THE THEATRE

The first building in England designed for the performance of plays—called, straightforwardly enough, "The Theatre"—was built in London when Shakespeare was still a boy. It was owned by James Burbage, father of Richard Burbage, who would become Shakespeare's lead actor in the acting company The Lord Chamberlain's Men. "The Theatre," consciously or unconsciously, resembled the yards in which traveling players had long plied their trade—it was an open-air polygon, with three tiers of galleries surrounding a canopied stage in a flat central yard, which was ideal for the athletic competitions the building also hosted. The innovative arena must have found an appreciative audience, for it was soon joined by the Curtain, and then the Rose, which was the first theater to rise in Southwark among the brothels, bars, and bear-baiting pits.

Even as these new venues were being built, a revolution in the drama itself was taking place. Just as Renaissance artists turned to classical models for inspiration, so English writers looked to Roman verse as a prototype for the new national drama. "Blank verse," or iambic pentameter (that is, a poetic line with five alternating stressed and unstressed syllables), was an adaptation of Latin forms, and first appeared in England in a translation of Virgil's *Aeneid*. Blank verse was first spoken on stage in 1561, in the now-forgotten *Gorboduc*, but it was not until the brilliant Christopher Marlowe (born the same year as Shakespeare) transformed it into the "mighty line" of such plays as *Tamburlaine* (1587) that the power and flexibility of the form made it the baseline of English drama.

Marlowe—who, unlike Shakespeare, had attended college—led the "university wits," a clique of hard-living free thinkers who in between all manner of exploits managed to define a new form of theater. The dates of Shakespeare's arrival in London are unknown—we have no record of him in Stratford after 1585—but by the early 1590s he had already absorbed the essence of Marlowe's invention, and begun producing astonishing innovations of his own.

While the "university wits" had worked with myth and fantasy, however, Shakespeare turned to a grand new theme, English history—penning the three-part saga of *Henry VI* in or around 1590. The trilogy was such a success that Shakespeare became the envy of his circle—one unhappy competitor, Robert Greene, even complained in 1592 of "an upstart crow...beautified with our feathers...[who is] in his own conceit the only Shake-scene in a country."

Such jibes perhaps only confirmed Shakespeare's estimation of himself, for he began to apply his mastery of blank verse in all directions, succeeding at tragedy (*Titus Andronicus*), farce (*The Comedy of Errors*), and romantic comedy (*The Two Gentlemen of Verona*). He drew his plots from everywhere: existing poems, romances, folk tales, even other plays. In fact a number of Shakespeare's dramas (*Hamlet* included) may be revisions of earlier texts owned by his troupe. Since copyright laws did not exist, acting companies usually kept their texts close to their chests, only allowing publication when a play was no longer popular, or, conversely, when a play was *so* popular (as with *Romeo and Juliet*) that unauthorized versions had already been printed.

Demand for new plays and performance venues steadily increased. Soon, new theaters (the Hope and the Swan) joined the Rose in Southwark, followed shortly by the legendary Globe, which opened in 1600. (After some trouble with their lease, Shakespeare's acting troupe, the Lord

pendeſt on ſo meane a ſtay . Baſe minded men all three of you,if by my miſerie you be not warn'd:for vnto none of you (like mee) ſought thoſe burres to cleaue : thoſe Puppets(I meane)that ſpake from our mouths, thoſe Anticks garniſht in our colours. Is it not ſtrange,that I,to whom they all haue beene beholding: is it not like that you,to whome they all haue beene beholding, ſhall (were yee in that caſe as I am now) bee both at once of them forſaken : Yes truſt them not : for there is an vp-ſtart Crow, beautified with our feathers, that with his Tygers hart wrapt in a Players hyde, ſuppoſes he is as well able to bombaſt out a blanke verſe as the beſt of you : and beeing an abſolute Iohannes fac totum,is in his owne conceit the onely Shake-ſcene in a countrey. O that I might intreat your rare wits to be imploied in more profitable courſes : & let thoſe Apes imitate your paſt excellence, and neuer more acquaint them with your admired inuentions . I knowe the beſt huſband of

Greene's insult, lines 9–14

Chamberlain's Men, had disassembled "The Theatre" and transported its timbers across the Thames, using them as the structure for the Globe.) Shakespeare was a shareholder in this new venture, with its motto "All the world's a stage," and continued to write and perform for it as well. Full-length plays were now being presented every afternoon but Sunday, and the public appetite for new material seemed endless.

The only curb on the public's hunger for theater was its fear of the plague—for popular belief held the disease was easily spread in crowds. Even worse, the infection was completely beyond the powers of Elizabethan medicine, which held that health derived from four "humors" or internal fluids identified as bile, phlegm, blood, and choler. Such articles of faith, however, were utterly ineffective against a genuine health crisis, and in times of plague, the authorities' panicked response was to shut down any venue where large crowds might congregate. The theaters would be closed for lengthy periods in 1593, 1597, and 1603, during which times Shakespeare was forced to play at court, tour the provinces, or, as many scholars believe, write what would become his famous cycle of sonnets.

THE NEXT STAGE

Between these catastrophic closings, the theater thrived as the great medium of its day; it functioned as film, television, and radio combined as well as a venue for music and dance (all performances, even tragedies, ended with a dance). Moreover, the theater was the place to see and be seen; for a penny

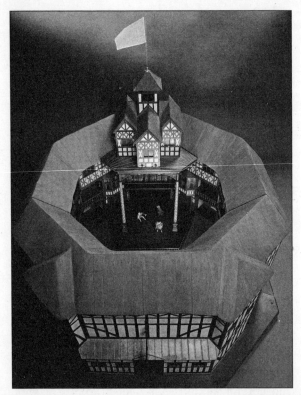

Famous scale model of the Globe completed by Dr. John Cranford Adams in 1954. Collectively, 25,000 pieces were used in constructing the replica. Dr. Adams used walnut to imitate the timber of the Globe, plaster was placed with a spoon and medicine dropper, and 6,500 tiny "bricks" measured by pencil eraser strips were individually placed on the model.

you could stand through a performance in the yard, a penny more bought you a seat in the galleries, while yet another purchased you a cushion. The wealthy, the poor, the royal, and the common all gathered at the Globe, and Shakespeare designed his plays—with their action, humor, and highly refined poetry—not only to satisfy their divergent tastes but also to respond to their differing points of view. In the crucible of Elizabethan theater, the various classes could briefly see themselves as others saw them, and drama could genuinely show "the age and body of the time his form and pressure," to quote Hamlet himself.

In order to accommodate his expanding art, the simplicity of the Elizabethan stage had developed a startling flexibility. The canopied platform of the Globe had a trap in its floor for sudden disappearances, while an alcove at the rear, between the pillars supporting its roof, allowed for "discoveries" and interior space. Above, a balcony made possible the love scene in *Romeo and Juliet*; while still higher, the thatched roof could double as a tower or rampart. And though the stage was largely free of scenery, the costumes were sumptuous—a theater troupe's clothing was its greatest asset. Patrons were used to real drums banging in battle scenes and real cannons firing overhead (in fact, a misfire would one day set the Globe aflame).

With the death of Elizabeth, and the accession of James I to the throne in 1603, Shakespeare only saw his power and influence grow. James, who considered himself an intellectual and something of a scholar, took over the patronage of the Lord Chamberlain's Men, renaming them the King's Men; the troupe even marched in his celebratory entrance to London. At this pinnacle of both artistic power and prestige, Shakespeare composed *Othello*, *King Lear*, and *Macbeth* in quick succession, and soon the King's Men acquired a new, indoor theater in London, which allowed the integration of more music and spectacle into his work. At this wildly popular venue, Shakespeare developed a new form of drama that scholars have dubbed "the romance," which combined elements of comedy and tragedy in a magnificent vision that would culminate in the playwright's last masterpiece, *The Tempest*. Not long after this final innovation, Shakespeare retired to Stratford a wealthy and prominent gentleman.

BEYOND THE ELIZABETHAN UNIVERSE

This is how Shakespeare fit into his age. But how did he transcend it? The answer lies in the plays themselves. For even as we see in the surface of his drama the belief system of England in the sixteenth century, Shakespeare himself is always questioning his own culture, holding its ideas up to the light and shaking them, sometimes hard. In the case of the Elizabethan faith in astrology, Shakespeare had his villain Edmund sneer, "We make guilty of our disasters the sun, the moon, and stars; as if we were villains on necessity." When pondering the medieval code of chivalry, Falstaff decides, "The better part of valor is discretion." The divine right of kings is questioned in *Richard II*, and the inferior status of women—a belief that survived even the crowning of Elizabeth—appears ridiculous before the brilliant examples of Portia (*The Merchant of Venice*), and Rosalind (*As You Like It*). Perhaps it is through this constant shifting of perspective, this relentless sense of exploration, that the playwright somehow outlived the limits of his own period, and became, in the words of his rival Ben Jonson, "not just for an age, but for all time."

Conclusion of the Sourcebooks Shakespeare
Hamlet: *Sir Derek Jacobi*

About the Online Teaching Resources

The Sourcebooks Shakespeare is committed to supporting students and educators in the study of Shakespeare. Visit our Shakespeare web site at http://www.sourcebooksshakespeare.com for additional materials and resources. To illustrate how the Sourcebooks Shakespeare may be used in your class, Jeremy Ehrlich, the head of education at the Folger Shakespeare Library, contributed an essay called "Working with Audio in the Classroom." The following is an excerpt:

One possible way of approaching basic audio work in the classroom is shown in the handout [on the site]. It is meant to give some guidance for the first-time user of audio in the classroom. I would urge you to adapt this to the particular circumstances and interests of your own students.

To use it, divide the students into four groups. Assign each group one of the four technical elements of audio—volume, pitch, pace, and pause—to follow as you play them an audio clip or clips. In the first section, have them record what they hear: the range they encounter in the clip and the places where their element changes. In the second section, have them suggest words for the tone of the passage based in part on their answers to the first. Sections three and four deal with tools of the actor. Modern acting theory finds the actor's objective is his single most important acting choice; an actor may then choose from a variety of tactics in order to achieve that objective. Thus, if a character's objective on stage is to get sympathy from his scene partner, he may start out by complaining, then shift to another tactic (asking for sympathy directly? throwing a tantrum?) if the first tactic fails. Asking your students to try to explain what they think a character is trying to get, and how she is trying to do it, is a way for them to follow this process through closely. Finally, the handout asks students to think about the meaning (theme) of the passage, concluding with a traditional and important tool of text analysis.

As you can see, this activity is more interesting and, probably, easier for students when it's used with multiple versions of the same piece of text. While defining an actor's motivation is difficult in a vacuum, doing so in relation to another performance may be easier: one Othello may be more concerned with gaining respect, while another Othello may be more concerned with obtaining love, for instance. This activity may be done outside of a group setting, although for students doing this work for the first time I suggest group work so they will be able to share answers on some potentially thought-provoking questions . . .

For the complete essay, please visit the web site. Additional resources are coming soon, including articles and essays, extended audio, a discussion forum, and more.

Acknowledgments

The series editors wish to give heartfelt thanks to the advisory editors of the series, David Bevington and Peter Holland, for their ongoing support, timely advice, and keen brilliance.

We are incredibly grateful to the community of Shakespeare scholars for their generosity in sharing their talents, collections, and even their address books. We would not have been able to put together such an august list of contributors without their help. First, sincere thanks to our text editor, Terri Bourus, for her thorough work. Thanks as well to Russell Jackson, Tom Garvey, Doug Lanier, and Andrew Wade for their marvelous essays. Extra appreciation goes to Doug Lanier for all his guidance and the use of his personal Shakespeare collection. We are grateful to William for his continuing guidance on textual issues, though any errors in this edition are ours.

We want to single out Tanya Gough, the proprietor of The Poor Yorick Shakespeare Catalog, for all her efforts on behalf of the series. She was an early supporter, providing encouragement from the very beginning and jumping in with whatever we needed. For her encyclopedic knowledge of Shakespeare on film and audio, for sharing her experience, for her continuing support, and for a myriad of other contributions too numerous to mention, we offer our deepest gratitude.

Our research was aided immensely by the wonderful staff at Shakespeare archives and libraries around the world: Susan Brock, Helen Hargest, and the staff at The Shakespeare Birthplace Trust; Jeremy Ehrlich, Bettina Smith, and everyone at the Folger Shakespeare Library; and Gene Rinkel, Bruce Swann, and Nuala Koetter from the Rare Books and Special Collections Library at the University of Illinois. These individuals were instrumental in helping us gather audio: Justyn Baker, Janet Benson, Barbara Brown, Nelda Gil, Carly Wilford, and Paul Brownstein, Sally Burton, and Barry Smith for the Burton audio. The following are the talented photographers who shared their work with us: Donald Cooper, Gerry Goodstein, George Joseph, Michal Daniel, and Carol Rosegg. Thank you to Jessica Talmage at the Mary Evans Picture Library and to Tracey Tomaso at Corbis. We appreciate all your help.

From the world of drama, the following shared their passion with us and helped us develop the series into a true partnership between the artistic and academic communities. We are indebted to: Liza Holtmeier, Lauren Beyea, and the team from the Shakespeare Theatre Company; Dana Kernich from AFTLS; Nancy Becker of The Shakespeare Society; and Santino Fontana. A special thank you to the 2006 *Hamlet* cast of Actors From the London Stage: Geoffrey Beevers, Anna Northam, Robert Mountford, Richard Stacey, and Terence Wilton.

With respect to the audio, we extend our heartfelt thanks to our narrating team: our director, John Tydeman, our esteemed narrator, Sir Derek Jacobi, and the staff of Motivation Studios. John has been a wonderful, generous resource to us and we look forward to future collaborations. We owe a debt of gratitude to Nicolas Soames for introducing us and for being unfailingly helpful. Thanks also to the "Speaking Shakespeare" team: Andrew Wade and Santino Fontana for that wonderful recording which will appear on the web site.

Our personal thanks for their kindness and unstinting support go to our friends and our extended families.

Finally, thanks to everyone at Sourcebooks who contributed their talents in realizing The Sourcebooks Shakespeare–in particular: Todd Green, Todd Stocke, Megan Dempster, Fred Marshall, and Michael Ryder. Special mention to Melanie Thompson, assistant extraordinaire for the Sourcebooks Shakespeare.

So, thanks to all at once and to each one (*Macbeth,* 5.7.104)

Audio Credits

In all cases, we have attempted to provide archival audio in its original form. While we have tried to achieve the best possible quality on the archival audio, some audio quality is the result of source limitations. Archival audio research by Marie Macaisa. Narration script by Tanya Gough and Marie Macaisa. Audio editing by Motivation Sound Studios, Marie Macaisa, and Todd Stocke. Narration recording and audio engineering by Motivation Sound Studios, London, UK. Mastering by Paul Estby. Recording for "Speaking Shakespeare" by Sotti Records, New York City, USA.

Narrated by Sir Derek Jacobi
Directed by John Tydeman
Produced by Marie Macaisa

The following are under license from BBC Worldwide Ltd. Permission kindly granted by Sir Derek Jacobi. All rights reserved.
Tracks 7, 19, 36

The following are under license from Naxos of America www.naxosusa.com
℗ HNH International Ltd. All rights reserved.
Tracks 3, 4, 6, 10, 16, 18, 20, 28, 31, 32, 34, 38

The following are under license from CBC Radio. All rights reserved.
Tracks 23, 26

The following are under license from Onward Production Ltd. All rights reserved.
Tracks 14, 29, 35

The following are selections from The Complete Arkangel Shakespeare ℗ 2003, with permission of The Audio Partners Publishing Corporation. All rights reserved. Unabridged audio dramatizations of all thirty-eight plays. For more information, visit www.audiopartners.com/shakespeare.
Tracks 9, 12, 15, 22, 25

Photo Credits

Every effort has been made to correctly attribute all the materials reproduced in this book. If any errors have been made, we will be happy to correct them in future editions.

Images from the 1934 production at the New Theatre directed by Sir John Gielgud and images from the 1958 production at the Shakespeare Memorial Theatre directed by Glen Byam Shaw are courtesy of the Rare Book and Special Collections Library, University of Illinois at Urbana-Champaign. Photos are credited on the pages in which they appear.

Photos from the Shakespeare Theatre Company's 2001 production directed by Gale Edwards are copyright © 2006 Carol Rosegg. Photos are credited on the pages in which they appear.

Photos from the 2000 film directed by Michael Almereyda, the 1996 film directed by Kenneth Branagh, the 1948 film directed by Laurence Olivier, the 1990 film directed by Franco Zeffirelli, the 1969 film directed by Tony Richardson, Sven Gade's and Heinz Schall's 1921 film, and Sara Bernhardt as Hamlet, are all courtesy of Douglas Lanier. Photos are credited on the pages in which they appear.

Photos from the Public Theater's 1971-72 production directed by Gerald Freedman, 1967-68 production directed by Joseph Papp, 1975-76 production directed by Michael Rudman, 1989-90 production directed by Kevin Kline are copyright © 2006 George E. Joseph. Photos are credited on the pages in which they appear.

Photos from the Royal Shakespeare Company's 1992 production directed by Adrian Noble, 1984 production directed by Ron Daniels, 1997 production directed by Matthew Warchus, 2001 production directed by Steven Pimlott, as well as, photos from the 2005 Northampton production directed by Rupert Goold, the 2006 Baxter Theatre Centre in South Africa production directed by Janet Suzman, the 1987 Royal Dramatic Theatre of Stockholm production directed by Ingmar Bergman, the 2003 Birmingham Repertory Theatre & Edinburgh International Festival production directed by Calixto Bieito are copyright © Donald Cooper. Photos are credited on the pages in which they appear.

Photo from the Brooklyn Academy of Music's 2002 production directed by John Caird is copyright © Richard Termine. Photos are credited on the pages in which they appear.

William Shakespeare's signature (on the title page) courtesy of Mary Evans Picture Library. Other images from the Mary Evans Picture Library used in the text are credited on the pages in which they appear.

Images from "In the Age of Shakespeare" courtesy of The Folger Shakespeare Library.

About the Contributors

TEXT EDITOR

Terri Bourus (Text Editor) is an Associate Professor of English at Indiana University Kokomo where she teaches Shakespeare, Renaissance Drama, and English Literature. Dr. Bourus has published widely on Shakespeare's texts and on Shakespeare in performance, including "Shakespeare and the London Publishing Environment: The Publisher of Q1 and Q2 Hamlet," "The First Quarto of Hamlet in Film: The Revenge Tragedies of Tony Richardson and Franco Zefferelli," and "'Enter Hamlet [reading a book]': Shakespeare's 'Other' Audience and the Publication of the Hamlet Quartos." Dr. Bourus is the recipient of several prestigious university teaching awards including the Amicus Award, the Indiana University Trustees Teaching Award, and the prestigious 2006 Claude Rich Excellence in Teaching Award.

SERIES EDITORS

Marie Macaisa spent twenty years in her first career: high-tech. She has a bachelor's degree in computer science from the Massachusetts Institute of Technology, a master's degree in artificial intelligence from the University of Pennsylvania, and worked for many years on the research and development of innovative applications of computer technology. A student and long-time fan of Shakespeare's works, she left high-tech and became the series editor of the *Sourcebooks Shakespeare* in 2003. She contributes the *Cast Speaks* essays for all volumes, writes the script and produces the accompanying audio, and is at work on the upcoming titles in the series.

Dominique Raccah is the founder, president, and publisher of Sourcebooks. Born in Paris, France, she has a bachelor's degree in psychology and a master's in quantitative psychology from the University of Illinois. In addition to the *Sourcebooks Shakespeare*, she also serves as series editor of *Poetry Speaks* and *Poetry Speaks to Children*.

ADVISORY BOARD

David Bevington (Series Advisor) is the Phyllis Fay Horton Distinguished Service Professor in the Humanities at the University of Chicago. A renowned text scholar, he has edited several Shakespeare editions including the *Bantam Shakespeare* in individual paperback volumes, *The Complete Works of Shakespeare*, (Longman, 2003), and *Troilus and Cressida* (Arden, 1998). He teaches courses in Shakespeare, Renaissance Drama, and Medieval Drama.

Peter Holland (Series Advisor) is the McMeel Family Chair in Shakespeare Studies at the University of Notre Dame. One of the central figures in performance-oriented Shakespeare criticism, he has also edited many Shakespeare plays, including *A Midsummer Night's Dream* for the Oxford Shakespeare series.

Essayists

Russell Jackson (*As Performed*) holds the Allardyce Nicoll Chair in Drama and Theatre Arts at the University of Birmingham (UK). From 1978 to 2004 he was a Fellow (and latterly, Director) of the Shakespeare Institute, the Stratford-based center for graduate studies in Shakespeare and his contemporaries. He edited *The Oxford Illustrated History of Shakespeare on Stage* (with Jonathan Bate, 2nd edition, 2001), two volumes in the *Players of Shakespeare* series (with Robert Smallwood for Cambridge University Press), and his second edition of *The Cambridge Companion to Shakespeare on Film* will be published in 2007. Since the mid-1980s he has worked as text advisor to Kenneth Branagh on stage and radio productions, and on all his Shakespeare films, and also on films by Oliver Parker (*Othello*, *An Ideal Husband*) and John Madden (*Shakespeare in Love*).

Thomas Garvey (*In the Age of Shakespeare*) has been acting, directing, or writing about Shakespeare for over two decades. A graduate of the Massachusetts Institute of Technology, he studied acting and directing with the MIT Shakespeare Ensemble, where he played Hamlet, Jacques, Iago, and other roles, and directed *All's Well That Ends Well* and *Twelfth Night*. He has since directed and designed several other Shakespearean productions, as well as works by Chekhov, Ibsen, Sophocles, Beckett, Moliere, and Shaw. Mr. Garvey has written on theater for the *Boston Globe* and other publications.

Douglas Lanier (*Hamlet and Popular Culture*) is Associate Professor of English at the University of New Hampshire. He has written many essays on Shakespeare in popular culture, including *Shakescorp Noir* in Shakespeare Quarterly 53.2 (Summer 2002) and *Shakespeare on the Record* in *The Black-well Companion to Shakespeare in Performance* (eds. Barbara Hodgdon and William Worthen, Blackwell, 2005). His book, *Shakespeare and Modern Popular Culture* (Oxford University Press), was published in 2002. He's currently working on a book-length study of cultural stratification in early modern British theater.

Andrew Wade (*Keeping Shakespeare Practical*) was Head of Voice for the Royal Shakespeare Company, 1990 - 2003 and Voice Assistant Director from 1987-1990. During this time he worked on 170 productions and with more than 80 directors. Along with Cicely Berry, Andrew recorded *Working Shakespeare*, the DVD series on *Voice and Shakespeare*, and he was the verse consultant for the movie *Shakespeare In Love*. In 2000, he won a Bronze Award from the New York International Radio Festival for the series *Lifespan*, which he co-directed and devised. He works widely teaching, lecturing and coaching throughout the world.

AUDIO CONTRIBUTORS
Sir Derek Jacobi (Series Narrator) is one of Britain's foremost actors of stage and screen. One of his earliest Shakespearean roles was Cassio to Sir Laurence Olivier's Othello in Stuart Burge's 1965 movie production. More recent roles include Hamlet in the acclaimed BBC Television Shakespeare production in 1980, the Chorus in Kenneth Branagh's 1989 film of *Henry V*, and Claudius in Branagh's 1996 movie *Hamlet*. He has been accorded numerous honors in his distinguished career, including a Tony award for Best Actor in *Much Ado About Nothing* and a BAFTA (British Academy of Film and Television) for his landmark portrayal of Emperor Claudius in the blockbuster television series *I, Claudius*. He was made a Knight of the British Empire in 1994 for his services to the theatre.

John Tydeman (Series Director) was the Head of Drama for BBC Radio for many years and is the director of countless productions, with fifteen Shake-speare plays to his credit. Among his numerous awards are the Prix Italia,

Prix Europa, UK Broadcasting Guild Best Radio Programme (*When The Wind Blows,* by Raymond Briggs), and the Sony Personal Award for services to radio. He has worked with most of Britain's leading actors and dramatists and has directed for the theater, television, and commercial recordings. He holds an M.A. from Cambridge University.

Tanya Gough (Audio Analyst) is the owner of the Poor Yorick Shakespeare Catalogue (www.bardcentral.com) and is on the editorial committee for the Shakespeare on Film portion of the Internet Shakespeare Edition at the University of Victoria. She taught English for four years in Japan and currently lectures in high schools and teacher training programs in Canada and the United States.

Joe Plummer (Audio Analyst) is the Director of Education for the Williamstown Theatre Festival and Assistant Professor of Shakespearean Performance with Roger Rees at Fordham University's Lincoln Center Campus. He has taught several Master classes on Shakespeare and Performance at Williams College and also teaches privately. Joe is currently the Artist-In-Residence and Director of Educational Outreach for The Shakespeare Society in New York City. He has taught acting for the National Shakespeare Company and for Brandeis University and has performed extensively in New York City and in other regional theaters.